# A Political Economy of Power

# OXFORD STUDIES IN THE HISTORY OF ECONOMICS

*Series Editor:*
Steven G. Medema, PhD, University Distinguished Professor of Economics, University of Colorado Denver

This series publishes leading-edge scholarship by historians of economics and social science, drawing upon approaches from intellectual history, the history of ideas, and the history of the natural and social sciences. It embraces the history of economic thinking from ancient times to the present, the evolution of the discipline itself, the relationship of economics to other fields of inquiry, and the diffusion of economic ideas within the discipline and to the policy realm and broader publics. This enlarged scope affords the possibility of looking anew at the intellectual, social, and professional forces that have surrounded and conditioned economics' continued development.

# A Political Economy of Power

## *Ordoliberalism in Context, 1932–1950*

Raphaël Fèvre

OXFORD
UNIVERSITY PRESS

OXFORD
UNIVERSITY PRESS

Oxford University Press is a department of the University of Oxford. It furthers the University's objective of excellence in research, scholarship, and education by publishing worldwide. Oxford is a registered trade mark of Oxford University Press in the UK and certain other countries.

Published in the United States of America by Oxford University Press
198 Madison Avenue, New York, NY 10016, United States of America.



Library of Congress Cataloging-in-Publication Data
Names: Fèvre, Raphaël, author.
Title: A political economy of power : Ordoliberalism in context, 1932–1950 / Raphaël Fèvre.
Description: New York : Oxford University Press, 2021. |
Series: Oxford studies history economics series | Includes
bibliographical references and index.
Identifiers: LCCN 2021025221 | ISBN 9780197607800 (hardback) |
ISBN 9780197607824 (epub)
Subjects: LCSH: Economic policy. | Economics—Germany—History—20th
century. | Historical school of economics. | Power (Social sciences)
Classification: LCC HC54 .F48 2021 | DDC 338.9009—dc23
LC record available at https://lccn.loc.gov/2021025221

DOI: 10.1093/oso/9780197607800.001.0001

# CONTENTS

# ACKNOWLEDGMENTS

This book on German ordoliberalism is largely based on a PhD dissertation that was completed in Lausanne, in October 2017. I wish to express my warm thanks to my co-supervisors, Jérôme Lallement and Roberto Baranzini, for their academic and personal guidance and for allowing me a viable compromise between freedom in the conduct of my research and the rigorous demands of intellectual work. I am also indebted to Richard Arena, Patricia Commun, Lisa Herzog, Harro Maas, and Emmanuel Picavet who examined my dissertation and contributed to shape its final version.

From 2012 to 2017, I have received the support of the University of Lausanne, where I enjoyed exceptional working conditions as a researcher and PhD student. I do remember as golden years this period spent at the Centre Walras Pareto. I learned more than I can tell in this remarkably fertile and inspiring environment, and all my gratitude and affection go to its members. I have a special thought for Michele Bee, Nicolas Brisset, Maxime Desmarais-Tremblay, Antoine Missemer, Thomas Mueller, François Allisson, and Nicolas Eyguesier, who maintained the uncertain but happy space between collegiality and friendship. They have been invaluable intellectual companions, initiating me to the subtleties of the academic environment and orienting the pursuit of my research. In Lausanne, I also benefited from the constant guidance and support of Pascal Bridel, Harro Maas, and Biancamaria Fontana. Bianca was particularly instrumental in generating (and nurturing) my interest in pursuing my academic work in Cambridge.

The manuscript of this book was written during an eighteen-month visiting fellowship at the University of Cambridge (funded by a postdoctoral Mobility Grant of the University of Lausanne). I was hosted by the Department of Politics and International Studies and benefited from the support of Clare Hall. The frequency and richness of intellectual exchanges, well beyond the usual disciplinary practices, make of Cambridge a remarkable place to pursue research in general and to work on the history of ideas in particular. I am most grateful to Duncan Kelly, who not only showed interest in my work from the start, but also was a constant source of support through our regular discussions over lunch at Jesus College.

I finished writing and polishing this book in Nice, where I joined the Groupe de Recherche en Droit, Economie et Gestion (GREDEG) at the Université Côte d'Azur in the Fall of 2020. Despite the restrictions due to the pandemic, my colleagues warmly welcomed me and helped me feel at home very quickly. I am thankful to Richard Arena, Nicolas Brisset, Muriel Dal Pont Legrand, and many others for their friendliness.

In recent years, I have benefited from numerous discussions on and around my work, feeding my reflection through casual talks, seminars, summer schools, international conferences, and workshops. The most regular of these meetings was the Albert Oliver Hirschman seminar led by Annie Cot and Jérôme Lallement at Université Paris 1—a hub of passionate debates from which I learned a great deal thanks to Cléo Chassonery-Zaïgouche, Aurélien Goustmedt, Dorian Jullien, Jean-Sébastien Lenfant, Erich Pinzon Fuchs, Matthieu Renault, Francesco Sergi, and all the members of the REHPERE team network. On many occasions, I also had the privilege to discuss my work with a number of specialists of ordoliberalism, such as Thomas Biebricher, Patricia Commun, Nils Goldschmidt, Harald Hagemann, Stefan Kolev, Daniel Nientiedt, Jean Solchany, and Keith Tribe, who offered me generous help and advice.

Finally, I wish to thank David Pervin and James Cook at Oxford University Press for adopting this project, and Steve Medema for welcoming it into the Oxford Studies in the History of Economics. I am particularly grateful to Steve and to the two reviewers for their encouraging and incisive suggestions. Biancamaria Fontana, Duncan Kelly, and Erwin Dekker were kind enough to read parts of the manuscript. I am indebted to them for being so characteristically generous with their time and for the acuity of their comments.

It goes without saying that none of this would have been possible without the loving support of my friends and family. I am especially grateful to my mother, Florence, who has constantly encouraged me in the pursuit of my studies as well as in my personal choices. I also owe her a taste for books and reading, without which writing a monograph on the history of ideas would have been clearly far less easy and enjoyable.

Through his incomparable wittiness, continuing support, and affection, Michele's contribution to all of this is immense: *per il suo sguardo che abbellisce ciò che abbraccia, possa un semplice silenzio esprimere la mia riconoscenza*.

—R. F.

Lausanne–Cambridge–Nice (2012–2021)

N.B. All translations from materials not already translated into English are mine. By and large, I have used existing translations while remaining free to amend them.

Chapter 5 of the book was first published as "Denazifying the Economy: Ordoliberals on the Economic Policy Battlefield (1946–50)," in *History of Political Economy* (Fèvre 2018c) but has been restructured differently in the book and augmented by the subsection "5.2.3 Toward a Consumer Democracy?"

# Introduction

## *The Making of Ordoliberalism*

In March 1950, German economist Walter Eucken traveled to England determined to disseminate the key ideas from his work through a series of lectures at the London School of Economics (LSE). Before he could deliver his fifth and final lecture, Eucken suffered a heart attack and died at the age of fifty-nine. Eucken never saw the publication of *The Foundations of Economics*, a translation of his 1940 magnum opus. Moreover, he could not react to the first occurrence of the neologism "ordoliberalism" (Moeller 1950), which characterized the intellectual project he shaped more than anyone else. In the first talk in his LSE cycle—later published as *This Unsuccessful Age* (1951)—Eucken noted with disarming simplicity, "I begin with the problem of *economic power*" (Eucken 1951, 31, emphasis in original). Eucken's seemingly ordinary sentence can be rephrased to capture the central argument of this book: for ordoliberals, *in the beginning was economic power*. More precisely, I will argue that the entire ordoliberal project, typically framed as a subvariety of liberalism, is better understood if considered as an autonomous form of economic knowledge driven by power issues. In short, the making of ordoliberalism from 1932 to 1950 coincided with the building of a *political economy of power*.

*A Political Economy of Power.* Raphaël Fèvre, Oxford University Press. © Oxford University Press 2021.
DOI: 10.1093/oso/9780197607800.003.0001

## I.1 ORDOLIBERALISM: FROM ACTUALITY TO HISTORY

In January 2016, Angela Merkel was invited to lecture at the University of Freiburg to celebrate the 125th anniversary of Walter Eucken's birth.[1] In her speech, the Federal Chancellor reaffirmed the importance of ordoliberal intellectual roots for contemporary Germany and, in particular, her "firm conviction" that the historical "ordoliberal principles" would have "neither lost their importance nor their relevance" (Merkel 2016). Angela Merkel's ordoliberal outlook is by no means unique among German politicians: the Free Democratic Party (FDP), the Christian Democratic Union (CDU), and, to a lesser extent, even the Social-Democratic Party (SPD) endorsed an orthodox ordoliberal line when addressing the Euro crisis (Dullien and Guérot 2012; Jacoby 2014; Uterwedde 2007). This reference to ordoliberalism has also resonated across the wide spectrum of German politics—albeit in a spirit of opposition to the CDU—from left-wing party leaders of *Die Linke* to the far-right of *Alternative für Deutschland* (Siems and Schnyder 2014; Havertz 2019).

Merkel's explicit endorsement of ordoliberalism is also shared by prominent European leaders such as Wolfgang Schäuble (2014), the former German Finance minister, or Mario Draghi (2013), President of the European Central Bank (ECB) from 2011 to 2019, in line with former (Tietmeyer 1999) and current (Weidmann 2013) presidents of the *Deutsche Bundesbank*. Beyond German borders, ordoliberalism has long been recognized as a major intellectual source that shaped the European Union from the beginning.[2] However, one issue still remains: How do we understand the recent revival of principles that has been at the heart of the

1. Freiburg im Breisgau is part of the Land of Baden-Württemberg and is located in the extreme southwest of Germany, at the foot of the Black Forest mountain range, a few kilometers from the borders of France and Switzerland. Eucken was professor of economics at the University of Freiburg from 1927 until his death.

2. Both the Treaty of Rome of 1957, which introduced a single market and the idea of free and undistorted competition, supplemented by the Maastricht Treaty in 1992, which established the Economic and Monetary Union, were partly shaped by ordoliberal ideas (Behrens 2015; Denord and Schwartz 2010; Ebner 2006; Mongouachon 2011; Strassel 2009; Warlouzet 2008). In the same way, the Stability and Growth Pact of 2011/2012 has been judged ordoliberal (Drexl 2011; Lechevalier 2015); it notably provided for a strong control of deficits and public debt in order to limit the discretionary budgetary policy of the Member States. If the ECB has been labeled ordoliberal (Dehay 1995, 2003), this perspective is now open to a more nuanced narrative (Bibow 2009, 2013). On ordoliberalism in relation to European economic policy, see also the collective volume edited dy Malte Dold and Tim Krieger (2019).

German Federal Republic's economy and politics since 1948 and a central part of Europe for many years?[3]

The sixtieth anniversary of the Treaty of Rome in 2017 did not coincide with sixty years of an ordoliberal Europe. Indeed, the European Union's economic policy embodied a "complex amalgam of nationally specific management traditions" around French indicative planning, which incorporates British and Swedish Keynesian poles as well as German ordoliberalism (Thompson 1992, 148). The 2007 financial crisis, and even more so the sovereign debt crisis that followed from 2010 to 2015, posed imperative challenges to the economic governance of Western countries in general and those in Europe in particular. Under German leadership, the European Union responded by restating a form of ordoliberal orthodoxy, culminating in a violent Greek episode. To some extent, the sovereign debt crisis marked a turning point at which ordoliberalism became the prevailing model for European economic policies and particularly at the expense of Keynesianism.[4] In other words, today's European Monetary Union (EMU) is allegedly locked in the ideological "iron cage" of ordoliberalism (Denord et al. 2015; Ryner 2015).

What are the central features of the current ordoliberal orthodoxy? Followers and critics of the ordoliberal Europe agree on its fundamentals, which center around three interrelated axioms.[5] The first axiom is that an

3. Merkel's praise of ordoliberalism during ceremonial occasions is not tantamount to engaging in actual ordoliberal policies. Clearly, the economic policy of West (and then reunified) Germany since 1948 has by no means followed a uniform path but has been marked by the ups and downs of ordoliberal-oriented policies. From mid-1960 to mid-1970 for instance, Keynesianism gained traction in West Germany due in particular to Karl Schiller, then Minister of the economy, who successfully set forth demand stimulus measures to cut the downturn of 1966–1967 (see Scherf 1986; Hagemann 2010). Yet, remarkably, and this is what interests us here, the dominant ordoliberal culture permeates the entire political sphere and has become an almost mandatory reference point for the German elite (Georgiou 2016, 67).

4. In contrast to this widely shared reading (Bibow 2018; Biebricher 2014a; Esch 2014; Ojala and Harjuniemi 2016; Olender 2012; Temin and Vines 2015), Brigitte Young argued that the ordoliberal influence on the European management of crises has been overestimated (2014a, 2015, 2018; Young and Semmler 2011). For instance, the unconventional monetary policy of *quantitative easing* pursued by the ECB since September 2014 would be much more interventionist (pragmatic/discretionary) than ordoliberal (rule-based) (Cerny 2016; Feld et al. 2015, 2017; Hien and Joerges 2018). In any case, the current crisis accompanying the global pandemic of COVID-19 is pushing European governance toward a more assertive Keynesianism, with unprecedented amounts of public spending.

5. Various versions of what Franz-Josef Meiers (2015, 11–14) termed the "categorical imperatives of ordoliberalism" can be found in the literature (Bonatti and Fracasso 2013, 1028–1031; Nedergaard and Snaith 2015, 1101; Ryner 2015, 281–282; Young 2015, 81–83).

independent Central Bank committed to price stability should manage monetary policy separate from national sovereignties. The second axiom involves the refusal to finance economic activity, even to stabilize the business cycle, through fiscal policy that might increase (public) debts. Ordoliberalism thus defined would exist at the heart of recent European policy, marked by monetary and fiscal austerity (Blyth 2013; Matthijs 2016; Biebricher and Vogelmann 2017).[6] Finally, a third axiom of contemporary ordoliberalism includes a defense of competition based on a structural supply policy as the primary tool to fight unemployment. This policy advocates the privatization of public enterprises and services, or legislative measures compatible with flexible labor. Collectively, these three objectives point to an economic policy by the rule (as opposed to discretion) in which the economic expert becomes predominant (in contrast to politics).

By its ability to shape public discourse and action, contemporary ordoliberalism is more concerned with a *political culture* than with its original *economic paradigm*. Thus, we face two objects of different natures, the former nevertheless with roots in the latter, in a relationship that has yet to be clarified. How can we explain that ordoliberalism may be a final survivor of the "third ways" from the postwar period and that it still makes sense to refer to this stream of thought today? A related question involves how ordoliberal thought has achieved such political longevity in spite of its inability to survive in contemporary economics.

This book's central hypothesis seeks the political robustness of ordoliberalism in endogenous factors or, specifically, in the ordoliberal approach and ideas themselves. First, answering these questions requires a clear conceptualization of ordoliberalism in its discursive context. Therefore, this book aims to restore the seminal ordoliberal project to its time and explain how it is the fruit of interwar doctrines, analyses, and debates across the field of social sciences in general and economics in particular. Defining ordoliberalism is tantamount to explaining how this identity played a *positive* role in founding a new political rationality and a *negative* one in marginalizing competing programs in the postwar period.

Through a study of the history of economic thought, this work aims to illuminate a subsequent political practice to observe how ideas "become effective forces in history," to borrow Max Weber's (1905, 48) formula.

6. Commentators pointed at the—mainly Protestant—ethical values underlying austerity: German inflexibility to "align responsibility with liability" (Schäfer 2016, 969–973) was seen as the action of "northern saints" conducting a "moral struggle" against "southern sinners" (Fourcade 2013, 625; Matthijs 2016, 376; Matthijs and McNamara 2015, 230).

A historical look at ordoliberalism will provide new insights on the principles at the heart of contemporary ordoliberal orthodoxy, such as the objectives of competition and price stability. This historical portrait will offer a singularly more complex—and, at times, conflicting—image than the alleged long-term continuity typically suggested.

Rebuilding the ordoliberal political economy requires that three preliminary issues be addressed. First, who are the authors who legitimately composed the corpus of the original ordoliberal project? Second, can they be brought together around common analyses and ideas despite their differences? Third, do these authors make it possible to identify the singularity of ordoliberalism as a current, a doctrine, or as a school of thought? The following sections in this introduction will answer these questions.

## I.2 WHO ARE THE ORDOLIBERALS? GENEALOGY OF A RESEARCH COMMUNITY

The neologism "ordoliberalismus" was coined in 1950, by the Tubingen economist Hero Moeller. Moeller was inspired by *Ordo,* an academic journal founded by Walter Eucken and Franz Böhm in 1948. Its editorial board included Wilhelm Röpke, Alexander Rüstow, and Friedrich A. Lutz, with Fritz W. Meyer and Hans Otto Lenel as editorial secretaries.[7] As a central place to promote ordoliberal ideas in the postwar period, *Ordo*'s advocates shared the "dogma of competition" according to Moeller (1950, 224). Nolens volens, Moeller's expression became authoritative, as indicated by the first monograph on the *Nature and Purposes of Ordoliberalism* (*Wesen und Ziele des Ordoliberalismus*) by Ernst-Wolfram Dürr (1954).[8] Years later, Böhm, Lutz, and Meyer (1961) made this neologism their own in the foreword to the twelfth volume of *Ordo*.

With the term "ordo," Eucken, Böhm, and others signaled their attachment to a tradition inspired by Augustine of Hippo (354–430).[9] As such,

7. *Ordo—Jahrbuch für die Ordnung von Wirtschaft und Gesellschaft* is still published today (http://www.ordo-journal.com/de/). Bönker, Labrousse, and Weisz (2001) traced the evolution of the journal through a bibliometric analysis of its contributors and articles subjects.

8. Articles by Carl J. Friedrich (1955) and Henry M. Oliver (1960a, 1960b) were among the first English-language works to mention a "German neoliberalism" and the "*Ordo* group."

9. Augustine developed the concept of "ordo" in Book XIX of *The City of God* (1998). "Ordo" refers to "the organisation of elements within a whole according to a hierarchical principle," it's an ideal of balance and measure (Bouton-Touboulic 1999, 297, 329–332).

*Ordo* resonates with one of Eucken's fundamental concepts: order (*Ordnung*). The concept of order can be interpreted in two ways in ordoliberal literature. On the one hand, it refers to different spheres of social life, such as the political, economic, or cultural; although distinct from each other, these are unified by similar internal principles of cohesion and necessity. Order was a way of thinking about reality that goes beyond disciplinary frameworks (Böhm 1950). On the other hand, the concept of order involves a duality: it serves to distinguish the "positive order" from the "natural order," terms that Eucken (1952, 372) considered born of the Enlightenment and imported into economic thought by François Quesnay.

The term "ordo" was also highly symbolic. In the context of the early postwar period, the reference to Augustine emphasized the Latin and Christian culture common to Europeans at a time when continental Europe lacked cohesion, to say the least. The ordoliberals' affirmation of their Christian roots—primarily Protestant, but also Catholic (see Krarup 2019)—provided a structure for western German political parties in the postwar period.

A study of ordoliberal thinking requires distinguishing between the authors and works that are internal and external to the concept; in short, drawing the boundaries of ordoliberalism. Three groups of authors can be distinguished within ordoliberalism: its founders, students (or followers), and satellites. Among the founders, there are two clusters. On the one hand, the economist Walter Eucken (1891–1950) and the lawyers Franz Böhm (1895–1977) and Hans Großmann-Doerth (1894–1944) initiated the Freiburg School (*Freiburger Schule der Nationalökonomie*). On the other hand, the cultural approach of Wilhelm Röpke (1899–1966) and Alexander Rüstow (1885–1963) also led to the first ordoliberals. Unlike the former, Röpke and Rüstow were forced into exile because of their liberal opinions and joined the University of Istanbul in 1933.[10] The Freiburg School also includes slightly younger followers: K. Paul Hensel (1907–1975), Friedrich A. Lutz (1901–1975), Karl Friedrich Maier (1905–1993), Fritz W. Meyer (1907–1980), and Leonhard Miksch (1901–1950). These students had completed their doctorate or habilitation theses and/or had a research assistant position under Eucken's supervision.

10. Turkey was a host country for many German-speaking scholars. They participated in the modernization of higher education in Istanbul. For instance, Röpke was one of the promoters of a Faculty of Economics independent of the Faculty of Law (Ege and Hagemann 2012, 961–963). In 1937, Röpke joined the Graduate Institute of International Studies of Geneva, where he held the chair of international economics until his retirement.

Finally, Ludwig Erhard (1897–1977) and Alfred Müller-Armack (1901–1978) on the one hand, and Heinrich F. von Stackelberg (1905–1946) on the other are considered "satellites" of ordoliberal thought because they are not strictly ordoliberals. The Minister of Economy and then-Federal Chancellor Ludwig Erhard and the academic Alfred Müller-Armack bore a political project based in part on ordoliberal ideas, which they renamed the "Social Market Economy" (*Soziale Marktwirtschaft*). Erhard and Müller-Armack were satellites who intervened *downstream* of ordoliberal thought, which contributed to its *political* shaping. In contrast, the market structure theorist Stackelberg acted as a satellite to intervene primarily *upstream* of ordoliberal thinking as a *theoretical* resource, as I will discuss in Chapter 3.

This partition has merit in renewing the coherence between the authors who are at the heart of this book, both founders and students, while delineating the satellites' external but no less decisive role in defining ordoliberalism's political and theoretical identity. Alternatively, ordoliberalism's temporal categorization can be outlined by three main stages, which are marked by different historical contexts. I have chosen to organize these around key dates and not in a purely linear manner: the outbreak (1932–1936), the blooming (1940–1942), and the acme (1948–1950) of ordoliberal thought.[11] The following chronological presentation highlights some of the works most cited in this book and frames some of its central questions.

Starting the history of ordoliberalism in 1932 raises the question of its *prehistory*. At this stage, two indications about the twenties are worth highlighting. First, this emphasizes the importance of certain academic socialization circles, such as the *Verein für Socialpolitik*, in which ordoliberals primarily interacted with such historicists as Werner Sombart and Arthur Spiethoff, but also with Austrians like Hayek, Ludwig von Mises, and Joseph A. Schumpeter. In 1922, and at Rüstow's initiative, Eucken, Röpke, and Lutz founded a subcommittee of the Verein called the "German Ricardians." Under Ricardo's patronage, Rüstow sought to bring together economists who wanted to revive economic theory as opposed to historicist canon, whether liberal or socialist (such as Adolf Löwe and Emil Lederer), although Austrian economists kept their distance with this project (Commun 2016, 24–27; Janssen 2009).

11. The secondary literature rather distinguishes two periods (Rieter and Schmolz 1993; Simonin 1999): from a separation between a phase of silent intellectual formation (1938–1945) which contrasts with that of public expression in favor of an economic and political project (1946–1966).

Second, the traumatic experience of German hyperinflation, which peaked in 1923, is noteworthy. Nevertheless, it would be incorrect to associate the ordoliberal aversion to price fluctuations with this single episode of *open* inflation because the *repressed* inflation of 1936–1948 in particular will occupy ordoliberal monetary concerns. However, hyperinflation has convinced the ordoliberals of the importance of price stability, not only for economic order, but above all for moral and social order as a whole. Stefan Zweig's analysis is particularly telling in its illustration of this idea; in *The World of Yesterday*, Zweig described the collapse of German society's values concomitant with the collapse of the paper mark's value:

> I have a pretty thorough knowledge of history, but never, to my recollection, has it produced such madness in such gigantic proportions. All values were changed, and not only material ones; the laws of the State were flouted, no tradition, no moral code was respected, Berlin was transformed into the Babylon of the world. (Zweig 1943, 313)

Dissatisfied with historicists' analyses of hyperinflation, the first ordoliberal generation sought to emancipate itself from their trained tradition, which was still fairly dominant in interwar Germany. Analyzing ordoliberalism as both a rupture from and continuity with the German Historical School presents tensions that will reoccur at different stages in the first three chapters of this book.

### I.2.1 The Birth (1932–1936)

The cornerstone of the history of ordoliberal political economy can be traced back to 1932, in which Eucken (1932b) published an important article to diagnose contemporary disorders, called "Structural Changes of the State and the Crisis of Capitalism" ("*Staatliche Strukturwandlungen und die Krisis des Kapitalismus*"). Eucken framed a long-term outlook to explain the driving forces behind the transition from laissez-faire liberalism to an interventionist reaction "born of a particular combination of economic interests, anti-capitalist sentiments, aspirations for a national policy and quasi-religious convictions" (Eucken 1932b, 306). The early thirties began with an unprecedented economic crisis, coupled with a political crisis of parliamentary democracy, which suggests the state's powerlessness in the face of the turbulent market economy. Germany was the European country most severely affected by the Great Depression, which began in the United States.

Given the scale of the crisis and the radical nature of the responses to it, the stakes were not only economic, but also political, social, and cultural. In a January 1935 lecture delivered to the Austrian Society of Economists in Vienna, Röpke (1936c, 1307) stressed that the end of the economic crisis lay in the establishment of new spiritual foundations to "morally reconcile the masses" with the liberal market economy. A few years earlier, Alexander Rüstow (1932, 183) was "convinced that it is not the economy that determines our destiny, but the State; and that the State also determines the destiny of the economy," in a presentation to the thirty-second session of the Verein für Socialpolitik. Thus, at the time of Eucken's 1932 article, Rüstow (1932, 183) voiced the need for "liberal interventionism," of which the existence of a "strong state" was the preliminary condition. The following year, Hans Großmann-Doerth (1933, 27) in his inaugural lecture at the University of Freiburg called for a "state that once again holds the power to impose its will," or a state that would be "free from the economy."

When ordoliberals called for a strong state, did this support the newly established National Socialist state following Adolf Hitler's appointment as chancellor in January 1933? More generally, what was the ordoliberals' position toward Nazism? A brief answer involves first noting the ordoliberals' various relationships with the National Socialist regime, which ranged from exile and open protest (Röpke and Rüstow) to a withdrawal and intellectual resistance that intensified beginning in 1942 (Eucken and Böhm).[12] Some ordoliberals participated in debates on implementing certain official economic reforms (Erhard and Miksch), sometimes accompanied by Nazi party membership and enthusiasm, at least in the early years (Müller-Armack, Großmann-Doerth, and Stackelberg). This theme is still controversial in recent historiography and some elements are subsequently addressed in the development of this book, particularly in Chapters 3 and 5.

In 1936, Franz Böhm, Walter Eucken, and Hans Großmann-Doerth signed a short text entitled *Our Task* (*Unsere Aufgabe*), which introduced the *Ordnung der Wirtschaft* collection, including contributions from Lutz (1936), Böhm (1937), and Miksch (1937b).[13] In fact, the foundations of the *Ordo* journal in 1948 were laid in 1936 with this series of monographic contributions, embodying what Franz Böhm (1957) retrospectively termed a "research and teaching community between lawyers and economists" at

12. On Eucken's resistance to Nazism, see in particular the volume edited by Nils Goldschmidt (2005a).

13. Apparently, Eucken wrote most of *Our Task* alone (Goldschmidt 2005b, 11). The English translation of this text by Alan Peacock and Hans Willgerodt was the opportunity to rename the text *The Ordo Manifesto of 1936* (Böhm, Eucken, and Großmann-Doerth 1936).

the University of Freiburg. *Our Task* was a programmatic, decisive text to illuminate the bases on which ordoliberals oppose historicism and how they view the scientist's role in the political sphere.

### I.2.2 The Blooming (1940–1942)

Published during the Second World War, Eucken's (1940a) *The Foundations of Political Economy* (*Die Grundlagen der Nationalökonomie*) and Röpke's (1942c) *The Social Crisis of Our Time* (*Die Gesellschaftskrisis der Gegenwart*) were the most authoritative works of ordoliberal thought, although very different in form.

As Eucken's book title suggests, the *Grundlagen* laid a foundation for the ordoliberal political economy. From an epistemological perspective, Eucken aimed to overcome the "great antinomy" between history and theory brought to the fore by the famous battle of the methods (*Methodenstreit*) between Gustav von Schmoller and Carl Menger. From a theoretical perspective, Eucken developed a typology to describe not only the different forms of economic orders or the administered versus exchange economies, but also the different forms of markets and monetary systems within the exchange economy. This perspective will reveal the role of Eucken's epistemological (Chapter 2) and theoretical ambitions (Chapter 3) in forming the ordoliberal political economy. This will also demonstrate the extent to which an analysis of economic power plays a decisive role.

In *The Social Crisis of Our Time*, Röpke adopted a much broader outlook than Eucken; although focused on economic issues, Röpke's reflections embraced a cultural challenge to modern Western civilization. *The Crisis of Our Time* is the first work in what Röpke considered as a trilogy published during the war (see Röpke 1942c, 1944b, 1945b). Rüstow (1942, 267) believed that together they "faced the same problem, but from a reverse perspective: while Professor Röpke insisted on the economic aspects, only scratching the surface of sociological issues, I focused on the field of sociology and the history of thought, briefly mentioning the economic aspects of our problem." This differentiation between economic, political, sociological, and legal arguments is one difficulty that this book will face.

During the war, the ordoliberal project of a "third way" (*dritter Weg*) increasingly developed. Did this third way synthesize laissez-faire and planning, or was this an alternative approach? How did the ordoliberals justify the impasse they sought to establish in the opposition between laissez-faire liberalism, on the one hand, and planning, on the other? Moreover, was power of the same nature, and did it lead to the same difficulties in the hands of private agents versus a state bureaucracy? Furthermore, how did state intervention—which "must not be in opposition to the functioning of the market mechanism or disturb the structure of the market, but on the contrary, maintain it" (Rüstow 1942, 281)—make it possible to overcome this impasse? Böhm (1942), Eucken (1942b), and Miksch (1942) were daily witnesses to the planned National Socialist war economy and voiced the competitive mechanism's potential as not only an economic instrument that contributes to efficiency, but also a political instrument that promotes freedom.

### I.2.3 The Acme (1948–1950)

The year 1948 was key for the ordoliberals in many ways. After the June 15 monetary reform established by the Allies, Ludwig Erhard, Director of the Administration of the Unified Economic Zone, promulgated price liberalization on June 20. In this context, the ordoliberals conducted decisive, expert work within political circles and in public opinion. As previously mentioned, the *Ordo*'s creation in the same year provided support for—and the beginning of an institutionalization of—ordoliberal ideas as this journal aimed to combine political militancy and scientific rigor. Lionel Robbins witnessed this twofold dimension when he wrote to *Ordo*'s editors that they had "succeeded in producing a journal which promises to be of absolutely first-class importance not only for professional economists, but also for all those who have the future of society of the west at heart."[14]

Until the early fifties, West Germany's economy was devastated and marked by chronic shortages and mass unemployment. Röpke (1950b) asked *Is the German Economic Policy the Right One?* (*Ist die deutsche Wirtschaftspolitik richtig?*) with the intent to push Erhard's market-oriented reforms and indicate that a return to administrative price-fixing, or planned resource allocations, would seriously undermine the country's economic recovery. However, 1950 was also marked by the deaths of Eucken at age fifty-nine and Miksch at age forty-nine, and thus ordoliberals lost not only their greatest contributor and one of its founders, but also two of its most active and influential members.

The posthumous publication of the *Principles of Economic Policy* (*Grundsätze der Wirtschaftspolitik*) presented Eucken's (1952) work to a

14. L. Robbins, letter to H. O. Lenel, September 21, 1948 [LSE Archive: ROBBINS/3/2/11].

wider audience and elevated him to an almost mythical stature as the gray eminence of the "economic miracle" (*Wirtschaftswunder*), of which Erhard was a leading political figure. Orphaned by some of its most important members (Eucken and Miksch), ordoliberal thinking was assimilated to Erhard and Müller-Armack's political syntheses, which marked a weakening of its original specificity. Therefore, the period of analysis in the book ends around 1950, with less interest in the dissemination of an intellectual heritage than in primarily reconstructing original ordoliberal ideas.

This presentation in three periods, from 1932 to 1950, is necessary to understand the constitution of ordoliberal thought. Nevertheless, this book will then offer a certain temporal coherence, justified by a demonstration of the centrality of the notion of power from the first to the last ordoliberal works.

### I.2.4 Crystallization of the Ordoliberal Project

This book gives a place of pride to the analysis of Walter Eucken's work, as his contributions played a central role in works by other ordoliberals and in the constitution of the ordoliberal political economy as a whole. In the search for a balanced approach, the book's narrative focuses on each member of the ordoliberal project.

In his *Foundations*, Eucken outlined a detailed scientific philosophy far beyond what any of the other ordoliberal authors contributed separately. In doing so, it is as though Eucken delivered a cornerstone of the *epistemological* and *theoretical* conceptions of ordoliberal thought as a whole. His students Friedrich Lutz (1940a, 1944, 1950) and Leonhard Miksch (1942, 1950b) confirmed this hypothesis, and the latter also specified that the *Foundations* were part of a

> joint work that has benefited from a rich mutual inspiration . . . through personalities involved for many years. Eucken did not build this community, and nothing would be more foreign to him. It has developed around him, like the crystal that represents the structure of the molecule that forms its nucleus. (Miksch 1950b, 289)

Thus, ordoliberalism was the result of a *crystallization* around a common project. Miksch mentioned that among these "personalities" not only the philosopher Edith Eucken-Erdsiek (Walter Eucken's wife), as well as Franz Böhm and Hans Großmann-Doerth, but also Friedrich Lutz, Karl

Friedrich Maier, Fritz Meyer, and himself were a part of this "circle." Hence others have claimed the *Foundations* as such; this book was also the product of the common spirit of Freiburg to a certain extent, to which everyone could then contribute in their own way, following—at least implicit—"divisions of labour" (Kolev 2017, 196–197). Outside the Freiburg school, Röpke (1942c, 1944a, 1963), Rüstow (1980), and, more unexpectedly, Stackelberg (1940, 1948), most enthusiastically welcomed Eucken's contributions.

If Eucken is the main character in this book's *dramatis personae*, Wilhelm Röpke is the other central figure and by far the most prolific ordoliberal author. His less systematic—but more comprehensive—views, coupled with an unparalleled sense of formula and the polemic, make Röpke's the strongest voice of ordoliberal ambitions for the social order as a whole.[15]

Certainly, ordoliberals do not constitute a "homogeneous group" (Young 2013, 38). However, non-homogeneity does not imply that each of these authors' individual contributions does not contribute to a common purpose that transcends their necessary heterogeneity. As André Piettre (1962, 339) noted, ordoliberalism exists in the "diverse expression of a common thought," and these diverse contributions to a *common project*—at times redundant, often complementary, and rarely contradictory—will emerge across this book. In short, to define ordoliberalism is to grasp what ordoliberals as a community of thought sought to achieve regarding a specific issue: the question of power, in this case. To meet this research goal means taking a new look at ordoliberalism vis-à-vis the current literature on the subject.

## I.3 COMPETING DEFINITIONS OF ORDOLIBERALISM

The growing literature on ordoliberalism invites two remarks. On the one hand, attempts to define ordoliberalism involve comparisons with other better-known schools of thought. On the other hand, these definitions provided in literature are heterogeneous, if not divergent. Although not mutually exclusive, the current definitions of ordoliberalism revolve

15. Röpke is the ordoliberal author who received the wider attention in the literature. For now, I shall only mention the three intellectual biographies in English (Zmirak 2001), German (Hennecke 2005), and French (Solchany 2015), as well as a recent collaborative volume that followed the 2016 symposium for the fiftieth anniversary of his death (Commun and Kolev 2018).

around three main interpretations: first, ordoliberalism as a part of the institutionalist paradigm; second, ordoliberalism as a kind of neoclassical synthesis; and finally, ordoliberalism as a variety of neoliberalism, and particularly as a variant of Austrian neoliberalism in the current prevailing interpretation.

According to the first interpretation, ordoliberalism consists of a comparative institutional approach to economic systems that parallels the French school of regulation (Labrousse and Weisz 2001). This form of comparative economics "starts from the thesis of the diversity of real economies" (Ananyin 2003, 6). Similarly, Karl Pribram had categorized ordoliberalism as an "organic economic science" (1983, 391). This first interpretation emphasizes what ordoliberal thought inherited from the German Historical Schools (Haarmann 2015; Peukert 2000; Schefold 1996, 2003).

The second interpretation maintains the institutionalist approach but instead focuses on a "synthesis of neoclassical and historical schools" (Priddat 2004, 71). This is what emerges from the work of Keith Tribe (1995): while offering a history of the various modalities of study of the economic and political order, from Cameralism to ordoliberalism, his work emphasized the ordoliberal use of neoclassical tools (Tribe 2001, 46; Hodgson 2001, 133). Following this argument, ordoliberalism is sometimes referred to as a "neo-institutionalism before the fact" (Bilger 1964, 117; Richter 2015); as a forerunner of "law and economics" (Grossekettler 1996; Nörr 1996, 2000; Yeager 2005; Hien and Joerges 2017); or as a "predecessor of the constitutional economy," according to Viktor Vanberg (1988, 1998, 2001; see also Leipold 1990). Vanberg described ordoliberalism as an "articulation of legal and economic perspectives," which "has as a common concern the constitutional foundations of an economy and a free society" (2006, 911). This last remark provides the basis for a transition from the second interpretation to the third.

The third interpretation specifies ordoliberalism's place within liberalism in general and within the neoliberal paradigm in particular. Eucken, Röpke, and the other ordoliberals participated in the Mont Pèlerin Society from its inception in 1947 as an integral part of the stories involved in the history of the "neoliberal thought collective" (Burgin 2012; Hartwell 1995; Mirowski and Plehwe 2009; Slobodian 2018; Walpen 2004). The literature examines the links and specificities of the ordoliberal approach within the various competing currents of ideas expressed by the Mont Pèlerin Society, of which Röpke (1961–1962) and Lutz (1964–1967) were presidents (Caré 2016; Kolev et al. 2020; Ptak 2009; Steiner and Walpen 2006).

Much of the recent work on ordoliberalism is engaged in a comparative study with Mises's and especially Hayek's views to clarify the link between ordoliberalism and Austrian economics.[16] Moreover, Hayek was a chair of economic policy at the University of Freiburg from 1961 until his retirement in 1967 (see Vanberg 2013). Scholars thus portray ordoliberalism as an "independent brand of liberal theory formation which can only be correctly understood and interpreted in the context of German-language traditions of economics and philosophy" (Goldschmidt 2013, 144). Undeniably, ordoliberals shared Mises's and Hayek's cultural background; yet, while common to some extent, Hayek in many ways does not deepen the Freiburg tradition so much as reorient it.[17]

Among the interpretations of ordoliberalism within neoliberalism, Michel Foucault's has received the most attention from social scientists. In *The Birth of Biopolitics* (2008), Foucault analyzed neoliberalism—or specifically, neoliberal "governmentality"—as "the way in which one conducts the conduct of men" (Foucault 2008, 186), as a government of life (hence the term "biopolitics"), and whose object is less the subject of law than the economic man, a rationally driven individual. Foucault devoted half his lessons to ordoliberalism before turning to the "entrepreneur of himself" model (Foucault 2008, 226), associated with Gary Becker's work and the Chicago School. In spite of a somewhat incomplete reading of the ordoliberals' original writings, Foucault offers a particularly penetrating analysis of Eucken's epistemology and suggests a remarkable interpretation of the ordoliberal as a project of society.[18] Foucault's ambition was less to understand ordoliberalism as such than to outline the transition from nineteenth-century classical-liberal governmental reason to a twentieth-century neoliberal government.[19]

Werner Bonefeld's *The Strong State and the Free Economy* (2017) was the first monograph exclusively devoted to ordoliberalism in a post-Foucauldian perspective. Bonefeld claimed that the ordoliberal argument would be less centered on economic policy and technique than on social control. Consequently, he contextualized ordoliberalism within the history of "authoritarian liberal thought" that goes from Benjamin Constant to

16. The literature is quite rich here (Biebricher 2014b; Blümle and Goldschmidt 2006; Bönker and Wagener 2001; Goldschmidt and Hesse 2013; Köhler and Kolev 2013; Kolev 2010, 2013, 2015; Kolev et al. 2020; Leen 2003; Meijer 2005; Nientiedt and Köhler 2016; Pongracic 1997; Wohlgemuth 2013; Wörsdörfer 2011, 2013b, 2014).

17. Erwin Dekker's perspective on *The Viennese Students of Civilization* (2016) offers new perspectives for discussions between Austrians and ordoliberals.

18. Critical reviews of the *Birth of Biopolitics* called into question Foucault's (lack of) first-hand use of primary sources (Lemke 2001; Tribe 2009; Wörsdörfer 2013a).

19. Following this Foucauldian heritage, François Denord (2007), Pierre Dardot and Christian Laval (2009), and Serge Audier (2008, 2012) have developed in many ways the French research on the history of neoliberal ideas, including ordoliberal ideas.

Carl Schmitt (Bonefeld 2017, 2). His perspective is chiefly that of political theory and political philosophy.[20]

By contrast, I aim at taking a step aside from the neoliberal perspective usually assigned to the ordoliberal authors. In my view, ordoliberalism is less a variety of neoliberalism than an original form of political economy—which is hardly saying that the ordoliberal discourse should be confined to the narrow disciplinary boundaries of economics, as this book will illustrate on various occasions. Previous studies finally gave too little place to ordoliberals' economic reasoning and how it took shape within public and academic debates of that time. However, this issue is crucial for two reasons. First, because it helps us to reconstruct the consistency that ties ordoliberal authors conceptually together. Second, it will also show that this paradigm, usually limited to an idiosyncratic Germanic framework, is actually in dialogue with the international developments of economic science.

This book will reexamine the Germanic context and heritage and its influence in the formation of an ordoliberal political economy, primarily through the reception of Karl Marx, Max Weber, Gustav von Schmoller, Werner Sombart, or Joseph A. Schumpeter. However, this study will also demonstrate that a certain international openness is necessary to rebuild the ordoliberal positioning in economics; this goes beyond a school of thought centered on national traditions, including works by Jean C. L. de Sismondi, Enrico Barone, Henry C. Simons, Oskar Lange, Edward Chamberlin, Joan Robinson, and John Maynard Keynes, among others.

The three main interpretations of the literature previously reviewed convey various definitions of ordoliberalism according to the authors and the works depicted in the analysis. Remarkably, the diversity of these definitions does not necessarily imply that some of them are flawed. Furthermore, observing ordoliberalism as a *political economy of power* will lead us to reconcile the apparent heterogeneity between the historicist-institutionalist and the neoclassical or liberal dynamics of ordoliberalism.

## I.4 TOWARD A POLITICAL ECONOMY OF POWER

Approaching ordoliberalism by considering it a "political economy" raises some concerns. It is neither a question of giving an approximate English translation of the expressions ordoliberals used in describing their own

20. See also the collective volume by Thomas Biebricher and Frieder Vogelmann (2017) and Biebricher's book on *The Political Theory of Neo-Liberalism* (2019).

discipline (such as *Nationalökonomie* or *Volkswirtschaftslehre*), nor of including ordoliberalism in the English (or French) tradition. "Political economy" seems to be the most appropriate term for the ordoliberal project and especially a broad study of the economic order in its relationship to society. In this perspective, political economy is less characterized by a technique or a specific set of tools than by an overall approach to the social sphere through the prism of economic issues.

As with liberalism, political economy is difficult to define. In contrast with the "scientific" or "analytical" character of economics, Schumpeter described political economy as a "comprehensive set of economic policies" built on a "certain unifying (normative) principles" that can "contain genuinely analytic work" (1954, 36). A certain tradition of thought belongs to political economy, as opposed to economics, if the following reasons are met. First, it admits that social, political, and other phenomena play a predominant role in the economy's functioning. Second, this tradition should place at the center of the relationships between actors a dynamic perspective of institutional change. Third, this tradition of thought reveals an interest in other social sciences and is not hostile to interdisciplinary reflections: political economy is a fundamentally *open* system (see Arena et al. 2009). Although the political economy is generally accompanied by a critical attitude toward economic theory thought as the only factor in explaining reality, it does not imply a rejection of all theoretical tools (Rothschild 1989). Thus defined, political economy has the advantage of not opposing or excluding economic theory, although it is considered as only one of its aspects, even if a central one.

As a political economy, ordoliberalism can be analyzed from four perspectives: it is an *epistemology* that specifies the canons of the formation of knowledge necessary to construct and interpret *economic theory*, which offers schemes of the causal and systematic relationships between different phenomena. From this point, the political economy aims to act on the existing state of affairs through an *economic policy* guided by theory. Finally, this logical sequence between epistemology, theory, and politics is conditioned by a vision of the world, a doctrine or more precisely what I call a "historical diagnosis."

The theme of power is also central to ordoliberal political economy. Referring to interwar ordoliberal thought, Franz Böhm observed that their main interest involves "the question of private power in a free society" (1957, 95). This objective was explicitly formulated in a contribution by K. Paul Hensel, Eucken's research assistant before the war. In *Ordo*'s fourth issue in the year following Eucken's death, Hensel noted:

> The general problem of order is thus determined by the role played by power—private or public—in people's ordinary life. Consequently, the antagonism of power must be the main subject of the whole theory of order (*Ordnungstheorie*), whose crucial problem consists in exploring how, in the face of this antagonism, the formation of equilibriums is thus possible within the political and economic relations between individuals. (Hensel 1951, 15)

The ordoliberals' keen interest in the theme of power is apparent in the semantic field mobilized in their works. The term "power" (*Macht*) can be found in a variety of forms in ordoliberal texts: economic power, monopolistic power, market power, the thirst for power, private and public power, power struggles, power groups and powerful groups, positions of power, the abuse of power, power constellations, power concentrations, and disempowerment.[21] These are a preview of the power-related terms that act as the basic grammar in this book.

In contrast to Max Weber, who defined power as the "ability of an individual or group to achieve their own goals or aims when others are trying to prevent them from realising them" (1956, 95), ordoliberals provided no explicit definition of power, whether economic, social, or political. This omission can be explained by the fact that power is itself the structuring issue of the ordoliberal political economy as a whole. All ordoliberal political economies can ultimately be read as an analysis of the power relationships in the economy and beyond:

> This word "power" has covered throughout the centuries, and in different parts of the world, widely varying facts, as has also the term "struggles for power." The economist's task is to get to grips with these facts, to distinguish them from one another, and to bring to light their economic and political effects. (Eucken 1940b, 272)

I suggest defining power from the ordoliberal perspective as *the capacity of an actor to determine the structure of a specific economic order*. Therefore, an individual—but most likely a group or an institution—has the power to *maintain* or *reshape* the economic process itself as well as the rules of the game, in local, national, or international contexts. This general definition preserves the heterogeneous nature of the sources of power, of its

21. In original German: *wirtschaftliche/ökonomische Macht, Monopolmacht, Marktmacht, Lust an Macht, private und öffentliche Macht, Machtkampf, Machtgruppen und machtvolle Gruppen, Machtposition, Machtstellung, Machtmißbrauch, Machtkonstellationen, Vermachtung, Machtballungen, Entmachtung.*

manifestations (whether intra- or extra-market), and of its consequences in the economic and political order (whether beneficial or harmful).

What I suggest and will try to show throughout this book is not merely that power was an important theme of research for the first ordoliberals. It is well known that Eucken, Böhm, Röpke, and the others dealt with questions of private and public powers, although the secondary literature explicitly dedicated to this theme is in fact quite scarce (Oswalt-Eucken 1994; Biebricher 2014b; Petersen 2019, chap. 2).[22] More essentially, I argue that the ordoliberals have built all the compartments of their political economy on the cornerstone of power issues and that this effort is precisely what makes the identity, unity, and originality of the old ordoliberal thinking. In the postwar period, the theme of power was gradually being overlooked by the next generation of ordoliberals.

Therefore, ordoliberalism is defined as a political economy of power because each of its elements—whether doctrinal, epistemological, theoretical, or political—confronts the notion of power. These four layers do not collectively address every aspect of ordoliberal thought but analyze it *as a whole*.

In Chapter 1 of the book, I will outline how ordoliberals have explored recent history through the lens of what can be called *institutional dynamics of power*. This ordoliberal doctrine or historical diagnosis was built around a causal link between historical liberalism in the nineteenth century and economic planning as developed in the first half of the twentieth century. Ordoliberals base their historical interpretation on an anthropological hypothesis in which the instinct to acquire power (or rent-seeking behaviors) is the driving force of mankind. To paraphrase Marx's famous formula, history for ordoliberals is the history of the struggles for economic power. In this sense, during its period of dominance, or roughly in the nineteenth century, historical liberalism pushed to the extreme its founding principles of economic freedom and state noninterference, leading to the general interest's subjection to private interests. Subsequently, the growing concentration of economic power after the First World War led the state's political and legislative decisions toward interventionism. In the final stage of the interwar period, planning completed this dynamic by centralizing economic power in the hands of the state, which largely took over production processes, the allocation of resources, and the distribution of income.

22. Pia Becker and Julian Dörr (2016) build on the ordoliberal analysis to develop a more comprehensive concept of power.

Rather than reflecting on the conditions that developed a competitive market economy, the ordoliberals analyzed what they perceived as the deleterious effects of certain types of economic systems (such as laissez-faire liberalism) for the entire political and social order. Therefore, ordoliberalism reflected on the link between the economic order and political models. This connection was decisive not only for the economy's function, but also because of its resilience in the face of private economic power.

In Chapter 2, I show that power to ordoliberals is the *source of an epistemological problem*. Eucken attempted to scientifically understand the driving forces underlying the economic order, or what he called the "actual economic reality" (*wirtschaftliche Wirklichkeit*). His ambition rested on a method to escape the given and immediate aspects of this reality, which seemed contaminated by vested interests. Thus, Eucken updated the old German methodological quarrel (*Methodenstreit*) with the intent not to settle the dispute between Gustav Schmoller and Carl Menger at the end of the nineteenth century but to overcome the terms of a debate he considered inconsistent with his epistemological problem. Eucken perceived Menger's dualist and a priori method as having lost all connection with reality in a theoretical monologue indifferent to the problem of economic power. Alternatively, Schmoller's empiricist method led him to a collection of facts contaminated by the opinions of the persons concerned, and therefore, Schmoller's understanding would depend on underlying struggles for power.

To resolve the great antinomy between theory and history, Eucken suggested articulating these two approaches by means of his theory of orders. Eucken aimed to apply theoretical analysis to the economic uses and abuses of power but without falling under the influence of the expression of vested interests.

In Chapter 3, I will highlight the sense in which power was an *essential object of the ordoliberal economic theory*. Ordoliberals studied the manifestations of power through the lens of the economic plan. This conceptual representation of economic action based on a set of theoretical and historical constraints allowed ordoliberals to arrive at an ideal-typical dichotomy between two economic orders at a macroeconomic level: a centrally administered economy on the one hand, and an economy of exchange on the other. With these two ideal-types, Eucken built a more refined typology according to the directions of the economic process, price mechanisms, legal property, the cooperation between firms and households, and the monetary system. Constructing this "morphological" theory led Eucken to take a stand relative to two of the discipline's great international discussions in the interwar years: the feasibility of a socialist calculation and the debate over imperfect or monopolistic market structures. The theoretical substance of these two debates closely relates to a political quest for the stability of the economic and social order.

The centrally administered economy is characterized by the strong influence of what ordoliberals perceived as illegitimate powers in the economic process. However, ordoliberals considered that markets within the exchange economy system itself were not free from power relations. This is precisely why Eucken offered a taxonomy based on twenty-five market structures ranging from a bilateral monopoly to full competition. Eucken also relied on the results of the mathematical economics of his time. Therefore, Stackelberg's contribution to an analysis of market structures without equilibrium, including oligopolies and bilateral monopolies, is indispensable in understanding the ordoliberals' literary marginalism.[23]

In Chapter 4, I analyze the ordoliberal political perspective and how ordoliberals formulated a new *social question* based on the collapse of human freedom and autonomy under rising private and public economic powers. Thus, ordoliberals regarded the dispersion of economic power within the economic process as key to overcoming this social question. Finding an answer to the social question required the institution and perpetuation of the competitive order by a strong state. Thus, the ordoliberal *economic policy aims to disperse economic power*. Ordoliberals considered competition as a formidable tool in disempowering private economic power and in regulating the social body. Tracing the various manifestations of economic power led ordoliberals to consider a broad program of economic and social policies that should be politically implemented by a strong state.

Constitutional principles should act as preventive measures to avoid the rise of private power, such as through monopolies or cartels. However, the dynamics of economic concentration could not be entirely prevented even when the economy tended toward a competitive order due to rent-seeking behaviors. This is why a permanent supervision of the economic order was always necessary to tame arbitrary power relationships. Ultimately, the ordoliberals imagined an Office of Competition Control that would compel monopolistic actors to behave in a manner analogous to that of an effectively competitive situation; this idea shaped the European Union's current antitrust law. With minimized economic power, individuals would be

23. This third chapter is by far the most extensive of the book. The reason for this sustained attention is twofold. First, although economic theory is only one aspect of a political economy, it is undeniably the heart of it. Second, and more importantly, the ordoliberal approached to economic theory has been neglected by the secondary literature in favor of more directly political themes.

both promoters of and subject to an expression of the volonté générale that directs the production process through consumer choices. The price system's proper functioning would limit both the individual and governmental capacity to shape the rules of the game over time. For ordoliberals, this set of constraints was a source of the greatest individual freedom compatible with a market economy and the key to solve the "new" social question.

The first and fourth chapters of this book adopt a transverse perspective relative to ordoliberals' contributions. In contrast, the two central chapters on the epistemological and theoretical dimensions of ordoliberalism more specifically address Eucken's contributions, which we recognize as essential to ordoliberalism as a whole. The last chapter builds on the systematic definition of the ordoliberal political economy to no longer directly question the *nature*, but rather the ordoliberal *posture* in the political context of the postwar period and how it has competed with the rise of mixed European economies.

Indeed, in Chapter 5, the last chapter of this book, I outline ordoliberal discourse in the early postwar period (1946–1950) and how it has gained traction on the political stage. I will also show that the ordoliberals sought to establish a *continuity* between the Nazis' economic order and the Western Allies' administration, and thereby confronted political authorities with the fact that proper denazification could succeed only if the Nazis' planning methods were rejected. This argument has been reconstructed around various kinds of documentation, including advisory reports, newspaper and magazine articles, and academic publications. Ultimately, the chapter contributes to not only restoring original ordoliberal ideas, and especially their critical scope, but also to providing a better knowledge of competing ideologies in an early Cold War context.

# CHAPTER 1
# From the Ashes of the Western Liberal Order

It might be too bold to claim that ordoliberals' insights regarding trends in the Western liberal order conveyed a historical philosophy per se, but this expression captures the spirit of ordoliberals' intentions. However, I suggest that ordoliberals formulated a "historical diagnosis," or a historical interpretation of the present that aims to reveal its ills and how to cure them.[1] The historical diagnostic shaped by Eucken and Röpke, among others, rested on an *institutional dynamic of power* because such power was the central factor in ordoliberals' explaining the transition from a primarily liberal economic order to planned systems in Western societies in general and in Germany in particular.

Ordoliberal literature is rooted in the economic, political, and legal events of the interwar period. The primary factors at this time include the cartelization of the German economy, a crisis involving parliamentary representative systems, and the development of the state's economic activities during a period of hyperinflation (1921–1924) and the Great Depression (1929–1932). However, the ordoliberal historical diagnosis aimed to encompass the modern era from the late eighteenth century. Ordoliberals perceived these interwar issues as the manifold factors of a generalized social crisis. Overall, this phenomenon would simultaneously affect all Western societies, albeit to varying degrees. Furthermore, it concerned the political, economic, and social spheres—and even the moral and

1. I borrow here the expression that Aurélien Berlan (2012) forged in his study on cultural criticism (*Kulturkritik*) and the founders of German sociology (Ferdinand Tönnies, Georg Simmel, and Max Weber).

*A Political Economy of Power*. Raphaël Fèvre, Oxford University Press. © Oxford University Press 2021.
DOI: 10.1093/oso/9780197607800.003.0002

spiritual—in organic relationships of mutual interdependence on domestic and international scales (Röpke 1942b). The generalized social crisis was ultimately considered a crisis of civilization, or a crisis of modernity itself marked by "massification" (*Vermassung*) and the loss of moral and religious values (nihilism), which exacerbated nationalism and the "will to power." Although this crisis is thematically and particularly present in works by both Wilhelm Röpke and Alexander Rüstow, it also infused ordoliberal reading altogether (Commun 2014; Fèvre 2015; Wörsdörfer 2014).

Given the scale and originality of the phenomenon described by the ordoliberals, the need for a new analytical framework to inform economic policy seemed imperative:

> The fast rise of technological progress, industrialisation, massification, and urbanisation is forcing us to pose economic policy problems differently. Yesterday's ideas are old and outdated. There is a gap between reality and economic policy ideologies, and appreciating this gap is vital to the success of economic policy. (Eucken 1951, 28)

At this stage, we are less interested in the symptoms of the crisis than in the causal explanations ordoliberals provided. Ordoliberals draw explanatory factors from the analysis of past and present European political and economic systems: particularly the "laissez-faire" liberalism of the nineteenth century and the planned economies of the first part of the twentieth century, whether in their Soviet, fascist, or, especially, national-socialist forms.

Ordoliberals have discussed their predecessors (such as Smith, Marx, and Schmoller) and contemporaries (Sombart, Schumpeter, or Keynes) in a similar perspective to Karl Marx, who sought in the English political economy a reflection of the state of capitalist relations. Eucken clearly evidenced this in his "Digressions on Ideologies," which closed his 1932 founding article entitled "Structural Transformations of the State and the Crisis of Capitalism." In this article, Eucken stated the following:

> Major historical processes are always accompanied by ideologies that wish to seem good and sensible. So it was with the reconstruction of the international system of states and the domestic state structure, whose decisive impact upon on the current situation of capitalism in the old capitalist countries was wrapped in ideologies that sought to justify and promote it. (Eucken 1932b, 69)

Despite the Marxist-like (materialist) formulation Eucken assumes in this passage, it is the last aspect of *promotion* or *encouragement* that takes precedence in an ordoliberal analysis. Thus, and in contradiction to Marxism, economic discourse occurred less as a legitimization of real conditions than as its architect. Accordingly, the ordoliberals considered that they must first and foremost win the "battle of ideas" to change the existing state of affairs. In the first half of the thirties, Röpke wrote many articles to invalidate the assumptions—and therefore, the political recommendations—of the theories of economic imperialism (1933, 1934b), fascist corporate economics (1935), and romantic socialism (1936b, 1936c).

Drawing parallels with Marx is not merely conjecture, as ordoliberals designated him a primary opponent in the context of the interwar period through his modern followers such as Sombart and Schumpeter. Ultimately, the ordoliberals aimed to intellectually resist what they called scholars' "anti-capitalist attitude," which found a particularly fruitful relay in the public opinion of the "masses" (Eucken 1932b, 58; see also 1932a, 1933; Röpke 1935, 85). Ordoliberal accusations lay less in the fact that planning would constitute a harmful application of Marxist principles than in the propagation of a mentality that eased its development. This is also what the ordoliberals described as a "relativist" and "fatalistic" intellectual attitude (Böhm et al. 1936, 18).[2] However, the final analysis indicates that the root causes of the rise of interventionism and economic planning are to be found in the inherent weaknesses of nineteenth-century liberalism and the idea of natural harmony that the Classics would have spread. In line with the central claim of this book, the starting point for the ordoliberal historical diagnosis must be sought in an analysis of power relations. As Eucken (1940b, 263) claimed, "to understand (*Verstehen*) the actual economic reality of the past, present, and probably throughout the future," it is necessary to "understand economic power and to perceive the striking uniformities in the processes of groups fighting for economic power."

## 1.1 AN ANTHROPOLOGY OF POWER

The economist's view of individual behavior is typically limited to a utilitarian optimizing calculation. However, ordoliberals' perceptions of human behavior were also based on an anthropological hypothesis, in that individuals are driven by a compelling lust for power.

2. The relativist or fatalistic approach was also directly related to the question of economic power since Böhm (1961, 36) considered a form of disciplinary bias: "doctrines that emphasize the study of historical development laws will tend to encourage the concentration of power, whereas the search for structural connections tends to favour a tendency towards greater freedom."

### 1.1.1 The Individual Lust for Power

Ordoliberals posited that the central principle of mankind involved a desire to acquire power. Thus, the struggle for power can be considered a driving force in the historical process. Furthermore, Eucken did not ask the question from a specific economic perspective, but within a global historical outlook:

> The pursuit of power is a vital instinct of man. At the same time, it is a larger and more constructive historical force. Sometimes at the service of a higher value. Often, however, the lust for power (*Lust an Macht*) is itself the origin of the will to power (*Willens zur Macht*). Frequently, the strongest individual is precisely the one who disregards moral and legal principles. (Eucken 1940c, 479)

Eucken borrowed Nietzsche's expression and embraced a perspective opened by the ideas of Schopenhauer and Spencer. As the first part of the quotation indicates, the quest for power can also lead to positive social outcomes. Moreover, what Röpke (1942b, 167) called the "natural conflict of interests" between producers and consumers, but also among producers within competitive markets, enables impersonal coordination through market mechanisms, in line with classic liberal views.

However, this "lust for power" for ordoliberals simultaneously involved the condition of possibility and the endogenous degenerative principle of a liberal market economy. In this sense, the search for rent and market power positions was a fundamental feature of the modern period and an instinct that the ordoliberal political economy had to address. Indeed, Eucken (1949, 222) stressed that there was "always" and "wherever possible" an "omnipresent, strong and irrepressible urge to eliminate competition and to acquire a monopolistic position." Concluding that "everyone espies possibilities of becoming a monopolist" (Eucken 1949, 222; see also Röpke 1942d, 169; Böhm 1947, 134). As individuals focused on their particular interests—and by doing so violated morality, freedom, and justice from an ordoliberal perspective—they undermined the foundations of a competitive order that safeguarded the general interest.

In ordoliberal thought, individuals' "lust for power" is a primary acting historical force. According to Eucken (1951, 38), "History was full of abuses of power. The possession of power causes arbitrary actions, threatens the freedom of individuals, and destroys mature and good orders." However, ordoliberals' perceptions of mankind were not solely reduced to an essentialist quest for power because their humanist (Kantian) and religious values

(Protestant, in particular) forbid such radical judgments.[3] Since the search for power is the central explanatory factor in the ordoliberal historical diagnosis, the ordoliberals sought to make their contemporaries aware of the fact that political, broadly institutional, and even ideological conditions can lead to particular individual behaviors among manifold potentialities. As Röpke noted, man would be "a crystal, whose feelings, instincts, and passions are the innumerable facets, some positive, some negative, some contributing to social integration and others to social disintegration, and which glitter *according to the feeling appealed by the circumstances*" (Röpke 1942d, 94, emphasis added).

Therefore, the individual's "lust for power" less involves an immutable essence of mankind than a normative principle that manifests itself as an adequate, valued, and gradually selected behavior. It emerges from ordoliberal works that the individual has been encouraged to seek his own interests and "abandon himself to the demon of his passion" (Böhm et al. 1936, 23). However, as long as this instinct is confined to the individual level, the compelling force of the competitive economic order prevails: the process of degeneration is initiated when a coalition of interests exists within groups. As Eucken (1951, 33) stressed, "group selfishness" rather than individual selfishness was at the center of the ordoliberals' interpretation of power relations.

### 1.1.2 Economic Concentration and Struggles for Power

According to the ordoliberals, the increasing concentration of economic power was a fundamental aspect of German economic history since the beginning of the twentieth century. This trend occurred due to "the increased importance of large companies, giant industries and monopolies of all kinds" (Röpke 1942b, 179; see also Eucken 1951, 31). Therefore, analyzing these "power groups" was an essential scientific task that Eucken believed was often neglected in academic studies. Historians and economists alike "seem always unable to appreciate how much economic history was full of brutal power struggles" (Eucken 1940b, 263–264).

From the economic theory perspective, economic power overlaps the market power resulting from specific supply or demand structures—such as monopolies, duopolies, or oligopolies, among others—which will be further discussed in Chapter 3. Röpke and Rüstow posited that companies' size

3. On ordoliberalism as a Kantian ethic, see François Bilger (1964, 126–131), Patricia Commun (2016, 77–78, 297–299), and Manuel Wörsdörfer (2010, 2013a).

was an inherent economic factor in firms' power, while Eucken perceived this as simply one among several explanatory factors, without any indication of necessity. In the political sphere, economic power groups then constrained and influenced the course of parliamentary or governmental decisions. Lobbying would ipso facto divert political institutions from their missions of general interest.

Politically, it was essential for discourse on the neoliberal anti-monopoly to clearly identify the origin of monopolies' formation: are they born from state action, or are they rather "spontaneous" structures that resulted from the competitive economic process itself? This question arose during the 1938 Walter Lippmann Colloquium (WLC) held in Paris.[4] Two contradictory positions were presented in a session entitled "Is the decline of liberalism due to endogenous causes?" that excluded a consensus among neoliberals. On the one hand, the French entrepreneur and essayist Auguste Detœuf argued that the concentration of companies and emergence of monopolies were phenomena intrinsic to the logic of liberalism as it has historically developed. On the other hand, Ludwig von Mises (see also 1949, 385, 716–717) claimed that only exogenous state action promoted the creation of cartels and monopolies. Therefore, the category of power was not analytically relevant without state intervention in Mises's conceptualization of the market economy, as Kolev (2013) stressed.

Röpke and Rüstow's positions in this debate were ambiguous. Even within his own books, Röpke mentions the inevitable development of monopolies while simultaneously noting the state's predominant role in the concentration of companies (1936a, 8; 1942b, 302; 1944a, 272). According to Röpke, concentration did not necessarily follow a logic of efficiency but was instead the result of internal and irrational psychological motives: size, power, and/or external political interference. The latter involved the artificial establishment of certain monopolies and indirectly misguided legislation, such as tariffs, quotas, and anti-bankruptcy laws, or those relative to patent, cartel, and public limited company laws. Similarly, Eucken pointed out that this concentration resulted from a mixture of "the pursuit of power, the tendency towards monopoly formation, and economic and legislative policy" (1950b, 13).

Ordoliberal literature presents two separate types of economic concentration. On the one hand, different firms could be legally and financially centralized under the same principal's authority, whether a natural or legal

4. Eucken was unable to attend the Colloquium to which he had been invited, probably because of the growing closure of the Third Reich's borders (see Kolev et al. 2020, 436). The proceedings of the WLC are available in English (see Reinhoudt and Audier 2017).

person, which gives rise to a monopoly (Röpke 1944a, 272). Therefore, this first type of concentration is characterized by the fact that "many works are carried out under a common direction" (Eucken 1950b, 10) following both a horizontally and vertically concentrated logic. This legal and financial centralization would be less an economic phenomenon than a managerial process of collecting productive forces under the same leadership of vertical and/or horizontal integration. On the other hand, the "internal technical centralisation of an operating unit" involved the question of firms' size (Röpke 1944a, 273). A technical concentration can follow a logic of efficiency, such as capital and technological progress, but Röpke insisted that firms had excessively grown beyond their optimal size; he posited that this explained why firms widely invested "the company's savings to self-finance its facilities beyond the limit set by the interest rate that would have been paid if the same capital had to be raised on the market" (Röpke 1942d, 229).

Regardless of whether ordoliberals perceived a company's monopolistic nature and size as two different phenomena, they are nevertheless linked as both phenomena are rooted in the desire to stabilize and acquire economic power. Furthermore, the surest way to eliminate any competitive threat involved conducting a "monopolistic war strategy," or absorbing other economic units to form trusts (Böhm 1961, 40–41). Here, Böhm highlighted an important point: it was less the concrete exploitation of a monopolistic power (e.g., through generating excessive profits) than the struggle for economic power (rent-seeking behaviors and their accompanying dynamic processes) that posed the most significant threat to the constitutional order and the democratic system. To an extent, the ordoliberals considered this struggle toward the monopoly as a social cost, or the destruction of value at the expense of efficiency as well as individual freedoms and eventually the democratic system.

The following section will demonstrate that the ordoliberal positioning followed a logic of criticism against deleterious liberal principles, distant from the more sympathetic appreciation of nineteenth-century liberalism that can be found in works by Hayek or Mises, for instance. Rüstow ferociously described the latter as a "paleo-liberal" in the margins of the WLC.[5] However, the intellectual critique of capitalism was occupied by historicism, close to Marxism. Thus, ordoliberals opposed Marxist views on the process of concentration, in that the emergence of monopolies, cartels, and

5. This pejorative term was later extended by Rüstow and Röpke to some of the Mont Pèlerin Society's members (Audier 2013, 19; Burgin 2012, 137). About the relationships between Mises and ordoliberals in general, see Stefan Kolev (2018a).

company mergers originated in the development of production techniques or, specifically, in the rise of technological progress inherent in the growth of capitalism.

### 1.1.3 Technical Progress as an Antagonistic Factor to Concentration

Eucken's article "Technique, Concentration, and Order of the Economy" ("*Technik, Konzentration und Ordnung der Wirtschaft*") was published in the 1950 issue of the journal *Ordo*. This article clarified the ordoliberal positioning in terms of a historical interpretation of capitalism's development relative to the theme of technological progress.[6] Furthermore, Eucken denied any causal link between the modern technological boom and the deterioration of competitive economic relations; therefore, he opposed the thesis that "the concentration of production and economic power derives from modern technology, and that with it the need for competition in the modern economy disappears" (Eucken 1950b, 4). This law of concentration was formulated in the wake of work by Sismondi, the Saint-Simonians, and Marx and is reflected in Schumpeter's contemporary writings.[7] This thesis, Eucken stressed, was also widespread in civil society and led to a political justification for cartel formation, ad hoc interventionism, and, ultimately, central planning. For ordoliberals, a causal relationship existed between concentration and competition, but, unlike Schumpeter's reading, technological development would drive competitive markets to evolve against monopolistic concentration. For Röpke (1936a, 7), it was clear that "the recent development in the technique of machinery has, in many directions, exerted even a lowering influence on the optimum size" of firms (see also Eucken 1950b, 5–6).

First, technological progress—and particularly in transport and telecommunications—has led to a decrease in the geographical distances between markets and, therefore, to a decrease in the local monopoly's power.

6. This text was also part of Eucken's posthumous book *Principles of Economic Policy* (1952, 225–240).

7. In essence, Marx's idea was that competition led to accumulation and thus to monopoly (large land ownership)—the completed form of the capitalist market economy—in a dialectical process (1844, 103). In *The Poverty of Philosophy* (1847), Marx noted that "competition was originally the opposite of monopoly and not monopoly the opposite of competition. So that the modern monopoly is not a simple antithesis, it is on the contrary the true synthesis. . . . Thus modern monopoly, bourgeois monopoly, is synthetic monopoly, the negation of the negation, the unity of opposites. It is the monopoly in the pure, normal, rational state" (206–207).

This phenomenon has functioned at the local, national, and even supranational levels by shaping a "*virtually*" unified global market (Röpke 1942d, 14, emphasis in original). Specifically, the labor market has experienced a thorough change in its structure. As Eucken (1950b, 6) noted, "workers now have the opportunity to choose from a large number of employees" and concluded that "competition, once rare in this field, is alive and well."

Second, Eucken (1950b) observed an intensification of "substitution competition," which resulted in a high elasticity of demand to the price of market goods. Consequently, even if a market structure was monopolistic, the possibility of substituting one good for another placed the monopoly in a situation similar to that of competitive markets. This type of substitution competition was chiefly encouraged by the emergence of new raw materials, such as plastics, petrochemicals, and textiles.

Third, technological progress resulted in greater adaptability in production. The faculty to adjust production must be defined, according to Eucken (1950b, 7) as "the ability for a company to transfer its production from one market to another." Although fixed costs increased in the modern period, this does not mean that it was impossible to reorient capital. On the contrary, for Eucken (1950b, 9), "fixed costs" did not coincide with "fixed production," and the German experience of rapidly reorienting capital for military purposes has reinforced him in this view.[8] While "the tension between growing competition and its opponents was a fundamental fact of recent economic history" (Eucken 1950b, 16), it is nevertheless necessary to discover the historical foundations of this tension. Based on the three previously mentioned arguments, the ordoliberals rejected an explanation of technological change in favor of one linked to the industrial dynamics of concentration, which had important effects on forming the political-economic order.

## 1.2 FROM HISTORICAL LIBERALISM TO ECONOMIC PLANNING: THE OTHER STORY OF THE GREAT TRANSFORMATION

The ordoliberal anthropology of power leads one to identify an institutional dynamic with a global explanatory scope, and thus, the following section

8. Already in the early thirties, Eucken (1932b) remarked that technological progress, innovation, and the emergence of new goods led to sudden changes in demand patterns as a result of increased competition (particularly in the machine processing, metal, precision engineering, textile, clothing, and food industries).

restores the ordoliberal narrative regarding this historical process. It is marked by a shift from the nineteenth century's politically and economically liberal attitude to the interventionism and economic planning that developed in the first part of the twentieth century. Ordoliberals discerned three successive periods (Eucken 1932b, 1951; Röpke 1942d). The mercantilist era of the seventeenth and eighteenth centuries was followed by a liberal age from 1815 to 1914, then by a stage of contemporary political experimentation that began in 1919. The following focuses on a two-phase presentation highlighting the transitions from one era to the other in general and the case of Germany in particular.

### 1.2.1 Historical Liberalism, Laissez-Faire, and the Crisis of Capitalism

The study of liberalism or capitalism particularly resonates in German circles. Following the writings of List, Marx, or the historical schools,[9] the ordoliberals were part of a long critical tradition, differentiated by their efforts to preserve the spirit of liberalism while radically dissociating themselves from its historical development.

Although Eucken sometimes used the term "capitalism" (*Kapitalismus*) in his writings, he was incredibly suspicious about this concept because he perceived capitalism as a false concept ideologically masking reality rather than revealing it. The notion of capitalism rested only on "a great historical fact"—the Industrial Revolution—which gradually spread to all economies worldwide (Eucken 1940b, 93). The problem with the term "capitalism" was that scholars hypostatically used it; capitalism essentially became a "personified substance" with its own properties of action, like a true and acting "living being" (Eucken 1940b, 330, n. 23). Again, Eucken found this attitude in certain scientific perspectives, such as those expressed by Marxists, Sombart, and Schumpeter, which were even more problematically infused in public opinion.

However, ordoliberals perceived economics as one of several factors that determine all realities of society, whether religious, social, or political. On the contrary, they believed the economy must be incorporated into a global process as simply one element included in relationships of equivalence and

9. By the end of the nineteen century, German academics widely rejected liberalism and socialism back to back. Contrary to the immediate impression, authors attached to the Socialism of the Chair (*Kathedersozialismus*), however, did not hesitate to distinguish themselves openly from the two programs, as Schmoller did (Nau 2000, 509).

interdependence. In this sense, the rejection of the capitalist concept was tantamount to rejecting Marxist materialism. Ordoliberals aimed at a multifactorial analysis of historical change:

> The phenomenon called today the "crisis of capitalism" can only be explained in a historical-universal perspective coupled with the analysis of *economic orders (Denken in Wirtschaftsordnungen).*[10] The vast revolution in economic forms which we are experiencing cannot be understood *simply* economically. . . . To enquire about the essence of "capitalism" is to frame the question unhistorically and far too narrowly. It is still more unhistorical to believe in some compelling process of development of the essence of capitalism. (Eucken 1940b, 95–97, emphasis in original)

Therefore, Eucken perceived the concept of capitalism as too reductive insofar as it ignores or refuses the influence of other spheres of society within the overall process. However, the concept is simultaneously too indeterminate as it does not accurately reflect the structures or forms of economic reality (e.g., if the economy is managed by competitive, monopolistic, or state-run processes). Eucken (1940b, 330) concluded that "concepts like 'capitalism' or 'socialism' are no substitute for the morphological study of the real economic world." From this perspective, let us now examine how the ordoliberals analyzed the development of the liberal period.

In the same vein as Eucken, Röpke also belittled the term "capitalism," which he considered too vague. Equally careful not to simplify it, Röpke defined capitalism as the "historical form of the market economy, or rather the overall historical combination in which it occurred in the nineteenth and twentieth centuries, but not to characterise the principle of order of the market economy as such" (Röpke 1944a, 33). Accordingly, Röpke (1942b) spoke of "*historische Liberalismus*," or "historical liberalism," which encompasses a particular experience while going beyond the empirical connotation of the term "capitalism."

The ordoliberals' denying of the term "capitalism" must be grasped through their opposition to historicism. Sombart's book *Der moderne Kapitalismus* helped to spread the use of the word at the turn of the century, although he did not coin the phrase. In line with all ordoliberals, Röpke understood historical liberalism as the market economy's material form in the nineteenth century, which for him approximated the laissez-faire approach

10. Literally "thinking in economic orders," i.e., thinking reality through the theory of orders (Böhm 1950).

assimilating the Manchester School's doctrine and utilitarianism. This also meant first and foremost "economic freedom, i.e. freedom of the market system based upon predominant competition" (Rüstow 1942, 268).

Ordoliberals perceived this laissez-faire liberalism as deviating from the original liberal doctrine formulated by Alexis de Tocqueville and Adam Smith. To some extent, the terms "capitalism," "*historical* liberalism," or "laissez-faire" ultimately tend to merge into ordoliberal writings and therefore are synonymous. These terms refer to different aspects of the same principles of economic organization and functioning that dominated European countries from 1815 to 1914. Thus, how did ordoliberals understand the relationship between the state and the market in the laissez-faire era? In short, what are the characteristics of this liberal period as it has historically developed? Eucken contradicted standard interpretations by insisting on legal support for the economic activities that "laissez-faire" liberalism promoted:

> It is usually said to have been a period of economic freedom from state influence . . . but this view is completely wrong. The early twentieth century was, in fact, a period when the state introduced legislation strictly defining and limiting the rights property, contract and association, as well as laws governing patents and copyright. At that time Germany, like other states, possessed a constitution designed to create an efficient machinery of state and to protect individual freedom. . . . The daily workings of every firm and household proceeded within the framework of legal norms laid down by the state, whether it was a question of buying or selling, being granting credit or engaging a worker. (Eucken 1951, 29)

What Eucken does not mention in this excerpt is that defining laissez-faire as a state governed by the rule of law (*Rechtsstaat*) also highlights this single approach's inadequacy in the state's role in a liberal market economy. Therefore, it was appropriate for ordoliberal thinking to determine "the truth and error in the liberal dogma of the automatic harmony of interests" (Röpke 1942b, 169).

While maintaining certain fundamental liberal principles, the ordoliberals sought to update liberalism, which required a distancing from liberalism as it has historically been achieved. Röpke insisted on one aspect that was widely accepted among ordoliberals: that they should not be "dogmatically tied to the economic programme of historical liberalism" as it is "not really possible to ignore the fact that the collapse of the liberal-capitalist world order was to no little extent also caused by its own deficiencies, misdirected developments and perversions" (Röpke 1942b,

142). As such, the ordoliberal project must be analyzed as a "fundamental revision" of liberal principles to inform the "renaissance of liberalism" in its political, ethical, and economic dimensions (Rüstow 1942, 278; see also Röpke 1944a, 33).

## 1.2.2 Grandeur and Misery of the Liberal Era

### *1.2.2.1 The Separation of the State and Commercial Spheres*

In Eucken's view, the mercantilist period resulted in the emergence of a dissociation—which induces a specification and rationalization of relations—between the spheres of the modern state and that of society (*Gesellschaft*). While this distinction was still fragile and imperfect, it developed according to a paradoxical historical trend that Eucken outlined: following the French Revolution, the "democratization" (*Demokratisierung*) of nation-states strengthened the individual's power over the state through universal suffrage, from which the state subsequently derived "new possibilities for the extension of its power" (1932b, 55). Nevertheless, the state has remained essentially absent from the economic sphere and from the market economy in its capitalist form, and particularly due to the influence of the precepts of separating—and restricting—powers at the center of the emerging political liberalism.

Nevertheless, some powerful groups in both the mercantilist and liberal eras forced the state to intervene in favor of their partisan interests through parliamentary assemblies. Furthermore, ordoliberals noted that "on a very large scale massive groups of economic power emerged, and these groups shaped the law (*Recht*) in a completely unilateral way" during the nineteenth century (Böhm et al. 1936, 17). On this point, one can find congruencies between the ordoliberal perspective and Adam Smith's.[11] Moreover, in *The Wealth of Nations*, Smith focused on the commercial sphere's deleterious influence on politics, therein increasing the spirit of conquest. Smith (1776, IV.iii.2) also mentioned the "spirit of monopoly," but this was not at the center of individual behavior as ordoliberals saw it; rather, Smith used it to specifically describe the "mean rapacity [and] the monopolising spirit of merchants and manufacturers," and especially in the context of the mercantilist period.

11. Several papers offer a comparison between Smith's ideas and that of the ordoliberals (Sally 1996; Klump and Wörsdörfer 2010; Bonefeld 2013a; Horn 2019).

Despite economic interests' influence on politics, the ordoliberals believed that the separation initiated in the mercantilist era between the state and economic spheres, which partially continued in the liberal age, was still firmly sealed. Therefore, this lobbying remained marginal at that time. In the nineteenth century—which was also identified as the "great liberal century"—international trade stability was predominant and ensured by peaceful diplomatic relations and formal and informal institutions prevailing between states through treaties and certain tacit rules. These conditions of cosmopolitan foreign policy in the sense of Kant provided a prosperous framework for the multiplication of trade, capital movements, and international divisions of labor (Eucken 1932b, 63–65; Röpke 1942d, 73–74). For the ordoliberals, it was subsequently England's international domination—the *Pax Britannica* (1815–1870)—that considerably contributed to capitalism's vigorous development in terms of increased wealth and industrial development, although Germany experienced this fallout later, beginning in 1850.[12]

### 1.2.2.2 *The Natural Harmony of the Classics Challenged*

Ordoliberals perceived the possibility of a new liberal agenda only through a distancing from historical liberalism. It is worth emphasizing the attention and scope with which ordoliberals have pursued this endeavor throughout their writings, as it is a part of their historical diagnosis. The first liberal authors were concerned with encouraging the dissolution of old feudal social structures to replace them with market relations, which were considered more egalitarian and therefore more just. The ordoliberals' beliefs highly paralleled the idea that "a free enterprise regime was necessary for a free, prosperous, and equitable society" (Van Horn 2009, 210). However, they noted that some liberal principles have undermined the foundations of the social order on which they were originally built. As such, Röpke replicated the reasoning he considered mistaken:

> The competitive market appeared to be a "philosopher's stone," which turned the base metal of callous business sentiments into the pure gold of common welfare and solidarity; social wisdom and morality were the surprising products

12. The *Pax Britannica* marked the British international domination in the military, political, and commercial fields. This domination resulted in certain advantages that are characteristic of peace periods, as, for instance, the development of trade, the spread of humanist and Christian values and education, etc. (see Gough 2014, 1–3).

> of countless individual actions not primarily commanded by either; and private vices were turned into public virtues. (Röpke 1942d, 67)

Röpke's last formula clearly referred to the subtitle of Bernard Mandeville's *Fable* (1714). From an ordoliberal perspective, the classics and their successors were wrong to consider the competitive market as a sociologically and politically autonomous institution. The market depends on its framework, which consequently influences and modifies it, as Rüstow (1942, 274) emphasized. However, the market could not provide the extra-economic framework of the moral and institutional conditions necessary for its function, nor was it able to spontaneously generate adequate economic regulations and particularly state regulations. Both shortcomings are particularly visible in Germany's national system as well as in international monetary systems (Miksch 1948, 322).

Therefore, laissez-faire have led to the destruction of economic freedom, in contradiction to its original objectives, due to currency fluctuations, the rationing of a productive supply, and inadequate labor legislation. The ordoliberals unanimously opined that historical liberalism had seminally failed as it did not seize the differences in nature between the internal mechanics of individual interactions (the process) and the "rules of the game" (*Spielregeln*) that govern this process:

> This was the mistake made in the principles and policies of the laissez-faire society or the free economy in the old style: It left both the battle for establishing the rules of the game, the framework of the forms of the economic order, as well as the daily struggle for quantities and prices, up to the individual. (Eucken 1949, 223; see also 1951, 93; Miksch 1948, 317; Röpke 1944a, 99)

No proper and legitimate intervention criteria have discriminated between the state's missions and private initiatives in historical liberalism; this doctrine opposed individuals to the central state instead of emphasizing what ordoliberals perceived as complementarity. In short, "the economic order and its shaping were not regarded as a special responsibility of the state" by the first liberals (Eucken 1951, 29).

From an internal liberal thought perspective, the originality of the ordoliberals' critique of laissez-faire was based on an attempt to discredit the private sector (or primarily landowners and captains of industry). As the economic order was "mainly left to private enterprise," it favored the development of monopolies (Eucken 1951, 30). As we have previously noted, ordoliberals referred to individual instincts—the instinct to seek power in the first place—as corresponding with human nature. Thus, they followed an argumentative line that on this point seems generally closer to Thomas Hobbes[13] than to the classical liberal tradition, and Smithian in particular, unlike the reading proposed by Helge Peukert (2000, 120). Smith was also criticized for having "largely overestimated the harmony of a self-regulated economy" (Miksch 1937a, 147), notably by postulating that such social harmony tended to merge with economic equilibrium in its contemporary sense (Miksch 1948, 316). For Röpke (1942b, 72), "the natural order"—understood as "the market automatically regulated by competition"—constituted a rationalist and naturalist dogma propagated by historical liberalism, which ultimately proved no different from social Darwinism.

In contrast, ordoliberals argued that the competitive economy was less a factor born from the functioning of markets' trade relations than the artificial product of civilization and its "advanced" values. Miksch (1948, 338) conveyed the market economy's fragility even more strongly in the aftermath of the Second World War, as did Böhm:

> A competitive economy never arises automatically, but is the *fruit of a highly developed social civilisation* and of a greater-than-ordinary exercise of *political will, love of liberty, and insight*. Only free communities can achieve this success. (Böhm 1954, 159, emphasis in original)

By a circular reasoning that places the economy of exchange at the center of the social edifice, the free society was consequently the cause as well as the result of the competitive order as conceived by ordoliberalism, with two consequences. First, this reasoning urges liberals to consider the competitive market as a necessary condition for a free society—but not sufficient and extremely fragile. Second, this circular causality will serve as an argument for defending a certain capitalist market model in the Cold War's East–West polarization, as discussed in Chapter 5.

13. In *Leviathan*, Hobbes (1651, chap. 11) was very clear about the role of power: "I put for a general inclination of all mankind a perpetual and restless desire of power after power, that ceases only in death." On the centrality of power in Hobbes, this "complex, rational passion, essentially comparative and strategic," see Pierre Dockès (2008, 127; see also Kurz 2018).

### 1.2.2.3 *Germany and Bismarck's Legacy*

From an ordoliberal perspective, Otto von Bismarck's accession to the post of Chancellor of the Empire in 1871 disrupted the balance between Germany's state and market spheres. First, from an incredibly feudalist perspective, Bismarck's protectionist policy would be the result of the "sacred union" between major industrial producers and political decision-makers (Röpke 1934a, 40). Second, and paralleling this economic policy of "national interest" and "reason of state" (Eucken 1932b, 56)—or even "brutal realpolitik" (Rüstow 1942, 277)—in the newly unified Germany, Bismarck in particular enacted protectionist measures and initiated a social policy. Both Eucken and Rüstow pointed to social insurance legislation as a guilty attempt to "reinforce the Reich by creating an interest on the part of the individual worker in its perpetuation," which led to the weakening of Germany's Parliament by "raising major economic issues on which there was no agreement within influential parties" (Eucken 1932b, 56). Indeed, Bismarck's social policy can be interpreted as a stabilization strategy to tame the rise of revolutionary sentiment and undermine some basic tenets of the Social Democratic Party's Marxist discourse (Abrams 2007, 40–41).

With such policies, Eucken argued that the Bismarckian state did not intervene against the capitalist economy as such, but rather encouraged and supported—though in a contradictory manner—some individual business groups. By doing so, the state itself became an actor in the "capitalist economic struggle" (Eucken 1932b, 57). Furthermore, the state's political institutions supported and participated in the development of private groups' interests, and, thus, they embraced an internal logic specific to the commercial sphere. In short, Bismarckian politics initiated a period in which "the *relation of state and economy gradually began to alter*, and the economy began to take the lead in their relationship" (Eucken 1932b, 56, emphasis in original). Following Eucken's views, the Bismarckian state was not yet an "economic state" (*Wirtschaftsstaat*).[14] However, Eucken stressed a process of self-destructing the state's authority through its economic decisions, which began at the turn of the century:

> The transformation of the liberal state into an economic state had great significance for the life of both *state* and *economy*. It has often been described how in this process the size of the state apparatus grew so extraordinarily, its budget swelled, interfering much more than hitherto in the provision of an individual's

14. Or "capitalist state" (Goldschmidt and Hesse 2013, 134).

> income through subsidies, duties, import prohibitions, quotas, moratoriums, its mediation and increased demand for tax revenue—state activity underwent a substantial expansion. . . . This process of expansion, a process that in the post-Bismarckian period was initiated and developed by the economy, did not result in the strengthening of the state, but rather by contrast in its weakening; bringing with it, indeed, even the danger of state dissolution. (Eucken 1932b, 59)

According to Eucken, the state would no longer act as a source in the decision-making process but tended to be "simply an instrument" of economic interest groups (Eucken 1932b). As such, it no longer acted according to the principles of state reason but met the anti-competitive requirements of certain private actors. At both the national and international levels, the state tended to merge with the interests of certain companies organized as cartels through a refined interventionist policy. Similarly, the "masses of workers and employees" urged the state to intervene in wage negotiations, in what Eucken called "labour market struggles" (Eucken 1932b, 57). In the facade of political decisions' primacy over the economic system's functioning, the emergence of powerful industries subsequently generated positions that threatened economic freedoms. Specifically, dominant industry positions carried political weight and guided (legislative) decisions in their support, which would tend to further strengthen power positions. This vicious circle continued until the rise of state interventionism in favor of particular interests (Eucken 1948a, 34; 1949, 223; Röpke 1942b, 32).

In short, "the democratisation of people and their passions, interest groups, and the chaotic forces of the mass" gained a decisive influence on foreign policy in the nineteenth century (Eucken 1932b, 63). From an ordoliberal perspective, it was not until 1931 and the end of the gold standard that the international political organization's last benefits were consumed (Eucken 1932b, 66; Lutz 1936; Röpke 1942d, 77–78; Rüstow 1942, 273). Ultimately, the divergence between political conditions and the real needs of capitalism resulted in the rise of economic states in the contemporary era of "experiments" (Eucken 1951, 30–32). This trend led ipso facto to the destruction of the state social organization of the market initiated during the historical liberalist period.

Placing the institution of the free and competitive market at the center of regulating the social process was a mistake that gradually eroded the moral reserves of both individuals and society, so much so that the system in place soon became unbearable. It was precisely the market economy "abandoned on its own" that was "dangerous and even untenable," leading individuals to reject "this organisation that has become odious to them" (Röpke 1944a, 71–72). Similar to Karl Polanyi's thesis developed in the same years as *The Great Transformation* (1944), civil society eventually defended itself against the market sphere's encroachment into all areas of social life through the phenomena of reappropriation and reinclusion. However, ordoliberals differed from Polanyi in that the latter emphasized these phenomena as a self-defense of society, while ordoliberals saw them as a catastrophe that culminated from a fundamental trend initiated by a faulty historical liberalism.[15] Furthermore, Röpke (1942b, 33) clearly specified that socialism was "essentially only the extremist continuation of a development which has already progressed far under a degenerated capitalist system."

Leonhard Miksch detailed the logical sequence from liberalism to interventionism—and ultimately, to planning—when he analyzed the decline of confidence in a competitive economy from both sides of the political spectrum. He offered yet another example of reflection that intermingles the state's effective actions and the struggle for ideas by presenting classical liberals and planners as two sides of the same coin:

> Trust in the eternal harmony of an economy free from state interference was gradually replaced by trust in the inevitable evolution towards a certain form of planning. . . . The generic idea of "economic freedom" has been totally reversed to become a war cry against the role of the state. The latter lost all right to impose itself as a regulatory force: it simply intervened randomly to satisfy the wishes of the participants, who were among the anonymous economic forces. Proponents of a planned economy generally share such a vision. They only distinguished themselves from the Liberals, defined in this way, by their opinion that the demolition of the competitive economy was not happening fast enough. (Miksch 1937a, 148)

The following section demonstrates that the type of causality between the two systems found in the ordoliberal diagnosis can be clarified by the power relations that reflect the dynamics between the economic and political spheres.

15. According to Polanyi, this movement was initiated by the fact that certain goods will be transformed into commodities, in particular through the transformation of elements that are not "produced for sale," namely labor, land, and currency. As Polanyi (1944, 148) noted, "liberal writers like Spencer and Sumner, Mises and Lippmann offer of an account of the double movement substantially similar to our own, but they put an entirely different interpretation on it"; what Quinn Slobodian (2018, 13) called the "crucial difference" in the "ends to which the market is being re-embedded."

### 1.2.3 The Economic State in the Age of Experimentation

According to the ordoliberals, the rise of Germany's "economic state" (*Wirtschaftsstaat*) at the beginning of the twentieth century marked a new stage in the relationship between markets and the state. This economic state was characterized by a confusion between private interests and the nation-state's general interest mission; the term itself covers different government practices, including "new forms" of money, market regulation, economic self-management, corporations, and planning (Eucken 1951, 28).

Specifically, Eucken blamed the economic policy pursued by Walter Rathenau[16] then Hjalmar Schacht[17] in Germany, as Eucken considered these two figures as the essence of the nation's new class of "experimenters" (Eucken 1951, 30). Furthermore, Röpke pinpointed the former's "engineer" and "technocrat" mentality (Rathenau), which would truly promote the "planned economy" (*Planwirtschaft*). According to Röpke (1944a, 144), "the fruits of this current of ideas" were eventually to be found in the type of National Socialist economic management. Thus, the ordoliberals constructed their historical analysis of the dynamics of power by closely observing recent German trends, which the ordoliberal founders experienced first-hand: first, in the twenties through industries' representative bodies (Rüstow and Eucken) and later by joining ministerial bodies (Rüstow and Böhm) or within circles of expertise as commissioned by executives (Röpke). This direct relationship with the industrial and political scene allowed ordoliberals to forge a common vision of crucial issues at the time, such as the proliferation of cartels, the Parliament's democratic functioning, and the state's economic interventionism.

#### *1.2.3.1 Das Kartellproblem (1897–1923)*

In the first half of the twentieth century, Germany was considered the land of cartels par excellence, beyond comparison with other European

16. Walter Rathenau (1867–1922), industrial leader, himself director of one of the country's largest industrial companies Allgemeine Elektricitäts-Gesellschaft (AEG) founded by his father, and politician, organized in particular the economic mobilization of war, relying largely on cartels. He then gained experience as Minister of Reconstruction of the Weimar Republic. A charismatic man of high intellectual, Jewish, and pan-Germanist culture, Rathenau was murdered in 1922 by nationalists (Barjot 2013, 1046–1047; Kitchen 2012, 204).

17. Hjalmar Schacht (1877–1970) was President of the Reichsbank (from 1924 to 1930; then from 1933 to 1939) and Minister of Economy of the Third Reich (from 1934 to 1937), in which posts he tried to promote a form of neo-Mercantilism (see Clavert 2009).

countries. This state of affairs was made possible by a complex combination of the interests of heavy industry, including large agrarian structures, with the hand of the government and the intellectual support of academics in general and economists in particular (Harding and Joshua 2010). To highlight the extent of the cartelization of the German economy, Robert Liefmann ironically noted that there was not only "a cartel for toilet paper, but also a specific cartel for 'crepe' toilet paper" (1927, 30).[18]

The cartelization of Germany took root at the end of the nineteenth century. The (Austrian) economist Friedrich Kleinwächter (1883, 143) was perhaps the first to document the growing number of cartels during the Long Depression (from 1873 to 1896), stressing that these cartels were the "children of misery" (*Kinder der Not*)—a term that has remained famous in the German-speaking world until today. The long-run historical trend of cartelization was central to forming the ordoliberal political economy. This helps us to understand why, for instance, Röpke (1942d, 224–225) noted that the growth of monopolies and cartels, as well as the size of firms and organizational costs, were two main factors to be observed if we seek the causes of a national economy's planning drift.

From 1875 to 1905, Germany passed from none to circa 400 cartels. Since then, the number of cartels increased exponentially to 1,500 cartels in 1923, and nearly 3,000 cartels a couple of years later in 1925.[19] Overall, the First World War was a favorable stage for an economic concentration in general and for cartels in particular. This great increase in the number of cartels took place especially in the heavy industries (iron, coal, steel, chemicals, etc.). Children of the concentration fueled by the war, these cartels not only resisted their necessary downsizing in the transformation process from a wartime to a peacetime economy, but they took advantage of the inherent instability of the early Weimar years. According to Eucken, the Socialisation Act of 1919 (*Sozialisierungsgesetz*) was the decisive act that brought German politics into the era of experimentation; at that time, syndicates acquired a "mandatory character" (Eucken 1951, 30–33; 1952, 172). These syndicates were larger than cartels, with a regional hierarchy

18. Robert Liefmann (1874–1941) completed his doctoral thesis under the supervision of Max Weber on the subject of cartels at the University of Freiburg in 1897 (see Grossein 2005, 923). He taught there as professor of economics from 1914 to 1933. Liefman wrote numerous authoritative works on the cartelization of the German economy. Anita Pelle (2016, 116) insisted on the links and similarities between Liefmann and the ordoliberal authors. During the war, Liefmann was deported; he died in a concentration camp in the French Pyrenees.

19. See Lee McGowan (2010, 47) and Jeffrey R. Fear (2008, 14). Eucken's writings (1951, 31–35) show he had a comparable scale in mind.

reporting to a central office, and included representatives of employers, employees, and consumers. Syndicates gained a form of socialization of "autonomous organs that are more or less politically controlled," labeled *Gemeinwirtschaft*, or "statism," or a collectively controlled economy (Nörr 2000, 152).

Among these syndicates' attributes, one finds the management of production (such as its output, quality standard, and boycott) and sales (such as prices, quotas, and distribution locations) on the market. According to Eucken (1951, 32), the 1919 decision consequently resulted in an ever-increasing agglomeration of economic power, in that "the old private power groups became compulsory corporations, thereby increasing their power, but they were in the future to have a socialised character." What was defended as common management for the benefit of all was perceived by the ordoliberals as the culpable collusion of employers and employees in a common spirit of monopoly, to the detriment of the rest of society and in particular to consumers as a whole.

In the early interwar period, the German economy faced the rise of cartels and a monetary crisis during a hyperinflation period. The Chancellor Gustav Stresemann introduced a 1923 decree aiming to combat "abuses" (*Mißbrauch*) of economic power positions in the market, or a dominant position in today's vocabulary.[20] To this end, the decree provided for the legal recognition—or compulsory transparency—of cartel agreements under government supervision. It also created a specific court institution (*Kartellgericht*) to address cartel abuses. From an ordoliberal perspective, the 1923 decree nevertheless confirmed a flaw in the February 4, 1897, judgment of the German Supreme Court (the *Reichsgericht*). The earlier decree authorized cartel agreements to restrict competition, guaranteeing specific protection vis-à-vis new entrants. In doing so, the Supreme Court embraced the views of industrialists who defended the possibility of lower prices in favor of the general interest, de facto supporting methods of economic struggle through discrimination by means of prices, boycotts, or sanctions. Such competitive impediments, based on a freedom of association, were quite at odds with the ordoliberal notion of better performance within competitive markets (Eucken 1951, 31; Böhm 1948).[21]

If Eucken, Böhm, and others revisited discussions on the 1923 ordinance, it was likely because these discussions were marked by "strong political and

20. A reproduction of the text of the 1923 decree (*Kartellverordnung*), translated into English, can be found in an appendix to Liefmann's book (1927, 351–357).

21. Recent literature tends to support the reading provided by the ordoliberals (Guesnerie et al. 2006, 36; Neumann 2001, 37).

economic resistance" (Marburg 1964, 83). In the face of the first decisions of the Cartel Court and the Ministry of Economy, which forced players to behave more favorably toward competitive market forms, the cartel representatives "denounced it as 'reactionary Manchesterianism' and, by contrast, praised the cartel principle as a higher form of economic development" (Eucken 1951, 34). In Germany, the "economic freedom" as enshrined in the Weimar Constitution must be understood as "the freedom of businessmen to choose between competition and monopoly," and indeed, "public opinion has grown used to this state of affairs, in which competition, restraint of competition, and monopoly enjoy equal rights" (Böhm 1954, 152–153).

Industrialists argued that cartels were a way to regulate competition compatible with market mechanisms. Cartels were required to protect small and medium-sized companies from international competition with large groups or for resilience against fluctuations in the economic cycle. Industrialists aimed to convince political and public opinion that private capital interests were *ultimately* compatible with that of the community (Liefmann 1927, 342–344; Pribram 1935, 5). In that spirit, the largest chemical manufacturers—such as Bayer, Hæchst, AGFA, and BASF—merged to form I. G. Farben in 1925. From an ordoliberal perspective, the 1923 ordinance was a complete failure.[22] Rüstow (1942, 275), who was nevertheless involved in its implementation, indicated his lack of conviction at that time—admittedly in the comfort of retrospective judgment. The 1923 *Kartellverordnung* was ineffective due to its inability to legally define when "abuse" occurred. The lawyers of Freiburg discussed this aspect in further detail (see Mongouachon 2011). Großmann-Doerth (1933) stressed the asymmetry between contractual parties accompanied by a "self-created law by the economy" (*selbstgeschaffene Recht der Wirtschaft*). Moreover, Böhm insisted that private law was unable to effectively assess the harm caused by dominant positions.[23] Second, and far from taking drastic control or dissolution measures, the Ministry of the Economy was satisfied with weak control in cartel policy. This (episodic) attempt to frame cartels was

22. It should be stressed that this observation of failure was decisive for understanding why ordoliberal economic policy in the field of cartels, or monopolies, favored a categorical refusal of their very formation, rather than a mere supervision, as Chapter 4 will explain in more details.

23. From 1925 to 1933, Franz Böhm worked in the Antitrust Control Department of the Ministry of Economy of the Republic of Weimar (Grossekettler 2005, 489). At the same time, Böhm wrote various articles, including "The Problem of Private Power" ("*Das Problem der privaten Macht*") and his PhD thesis on *Competition and Monopolistic Struggle* (*Wettbewerb und Monopolkampf*), which earned him a university position in Freiburg (Böhm 1928, 1933).

ultimately anecdotal in the long-run German tradition. According to Böhm (1954, 144), this history was marked by a persistent tendency in favor of cartelization, in industrial and political circles as well as civil society.

Under these conditions, the cartel community did not experience any opposition to the state supervision and control from which it believed it could benefit. The number of cartels—as with the concentration process in general—continued to experience strong growth. The ordoliberals perceived the economy's cartelization as not only harmful to the market sphere, but also contaminating the political sphere, including the legislative and executive branches, by taking over "the formation of the *volonté générale*" (Böhm 1966, 64).

This subsection devoted to the question of cartels in Germany demonstrates that the ordoliberal historical diagnosis particularly underlined how legislative measures proved incapable of stemming the dynamics of power concentration, although they did not provoke it. According to the ordoliberals, this faulty legislation was one cause of global political powerlessness to resist pressure from economic power groups, and particularly relative to the type of democratic representation.

#### *1.2.3.2 Economic Interests in the Parliament (1924–1932)*

Following deep tensions in the political life of the Weimar Republic's formative years (1918–1924), the aftermath of Germany's 1923 hyperinflation was marked by a relative calm.[24] However, as early as 1929, the Great Depression undermined the German Republic's fragile democratic foundations. In a manner particularly exacerbated since the early thirties, the representative parliamentary system was collectively in a debate between attempts at rehabilitation and categorical rejection (Baume 2006); the ordoliberal discourse belongs to the second class. Ordoliberals' apprehension of the rise and increasing concentration of economic power in society led them to reject certain political institutions considered too permeable by pressures from the private sphere. It was not exclusively a question of considering power from an economic perspective, but rather of understanding its dynamic relationships with the entire social sphere. Specifically, understanding economic power in all its aspects also required

24. To speak of tensions here is an understatement, given that the situation has regularly come close to civil war. We have only to recall failed coup attempts (including that of Hitler in 1923) and insurrectional strikes, but also the almost four hundred assassinations perpetrated—more than 90 percent by the right—on a political basis, including those of Rosa Luxembourg and Rathenau already mentioned (Mosse and Magyar 1999 chap. 7; Solchany 2003, chap. 1).

an examination of "the influence of certain groups of economic power on the legal system" (Eucken 1948a, 32). The pluralistic expression of political parties within a representative parliamentary embodied the medium par excellence of this "influence" that ordoliberals condemned.

Without disclosing precisely all the mechanisms of propagation, the ordoliberals argued that the construction of economic power will generate pressure groups. The ordoliberals saw this trend as a "refeudalization" of politics by economics in industrialized states (Böhm 1961, 36), in violation of the democratic principles that had first empowered the market process:

> For instance, let us take a country where a parliamentary democracy is in place. Its economic order, . . . whose production process was initially dominated by competitive markets and thus the formation of a system of competitive prices, is being transferred to groups of monopoly powers, or partial monopolies, in different industries. . . . As time goes by, the character of democracy is gradually eroding. Of course, economic interests were already being asserted in Parliament at a time when the competitive market was dominant, for example, those of farmers. . . . But in the new situation, monopolies exert much greater political influence because of their economic power. (Eucken 1948a, 31–32; see also 1940b, 31)

It is conceivable that by strengthening their financial weight or vital nature for certain employment areas, some companies (or sectors) could acquire significant bargaining power over the ruling political/administrative class. Formally, the two dimensions of power—economic and political—were therefore related by a vicious circle, in that monopolies' and cartels' emergence was based on internal conditions (individuals' desire for power) and external conditions (faulty legislation). As they grew (e.g., in capital or market share, among others), pressure from these economic power groups could then impose ordinary or extraordinary legal measures in their sole interest, external conditions then strengthened, and the cycle progressed.[25]

However, economic interests were exercised well beyond the political sphere to participate in the ideological formation of both scientific and public opinion.[26] Support from some experts and intellectuals considerably reinforced the legitimacy of power groups' demands at the collective societal level. According to Eucken, the "intellectual history of mankind"

25. From an ordoliberal point of view, it was the holders of economic power who have the greatest influence on the behavior of elected officials. Later, constitutional economics extended the analysis of strategic behavior to the study of public choices, particularly through the analysis of electoral cycles.

26. On the involvement and place of economists in the Reichstag from 1867 to 1918, see Harald Hagemann and Matthias Rösch (2005).

coincided with demands to "secure and claims to power by means of ideologies" (Eucken 1940b, 29–30; see also Röpke 1936c, 1301). In this sense, economic power was a commanding engine of institutional change in a way that favored monopolistic practices and positions and therefore deleterious to the competitive order. The ordoliberals' extreme discomfort with parliamentary democratic regimes was undoubtedly rooted in the political and economic experiences within the Weimar Republic.

Such representative institutions as parliaments faced public demands for economic and social intervention on a scale never before achieved in times of peace. This was a recurring issue not only in Germany, but also throughout interwar Europe (Lindseth 2004, 1355; Hobsbawm 2014, 156). For example, if representative parliaments had been associated with the liberal state of the nineteenth century, and particularly in England in the face of increasing administrative power to formulate laws, they were perceived in Germany as a place in which partisan interests were expressed, which led to a decision-making deadlock. In contrast to the Anglo-Saxon liberal political thought, in which a pluralism of opinion promotes the debates necessary for consensus, ordoliberalism shared an anti-pluralist position (Megay 1970). In line with continental European tradition, the concept of the common good was supposed to stem from general will.

Based on the Italian fascist and German National Socialist examples, Rüstow established a causal link between asserted economic power, parliamentarianism synonymous with a politically weak state, and the struggle of parties for power until a single political party's totalitarian seizure of power:

> The democratic parliamentary structure of some economically leading states caused the economic corruption to spread to the internal policy of the state, to political parties, and to the *parliamentarism* itself. The political parties were slowly transformed into parliamentary agencies of economic pressure-groups and were financed by them. Not a single one of these parties or groups which supported them was at first able to win a parliamentary majority by its own strength alone. . . . A coalition of several parties was therefore necessary. A crisis of *parliamentarism*, a crisis indeed of the state itself, was the unavoidable consequence. . . . Their parliamentary tactics consisted in abusing the rules of liberal *parliamentarism* for the purpose of weakening democracy and its organs. . . . The consequence was that in Italy and Germany . . . the game of pluralism ended in a totalitarian one-party dictatorship. (Rüstow 1942, 276–277, emphasis in original)

As previously mentioned, ordoliberals faced economic instability—hyperinflation and an economic crisis—and the political instability of the twenties and thirties, which ultimately gripped the democratic character of the Weimar Republic. From 1930 to 1932, the political regime could still be described as "semi-parliamentary" under Heinrich Brüning's chancellery. However, with its successor Chancellor Franz von Papen, the executive branch remarkably influenced both positive and negative functions of the Reichstag; von Papen governed by legislative decree to bypass parliamentary procedure. This authoritarian drift paved the way to "unify all executive and legislative power permanently in the hands of the Chancellor-Führer, Adolf Hitler," synonymous with the final collapse of the Weimar Republic (Lindseth 2004, 1371).

In apparent opposition to the ordoliberal observation, it should be noted that from Brüning to von Papen, the weakening of the Reichstag's role did not result in a distancing of politics from economic interests; in contrast, Brüning's and von Papen's policies reflected the concerns of these interest groups (Petzina 1969, 65–70). Indeed, both Chancellors relied deeply on "expert circles" and informal councils, composed primarily of members of heavy industry and banking, the army (*Reichswehr*), or the great agrarian nobility (*Junkertum*).[27] Although ordoliberals placed high expectations on the "policy of experts" derived from men of science, they refused to perceive practitioners as potential trusted advisers, as the latter were deemed incapable of divesting themselves of their private interests.

### *1.2.3.3 Nazi Economic Planning (1933–1938)*

In the ordoliberal diagnosis, the strengthening of the economic power of cartels (or large industrial groups) coupled with the pluralistic expression of interests—in Parliament as well as in the sphere of government—led to the multiplication of ad hoc economic and legislative measures. These measures, also called "punctual" interventions by Eucken, achieved certain specific objectives, such as full employment. However, these same measures prevented a coherent, systematic treatment of the economic process and thus led to a disordered price system for ordoliberals.

In the face of growing economic instability, the state had to increase and intensify the scope of its interventions in the economic process. In doing so, it went so far as to profoundly change the economic order in favor of a

27. Röpke participated in the Brauns Commission settled by the Brüning government in 1931 to resorb massive unemployment. Mocked as a "Professor commission," it was actually mainly composed of senior civil servants, and Röpke's plea for a proto-Keynesian recovery policy was actually neglected (see Röpke 1931). On this episode and Röpke's arguments, see Klausinger (1999), Commun (2018), and Fèvre (2018b).

centrally planned system in which monetary prices were no longer decisive in the resource allocation process. Therefore, this era of experimentation was marked by a transition from an interventionist economic state, which was still part of the "exchange economy" (*Verkehrswirtschaft*) to a "centrally administrated economy" (*Zentralverwaltungswirtschaft*), by nature foreign to the competitive order. Eucken's morphology of the economic order will be considered in Chapter 3.

As Hitler seized power, the National Socialists demonstrated their support for the world of industry, particularly by consolidating the state's right of control over companies' entry into and exit from cartelized markets. Simultaneously, the Nazis increased the Ministry of Economy's power over the cartels as the state empowered itself to "make strategic use" of cartels for political purposes (Hesse and Roelevink 2015, 197). Böhm (1954, 163) noted that, in particular, the Ministry of Economy was "authorised to force independent firms to join a compulsory cartel, or to make outsiders adhere to a private cartel, if he deemed this to be in the public interest." The National Socialist argument was a part of a broader *process of rationalization* of the economy that it completed. Although this process was not newly established, it gradually took on new proportions in Germany.[28] This coincided with a public debate, conducted through what Röpke (1936c, 1301) described as an "ideology," intensely mobilizing such terms as "market organization," "economic stabilization," and the "managed economy"; protecting against "unfair competition"; or even calling for the "general interest before private interest." This state of mind was typical in the interwar period of confidence in the capitalist system's inevitable shift toward state socialism. This was enabled in Germany by the ever-increasing concentration and socialization of economic units.

In National Socialist Germany, purported cartel organizations were still formally in charge of production decisions. However, Eucken drew our attention to the profound underground upheaval that was nevertheless at work, in contrast to the apparent continuity from the Weimar Republic to the Third Reich:

> In 1930 cartels were associations of independent undertakings for purposes of excluding competition; this means that they belonged to an exchange economy. In 1940 cartels were mainly instruments of the central economic administration.

28. The example of the central planning of the Russian socialist system was the driving force behind this line of reasoning and inspired and strengthened the discourse of the German SPD.

> Although they have retained something of their original purpose, their role had changed regarding the economic order. (Eucken 1940b, 225)

From 1932 to 1933, the economic order still resulted from a combination of the two pure forms. As early as 1936, however, Eucken (1948c, 79–80) considered that the centrally administered economy began to dominate the exchange economy in forming the economic process. This period coincided with the beginnings of large-scale Nazi economic planning, put in place by Hermann Göring in the form of a "quadrennial plan" (*Vierjahresplan*).

As cartels followed a process of socialization and prioritization, it became increasingly clear that they operated as structures subordinate to the state leadership, to serve objectives set by the government. Therefore, tensions in production or social conflicts—or such exogenous objectives as military expansion—were triggering factors to achieve the final step of complete state socialization. After the cartels had continuously gained political influence for a period of time in the form of accommodating legislation, the state finally took over the direction of the entire economic process within reach. This ultimately resulted in a transfer of the ability to establish economic plans, individual or collective, from such voluntary or mandatory organizations as cartels to the next level: the Ministry of Economy.

In summary, the German economic order transitioned from an exchange economy dominated by monopolistic tendencies to a centrally administered economy. Syndicates, unions, cartels, and major group leaders merged into the core public administration itself, from which they continued to exercise power in a special combination with departmental administration (Eucken 1951, 36; see also Miksch 1948, 321–322). As cartels were deprived of fundamental productive decisions, they abandoned their status as economic units, in the strongest sense of the term, to operate as mere management bodies. As Böhm mentioned,

> In October 1936 a price freeze order was issued . . . and this law abolished the price system as a means of economic guidance. The government saw itself therefore obliged to allocate raw materials, semi-manufactured goods, labour, credits, etc., i.e. to go over to a comprehensive compulsory planned economy. The cartel administrations were turned into semi-official public offices, a measure that increased their prestige. (Böhm 1954, 163)

Eucken obviously said nothing about the experience of the National Socialist-planned economy in his 1932 article, "Structural Transformations of the State and the Crisis of Capitalism." However, as Eucken (1932b, 69) stressed that "the masses exert great influence in Germany over the state and its economic policies, whereas the Russian state is entirely separated from them," one may wonder whether the problem of private power exercised in society can be solved by the centralized planning state. In other words, does the "pre-eminence of the central government in economic decisions [allow] the balance of power to be maintained" (Eucken 1948a, 32), as it can be in an exchange economy dominated by a competitive order? Such a question by Eucken was purely rhetorical. Eucken (1951, 37) later commented on the disastrous Third Reich economic experiment by noting that "power remains power whoever may exercise it," and it was in fact "in public rather than private hands that power reaches its zenith."

To fully understand the meaning of Eucken's quote, one must consider it through the dynamics of power highlighted thus far in this Chapter. Public power was the most damaging, as it inevitably and logically comes with a concentration of economic power derived from the behavior of private actors. The merger—or rather, the abandonment—of the private economic power exercised by cartels and large industrial groups in favor of public power completed the logic of concentration initiated by individual instinct in a form of deleterious amalgam: the state is economic, and the economy is bureaucratic. The ordoliberals perceived this as a reciprocal weakening of both spheres: a loss of legitimate authority for the state and the market's inability to satisfy consumers' needs. Thus, we can now fully understand Eucken's (1932b, 70) characterization of the "total economic state" as intimately "weak."

The ordoliberal *institutional dynamics of power* outlined the transition from the nineteenth-century liberal order to the National Socialist years' economic planning. In doing so, ordoliberals built a causal sequence rooted in a historical narrative. However, ordoliberals did not consider this narrative as necessary nor as an inescapable process; on the contrary, ordoliberals' political economy was designed to oppose the laws of development formalized by Marxists and historicists.

## 1.3 THE ORDOLIBERAL MANIFESTO OF 1936: SCIENCE BEYOND RELATIVISM AND FATALISM

Familiar with the politics during the Weimar period, the ordoliberals witnessed the establishment of a centralized (Nazi) economic administration order that completely opposed their competitive ideal. An analysis of the deleterious principles of historical liberalism toward this state of affairs functions as a safeguard against any determinism or defeatism in ordoliberal thought. In contrast, this experience convinced ordoliberals that the battle for societal reform must be won in terms of ideas. Regarding the power of interests and the ideologies that were—knowingly or unknowingly—favorable toward such interests, the ordoliberals opposed the formative capacity of scientific reason.

### 1.3.1 The Battlefield: The Market of Ideas

In 1936, Franz Böhm, Walter Eucken, and Hans Großmann-Doerth signed a brief programmatic text entitled *Our Task* (*Unsere Aufgabe*). The year 1936 coincided with Göring initiating his quadrennial plans, as previously noted, which was likely a factor to be considered in the timetable for drafting the "ordoliberal manifesto." However, the general purpose of this text remained incredibly abstract and made obscure references to current events. Essentially, this manifesto embodied the leitmotif of the ordoliberal political economy: to transform effective reality following the precepts science has assigned it. Accordingly, Eucken (1951, 83) later called "economic thinking" a "political-economic force," in the sense that it "determines and orientates economic and political action."

Indeed, from an ordoliberal perspective, only science is "capable of being a spiritual and moral power" (*geistig-sittliche Macht*), of being a "guiding potency" of political action rather than subordinate to it (Hensel 1951, 16).[29] Hence, the "strong" in the ordoliberal sense were not those who abandoned themselves to the search for power (or the will for power), as he or she would be "intimately weak," but individuals who call upon reason:

> The strong man feels his strength increase whenever he is able to apply reason to illuminate the darkness surrounding the acting agent and to the exercise of his power. Using this conviction as our point of departure, which is based on historical experience, we wish to bring scientific reasoning, as displayed in jurisprudence and political economy, into effect for the purpose of constructing and reorganising the economic constitution (*Wirtschaftsverfassung*). (Böhm et al. 1936, 23)

The act of faith in favor of scientific reason was all the more essential to the ordoliberals as it remedied the contemporary political rationality conveyed through various ideologies. Ordoliberals argued that their political

29. Hensel took up almost word for word the expression of the ordoliberal manifesto: "*eine geistliche und sittliche Macht*" (Böhm et al. 1936, 22).

economy could cure a deeply irrational political reasoning. A year before the publication of *Our Task*, Röpke (1935, 94) focused on this aspect with an Italian example: "the fascist government is so irrational that it brings different objectives into conflict with each other, thus generating results that are not desired by the government itself" (see also Eucken 1932b, 69–70). The intellectual positioning of ordoliberalism within idealistic philosophy has two primary and related consequences. First, ordoliberals sought to change the economic order through rational discourse, even in defiance of material conditions. Second, this rational discourse would be a prerogative for scientists, who therefore have every authority to discover a certain precedence in the sphere of political decision-making.

### 1.3.2 The Weapons: Scientists to Guide Policy

The defeat or renunciation of scientific thought in the face of contemporary challenges would leave the field open for the development of interest groups' ideologies to guide political decisions. Indeed, ordoliberals typically perceived the rise of "conservative radical" intellectual groups such as the *Tat-Kreis* as a product of this trend (Röpke 1934a, 22–23; Böhm et al. 1936, 19). The members of the *Tat-Kreis* belonged to the "conservative revolution" movement. Although disparate, this expression referred to authors who shared at least two beliefs (Dupeux 1992; Staudenmaier 2014): first, a confidence in the irreducible specificity of the German being; second, a confidence in the durability of conservative values linked to the state, the nation, the people, and the German "race." Ordoliberals perceived the temptation of politics' primacy over economics—*der Primat der Politik über die Wirtschaft*—as a central conservative component, or of "fascist economics," as Röpke (1935, 94) phrased it. The thinkers in the conservative revolution assigned to the state a fundamental and leading role of ruling every other sphere, especially the economy. This conservative plea for a planned organization in the hands of a few large industrial groups did not sit well with ordoliberal discourse and was regularly denounced by Lutz (1933), Röpke (1945a), and Eucken (1946b).

Recovering the formative capacity of political economy and legal science—to emerge from the crisis of civilization as portrayed by the ordoliberals—required the awakening of an elite group of scientists, journalists, and magistrates. In short, the ordoliberals advocated the return of the "clerks," an expression that Röpke (1944a, 200–213) borrowed from a popular essay by Julien Benda (1927), the French intellectual. The ordoliberal manifesto was built around similar considerations and opened with an apology of the figure of the scientist. As ethics would allow scientists to extricate themselves from the daily struggles of partisan interests, scientists would be the only admissible guides to political action. The ordoliberals' optimism and confidence in science were not supported by a proper demonstration; rather, they noted that

> Men of science, by virtue of their profession (*Beruf*) and position being independent of economic interests, are the only objective, independent advisers capable of providing true insight into the intricate interrelationships of economic activity and therefore also providing the basis upon which economic judgement can be made . . . about economic measures appropriate in particular circumstances. (Böhm et al. 1936, 15)

The ordoliberal manifesto closed with one condition absolutely necessary for a return to grace for the formative capacity of the human sciences, such as the political economy and legal doctrine: "The collaboration of the two sciences, which in this respect still leaves much to be desired, is clearly essential (Böhm et al. 1936, 25). Ordoliberals called for interdisciplinarity in contemporary terms. This was less the division into the disciplinary, specialized knowledge that ordoliberals questioned than the difficulty of conducting a constructive dialogue among scientific results. Indeed, if the "division of the humanities . . . has proved to be untenable," it was precisely to the extent that "whenever the subject demands the use of both [sciences], then this must be done." However, each science "must preserve its individuality if it is to achieve anything" (Böhm et al. 1936). Such a declaration, although vague, was thus foreign to economics' imperialism over other disciplines and must be considered relative to the emergence of scientific specializations in the interwar period.[30]

It should also be noted that a form of hierarchy between the disciplines of economics and law emerged from ordoliberal writings. For instance, Böhm's primary ambition involved translating the main principles of political economy into legal semantics. One of the ordoliberals' main concerns included conveying the Courts of Justice's decisions through political economy: "The problem of understanding and fashioning the legal instruments for an economic constitution can only be solved if the lawyer avails himself of the findings of economic research" (Böhm et al. 1936, 24).

*Our Task* was above all a polemical text, concerned to position the ordoliberal discourse within the academic and political fields. As such, the

30. The publication of the ordoliberal manifesto came a year after Edmund Husserl's acclaimed 1935–1936 conferences on *The Crisis of European Humanity and Philosophy* (1970). Husserl discussed the role of science in society, considering the "necessity" but also the "danger of specialisation" of disciplines.

manifesto was centrally a violent charge against the German intellectual milieu. Ordoliberals claimed "historical fatalism" was a "sign of weakness" from some intellectuals, asking: "How can the intellect shape events when it accepts them as inevitable?" (Böhm et al. 1936, 19–20). Ordoliberals pointed to the German Historical School in particular, as Historicism was blamed for having deprived legal science (*Rechtswissenschaft*) and political economy (*Nationalökonomie*) of the theoretical tools necessary for these two disciplines to practically contribute to society. Historicist works by Friedrich List, and especially Friedrich von Savigny, were blamed for fostering the development in contemporary times of an "atmosphere" impregnated with "fatalism" and "relativism" regarding historical developments (Böhm et al. 1936, 18).[31]

Endorsing a liberal position in favor of economic competition in Germany between the two world wars was brave, to some extent. Röpke and Rüstow paid the price for their opinions and were forced into exile. However, it should also be noted that by basing their analyses on a rejection of both Anglo-Saxon liberalism and Marxist socialism, Böhm, Eucken, and Großmann-Doerth weighed such risk-taking by attacking two streams of ideas already largely in disgrace under Hitler's regime. In this sense, a criticism of the intellectual milieu remained incredibly abstract—which was likely a necessity at the time. Ordoliberals' criticism targeted figures from the past (Savigny) or already under the Nazi regime's yoke of criticism (Marx). Even when ordoliberals attacked historicism—and specifically Werner Sombart, whose work experienced a brief revival under National Socialism (Hagemann 2016, 228)—it was in the form of a Marxist epigone.

### 1.3.3 An Alternative to the Marxist-Historicist Diagnosis

Although fatalism and relativism were not synonymous in the ordoliberal manifesto, they specifically interacted in many ways. Sombart's "relativist and fatalistic attitude" embodied a synthesis of these two trends in contemporary scientific circles (Böhm et al. 1936, 18). Beyond elitism, ordoliberals argued that the combination of relativism and fatalism permeates society as a whole. According to them, German public opinion had to be cured from a Marxist style of thinking.

31. Friedrich Carl von Savigny (1779–1861) had a profound and long-lasting impact on German legal doctrine by insisting on "a historical identity of law linked to the people" (Rabault 2016c, 21; see also Zimmermann 2013, 98–99).

As the ordoliberals transposed Marx's legacy into Sombart's reading, they rejected the idea of a "social, political, and spiritual superstructure" that was only a reflection, with no effect on the economic infrastructure (Böhm et al. 1936, 19–20). Ordoliberals also did not share the existence of laws of development marking the inevitable end of capitalism (Eucken 1932b, 54–55; Röpke 1936a, 13; 1940, 59). Furthermore, Röpke (1934b, 55) opposed supporters of imperialist economic theory, such as Rosa Luxembourg or Rudolf Hilferding, who perceived "modern imperialism as a [necessary] political consequence of the economic structure of capitalism." Law for ordoliberals was a priori creative, and not only an a posteriori justification. This was not as much because the law sanctions private property—and therefore collective ownership would change something about it—but more fundamentally because legal decisions related to the question of market structures were the most appropriate way to define the economic order:

> After the First World War, when many cartels and combines were being formed, the economic order changed its structure. . . . After 1933 new elements of centrally administered economy emerged. But the same law of property was in force the whole time. To conclude that law of property is unimportant for the economic system would certainly be mistaken. But the form of an economic order is not determined by the law of property. If the Supreme Court of the Reich, for example, at the end of the last century had not confirmed the legality of cartel agreements [in its 1987 judgment], the development of cartels in Germany would not have followed the course it did. (Eucken 1940b, 86)

With Sombart's death in 1941, Schumpeter fueled an ordoliberal criticism of economic and political fatalism. Although important parallels exist between Schumpeter's historical reading and that of the ordoliberals (Meijer 2005, 147–148), the conclusions mediated by specific relations to determinism proved to be radically antithetical. Indeed, in *Capitalism, Socialism and Democracy*, Schumpeter (1942) wondered whether socialism would replace capitalism and, with it, economic liberalism. His study presented a clear, radical conclusion: if capitalism can't survive, Schumpeter believed, socialism certainly can.

The problem of the inexorability of economic socialization, and particularly among firms, was closely linked to the question of forming monopolies and goes beyond Schumpeter's analysis. The debate about the "necessity" or "desirability" of cartels in Germany and of economic concentration in general was far from specific to the interwar period. When the liberal economist Edgar Salin stood in the early sixties in favor of economic concentration to improve the competitive economy's performance—and specifically, to resist the pressure of communist planned economies—*Ordo*'s editors opposed Salin's argument by making a statement similar to those made by the ordoliberal founders of this journal some thirty years earlier.[32]

## 1.4 CONCLUSION: AN INSTITUTIONAL DYNAMICS OF POWER

By stressing the importance of an anthropological hypothesis in the ordoliberal political economy, we emphasized that power relations were key in ordoliberals' historical interpretation. The extent of industrial cartelization in modern Germany helped to interpret the omnipresent theme of economic power in ordoliberal discussions. If ordoliberals insisted on power groups' decisive role in the dynamics of the economic order, they also nevertheless rejected the inevitable tendency toward economic concentration. The forces that contributed to developing competitive economic relations, such as increasing technological progress, paved the way for a positive ordoliberal economic policy.

During the Second World War, Eucken (1942b, 37) outlined the impasse that had entrapped the German economic order: "Here the administered economy, whose replacement is necessary, there the group anarchy of the 'free' economy, which leads to high tensions and heavy damage." Based on the historical diagnosis of the economic experiences of the Weimar Republic and subsequently National Socialist Germany and faced with the degeneration of nineteenth-century liberal capitalism that finally paved the way, Eucken rhetorically asked: "Is there a third way (*dritter Weg*)?"[33]

By underlining the causal process between liberalism and planning at the heart of the ordoliberal historical diagnosis, we can understand why a median path—or a mixed economy (or corporatism) *between* liberalism (or capitalism) and planning (or communism)—cannot represent an adequate solution from the ordoliberal perspective because the question of power as proposed is not then resolved. In following this reading, societies would simply exist in a highly unstable transition period from private economic interests concentrated in the form of a group to public economic power, which combines large conglomerates and a bureaucratic state administration.

32. See the account by Theodore F. Marburg (1964, 99).

33. Röpke (1940, 24; 1942b, 43; 1944a, 38) used several terms and spoke of "constructive liberalism" or "economic humanism," but also preferred to speak of a "third way."

The core mechanism of the ordoliberal diagnosis can be described as an *institutional dynamics of power* that sought to explain the causal sequence from liberalism to planning. Considering power relations as a driving force behind this dynamic makes it possible to both simultaneously and endogenously account for the formation of legislative decisions and the economic process's direction. By the same explanatory scheme, the ordoliberals designated historical liberalism and modern planning as two irrational tendencies that merely express the same disorder, albeit in various forms. Historical liberalism in the ordoliberal narrative has pushed to the extreme its founding principle of economic freedom and non-state interference. Consequently, planning has carried through its principle of taking charge of the production process and allocating resources. This double tendency presented itself as an ordoliberal, idealist counterpart to dialectical materialism in the historical economy of discourse.

We worked to clarify the ordoliberal conception of scientists' role in society and in the design of the economic order in particular. It is the awareness of the need for a deliberately constructed order, and not a spontaneous one, that led the ordoliberals to not only formalize an economic constitution, but also recommend certain specific economic policies—first, to promote and defend the competitive order. By affirming political voluntarism, the ordoliberals opposed an idealistic response to the Marxist materialistic reading. Nevertheless, the ordoliberals owed much to Marx and the Historical Schools. More than a neglect of historicists' research program, ordoliberals "reoriented" its basic tenets.

# CHAPTER 2
# Science Against Interests

We cannot understand ordoliberalism apart from the philosophy of science underlying it. In this respect, Walter Eucken's contributions are pivotal. Indeed, in his book *Die Grundlagen der Nationalökonomie* (1940a), which can be literally translated as *The Foundations of Political Economy*, Eucken proposed a new methodological framework for the German political economy. Recent studies have interpreted Eucken's research as an attempt to solve the German methodological dispute initiated by Gustav Schmoller and Carl Menger at the very end of the nineteenth century. Although this ambition has been widely recognized, Eucken's methodology does not end with the *Methodenstreit*. In fact, this step was not the central objective of Eucken's work: indeed, the introductory alert in the preface—"this book is not a methodological book" (Eucken 1940a, ix)—would remain sibylline.

In *Foundations*, Eucken intended to overcome a twofold obstacle—ontological and epistemological—to which economic knowledge would be captive. On the one hand, the ontological obstacle designates the fact that, by the very nature of economic phenomena, the researcher is faced with the "great antinomy" (*Große Antinomie*) between the historical-individual and the theoretical-general aspects of the systematic understanding of these phenomena. On the other hand, the epistemological obstacle means that Eucken's approach aimed to rid scientific knowledge of the influence of ideology that is driven by interest groups of power. In a telling metaphor, Eucken (1940b, 264) invited economists to perform the difficult task of drawing back "the curtain interested ideologies used to veil the concentration of, and struggle for, economic power." In short, for Eucken, power was simultaneously the object of economic analysis and the central obstacle in the way of the pursuit of scientific, economic knowledge. This second

*A Political Economy of Power.* Raphaël Fèvre, Oxford University Press. © Oxford University Press 2021.
DOI: 10.1093/oso/9780197607800.003.0003

obstacle—epistemological—is usually neglected in the current literature. However, it is essential to understanding Eucken's approach as well as the whole of ordoliberal political economy.[1]

To overcome this twofold obstacle and thus scientifically (re)found political economy, Eucken relied on the philosophical discourse of his time. The rise of neo-Kantism marked the German intellectual context at the beginning of the twentieth century and, within it, the work of Walter Eucken's father.[2] Although forgotten today, Rudolf Eucken was a prominent philosopher at the time and was awarded the Nobel Prize for literature in 1908, for his development of the philosophy of life (*Lebensphilosophie*). Equally influential to Walter Eucken's methodology was Edmund Husserl's transcendental phenomenology. Husserl was personally and intellectually close to the Eucken family. Walter maintained friendly relations with Husserl from his appointment as professor of political economy in 1927 at the same University of Freiburg im Breisgau (Klump 2003, 149).

By the beginning of the twentieth century, the philosophical and economic literature was not as hermetic to each other as one might think in retrospect. Proof of this was the work by Max Weber, one of Eucken's predecessors at the Chair of Economics at the University of Fribourg from 1893 to 1896 (Tribe 1995, 82). Eucken maintained a tenuous companionship with Weber's epistemology, particularly in relation to the concept of ideal type (*Idealtypus*). This proximity maintained by Eucken contrasted with the intellectual detachment from Weber marked by economists like Joseph A. Schumpeter (although personally close to Weber) or Ludwig Mises in the early interwar period—a withdrawal that "reflects the turning point in political economy in less than a generation and the misunderstanding of the importance of Weber's work" (Bruhns 1996, 1260). Overall, the plural philosophical references that Eucken mobilized anchored his

1. Eucken did not use this terminology, even if he spoke in terms of "obstacle" (*Hindernis*). Here I freely draws on Gaston Bachelard's definition of the "epistemological obstacle" as a difficulty "in the very act of knowing." In fact, "an epistemological obstacle is embedded in the unquestioned knowledge" of the researcher—it is of the order of "instinct" (Bachelard 1938, 13–15). By contrast, this study terms the "ontological obstacle" as a difficulty "external" to the scientist, one that is based on "the complexity and transience of the phenomena." On Eucken's epistemological obstacle, see also Fèvre (2020).

2. The neo-Kantism movement was attempting to revive philosophy of science building on the Kantian intention of reconciling rationalism and empiricism. The term "neo-Kantism" designates not only authors of the Marburg School (such as Hermann Cohen, Paul Natorp, and Ernst Cassirer), but also Heinrich Rickert and Wilhelm Windelband. Eucken cited the last three in his *Foundations*.

work within a specific tradition that was alternative to historicism while foreign to positivism.[3]

## 2.1 POWER AS A CENTRAL EPISTEMOLOGICAL QUESTION

### 2.1.1 *Foundations*, an Anti-Treatise of Methodology?

The preface to the original German edition of *Foundations* provides a useful starting point for understanding the nature of Eucken's epistemological project. This first preface (dated November 1939) is translated and reproduced here in its entirety:

> This book is not a methodological book. Its subject of study is the effective economic reality. The overwhelming proliferation of methodological reflections is a sign of disease for any science, although no science has ever been cured by methodology alone. The vital scope of the questions addressed to political economy is characterised by internal insecurity, distance from life itself and fragmentation which—despite many major particular results—prevail within it. Therefore, it is necessary to rethink the concrete problems it has to solve from the beginning. The purpose of this book is to penetrate into the effective economic reality in order to understand it scientifically. (Eucken 1940a, ix)

Eucken's opening statement against a purely methodological reading of his work can be understood as a desire to mark his originality within the field. In a book review for *Economica*, Friedrich Lutz (1944, 210), Eucken's former student, stressed the absence of "endless abstract discussions" on induction and deduction, as well as on whether economics was a social or a natural science. Despite this and "the author's [Eucken] denial," the book was, at least, "partly a treatise on methodology" to Lutz's own admission. However, the issue is not so much the veracity of Eucken's statement in this incipit as its overall significance in the economy of his discourse.

3. The philosophical investigation in this chapter is limited to the comprehensive exposition of Eucken's epistemology regarding the specific theme of power. Specifically, this is neither a systematic analysis of its sources nor a critical evaluation of its interpretations and uses. The secondary literature already offers significant contributions in this regard. In particular, Nils Goldschmidt (2002, 2013) as well as Rainer Klump and Manuel Wörsdörfer (2011) provided comprehensive accounts of the links between Husserl, Rudolf, and Eucken (see also Campagnolo 2003; Goldschmidt 2003; Herrmann-Pillath 1991, 1994; Miettinen 2016; Oksala 2016; Weisz 2001; Wörsdörfer 2011).

The expression "effective economic reality" (*wirtschaftliche Wirklichkeit*) was far from anecdotal since Eucken used it abundantly throughout the *Foundations*.[4] Moreover, this term appeared in the first lines of the editors' foreword in the first issue of the journal *Ordo* (Eucken and Böhm 1948, vii).

Thus, in this preface, Eucken stressed the opposition between artificial methodology and a study of reality that may seem partially forced. Specifically, he noted the gap between the "constantly metatheoretical" discourse that deals with preconditions and conceptual elaboration rather than actual engagement (Campagnolo 2004, 165). In doing so, Eucken rejected a certain tradition of historicism in favor of Weber's project (1904), regarding social science as a "science of reality" (*Wirklichkeitswissenchaft*). Eucken's theoretical research aimed "to be an instrument of knowledge, not its object" (1940b, 301). Nevertheless, Eucken stressed that "experience and even everyday experience (*Alltagserfahrung*) is impossible without concepts" (1940b, 24). Thus, any knowledge of reality is mediated by concepts (*Begriffe*) in the Kantian sense of a priori. The economist must, therefore, investigate facts through concepts, not concepts directly.

Moreover, in Eucken's view, these concepts that economists necessarily employ (e.g., work, production, prices, etc.) do not need a priori scientific definition. They are borrowed from the understanding derived from ordinary life, however unsatisfactory that immediate understanding may be. It is ultimately the starting point and necessarily provisional. However, it is essential to preserving the link between actual problems rather than rushing "into darkness and inner speculation" (1940b, 25). Hence Eucken (1940b, 28) called for a return to "things" (*Sachen*)—as opposed to "words" (*Worte*)—as the source of a proper economic conceptualization.

### 2.1.2 Everyday Experience and the Five Aspects of the Economic Problem

Eucken (1940b, 17) opened his *Foundations* with two unexpected references: Hippolyte Taine, on the one hand, and René Descartes, on the other. From Taine, Eucken borrowed his warning from a culture (therefore, science) that no longer looks directly at facts but rather focuses on representations and "meaningless conceptual systems" (i.e., science that

4. *Wirklichkeit* is consistently translated here as effective reality, to differentiate it from *Realität*, which means the level of factual experience (specific to historicism). Eucken, instead, aimed at the theoretical structuring principles of reality.

no longer asks decisive questions). From Descartes, Eucken borrowed the "universal doubt" and the cogito.[5] Moreover, Eucken placed himself in Descartes' thought experiment: facing a stove that heats a small room, he determined to question reality. Eucken questioned the objective characteristics of the stove (production and use), thereby approaching what has been described as phenomenology of the economic system (see Herrmann-Pillath 1994):[6]

> What is the material out of which the stove is constructed, asks the scientist. This question alone gives rise to a host of others which lead back to atomic physics. Why does this stove produce a certain amount of calories? This leads us on to the theory of heat. *Our* questions are different. Why was the stove produced at all? Why was it set up in this particular room? Simple questions—seemingly. (Eucken 1940b, 18, emphasis in original)

In Eucken's view, science emerged from researchers' will to question reality from a certain viewpoint: the type of question defined the scientific field that emerged. In support of his claim, Eucken explicitly relied on a statement by Weber at the first congress of German sociologists (*Deutsche Gesellschaft für Soziologie*) in 1909: "'Economy,' then, is something we select from out of the variety of our experience, a point of view that we adopt when we are faced with particular sorts of problems" (Weber, quoted by Eucken 1940b, 319, n. 1). Eucken (1940b, 18) formulated a series of related questions before setting out the central concern that the economist should address based on experience: "How is this process with its far-reaching division of labour steered (*Lenkung*) in its entirety so that everyone comes by the goods on which each human existence depends?" In other words, Eucken aimed at addressing the question of the "internal relations of daily economic life" (1940b, 102).

According to Eucken (1940b, 9–22), answering this question concerned five aspects of the economic process: (1) the alternative use of scarce resources to satisfy needs, (2) the distribution of income, (3) the orientation of the production structure by savings or investment (their temporal

5. Behind the reference to Descartes, however, emerged the shadow of Husserl. Indeed, Husserl built on Descartes to shape his concept of suspension of judgment. Like Husserl's *Epochè*, Eucken aimed to adopt a disinterested and impartial view of economic reality (Klump and Wörsdörfer 2011, 556).

6. To what extent Eucken's methodology was actually satisfying the canons of Husserl's phenomenology is beyond the scope of this study (see Miettinen 2016). The very possibility and desirability of a phenomenological analysis of the economy is, however, a subject of interest today (Düppe 2011).

aspects in particular), (4) the choice among production techniques, and (5) the spatial distribution of production at the national and international levels (see also Kuhnert 2008, 5–7). The term aspect—or "faces" (*Seiten*)—is important. Eucken emphasized that these five aspects represent five distinct components and ways of examining the same fundamental problem. They are, therefore, interdependent within the single and "overall social process of the economy" (Eucken 1940b, 23).

Eucken conceded that many economists before him had perceived these questions in a similar way, but they would often fail in formulating them. Eucken warned against definitions of economic science based on separate spheres (production, distribution, consumption, and exchange), as propagated by Jean-Baptiste Say following his *Cours complet d'économie politique pratique* (1828). Such an approach would be incorrect because it would make the economist lose sight of the "unity of economic activities" (Eucken 1940b, 26). Eucken hammered this point: "Since there are no independent spheres in the economy, there should be no separate theories, but only a whole: one problem and one theory" (1940b, 26). In contrast to Say, David Ricardo would have known how to recognize the unity of economic phenomena. However, Eucken stressed that this was at the cost of major impasses, particularly concerning the role of time and space in the economic process. This faulty Ricardian conception of theory would have infused the work of the Lausanne School (Léon Walras and Vilfredo Pareto).

Experience, according to Eucken, must provide the initial impetus for scientific work by isolating the endemic problems of the different sciences in general, especially of economics. To do this, questions could be formulated ex materia from a surmise. Starting from categories and definitions constructed a priori would entail a biased approach to the problems raised by economic analysis. Thus, Eucken (1940b, 304) insisted that "we do not impose our system on the facts, but we find it in the facts." A scientific definition would then be the "summary," the result of "the progressive analysis of things," or the "factual analysis" (*Sachanalyse*) by science, and not one of its assumptions (1940b, 301). Eventually, one may arrive at a definition that can then be made available for new studies: each concept would undergo a cumulative process rising from ordinary intuition up to a scientifically based proposal.

However, based on an analysis of the facts, Eucken's return to experience was not a justification for naïve empiricism. Eucken was particularly explicit on this subject, claiming that empiricism weakens science because it condemns it to captivity by the ideological judgments from interest groups, which is precisely what he aimed to overcome.

### 2.1.3 Science Facing Interests

To approach the effective economic reality, the economist must, therefore, rely on daily experience (*Alltagserfahrung*). However, in doing so, Eucken warned us that the individual—the worker, the entrepreneur, the politician, or the economist—was inclined to adopt a biased perspective, being himself a part of the economic system. In this respect, we are dealing again with the interpretative key to ordoliberalism proposed in this book (the question of the power exercised by individuals or groups) in the form of an epistemological obstacle:

> There is not only the fundamental problem of the economy that emerges from the experience of daily economic life. In the same economic life, there is also a unique tangle of opinions and ideologies on economic issues. This everyday economic experience in which we all share may thus be regarded in two ways. It provides the initial impulse for asking significant questions that call for an urgent response; and at the same time puts a considerable *obstacle* (*Hindernis*) in the way of our finding really useful answers. (Eucken 1940b, 28, emphasis in original)

Eucken seeks to ensure a strict separation between the knowing subject, on the one hand, and his object, on the other hand, that invalidates pure empiricism. Accordingly, empiricism would amount to the faulty reproduction of the expression of interests within the scientific discourse. In short, empiricism maintains a double illusion. First, individuals are not always able to properly assess what is really in their interest because they find themselves indistinguishably intertwining "real interest" and "presumed interest" (Eucken 1940b, 28–29). Eucken used the example of the entrepreneurs who, in 1922–1923, urged—successfully—the *Reichsbank* to pursue a cheap credit policy, which was extremely unfavorable due to hyperinflation. Second, Eucken perceived the individual as subject to what Hayek termed the pretense of (common) knowledge. In other words, their opinions always go beyond their situation so to project themselves onto the economic process but without grasping "the social economy in its overall configuration" (Eucken 1940b, 29).

At the individual level, though, interest opinions are only marginally problematic for Eucken (1940b, 32) since they are still "fragmented" (*zersplitterten*) among the population. These individual opinions may even be relevant within their field of limited expertise. However, the strongest version of Eucken's epistemological obstacle comes to the fore with the formation of "closed ideological groups," which, as "power groups," were armed for "economic struggle" (Eucken 1940b, 29).[7]

According to Eucken (1940b, 31), economic theory itself would not be free from ideological usage. First, a theory could be proposed for the benefit of political interests, as was the case with the doctrine of free trade in the nineteenth century. Second, an ideological argument could also be accepted as part of a theory. Eucken (1940b, 321) claimed that this problem, which was perceived by the first economists like François Quesnay and Adam Smith in their charge against mercantilism, would be increasingly less recognized by modern economists (with the notable exception of Karl Marx):

> Many economists have not yet recognized the decisive importance of their task for everyday economic life. Even in writings on methodology, the subject is generally overlooked, or only superficially addressed, without its basic importance being made clear. Often, biased ideologies are not seen for what they are, in spite of the ponderous concentrations of power operating behind them. (Eucken 1940b, 32–33)

After such a negative depiction, one might wonder how the economist could overcome this fundamental subjectivism. Could the economist even stand above the expression of interests to scientifically grasp the economic reality? Eucken aimed at providing a positive answer to this question, as opposed to the approach he depicted as negative (inspired by Marx). What Eucken sought with his *Foundations* was a fundamental criterion for determining the intrinsic value of a proposal on the economic world, knowing that any proposal was the result of interests:

> It is not that what we have learned from our everyday experience must be wrong because of the expression of particular interests. It may be either true or false. To decide that, we must find a strict criterion and a scientific method. (Eucken 1940b, 32)

7. In some passages, Hutchinson's English translation of Eucken's book is questionable. For example, he suppressed several direct quotations from Schopenhauer from the original text in his translation (compare Eucken 1940a, 11, to 1940b, 29). Moreover, he provided approximate and condensed translations, drawing the text toward a contingent interpretation of the passion–interest relationship, which seems more appropriate to the English political economy than to Eucken's demonstration, for whom the expression of interest is both the source of economic activity and its essential problem (see Chapter 1).

The internal link to the fundamental problem of the economy is made explicit here. Indeed, to adequately understand the five aspects of this problem (described earlier), it is necessary to go through the (phenomenal) experience of the economy, a form of return to things. The researcher is then subject to the contamination of science by vested interests, characteristic for Eucken of an empirical approach.

This first section emphasized the phenomenological (rather than methodological) nature of Eucken's *Foundations*, which highlighted the existence of an epistemological problem at the root of any scientific approach and thus the imperative need to detach scientific production from any ideological process. In the conclusion of his *Foundations*, Eucken (1940b, 305) highlighted that "overcoming (*Überwindung*) opinions and ideologies is an essential task of political economy" but that this task required "strict adherence to the idea of truth." Escaping this pitfall would require a specification of the scientific methodology, thereby grasping the dual nature of political economy.

## 2.2 THE SINGULARITY OF POLITICAL ECONOMY AS A SCIENCE

### 2.2.1 "The Great Antinomy" Between Theory and History

According to Eucken, any economic issue must be considered directly from its daily distinctiveness and randomness (i.e., in its "historical-individual" aspect). Eucken emphasized that every economic framework was "in itself History" and thus was "part of the overall process of historical being and becoming" (1940b, 34, 37). Nevertheless, Eucken claimed that the economist's work was different from the work of the specialized historian. The singularity of the economist would be explained by the general rules that govern the economy (these theoretical rules will be explored in Chapter 3). Accordingly, the economic process is not a historical object of the same nature as "wars" or "diplomatic negotiations" (1940b, 39). Any causal explanation in political economy requires an understanding of the connections and systematic relationships between facts, which are invisible to those who only compile these facts. This situation is what Eucken called the "theoretical-general" aspect of economic science.

Economic activities inevitably appear in a particular and contingent form, but at the same time are ruled by certain general principles that are universally valid. Thus, a simple collection of facts would only confuse the economist in a "chaos of details" (1940b, 41). It would leave the economist unable to perceive the internal relationships expressed. Eucken argued that both the historical and theoretical aspects of the economic problem must be addressed together from the beginning of the scientific inquiry:

> The theoretical questions do not come at the end of our science, and the theoretical propositions which we have to seek are not simply a distillation of experience. . . . It is not any doctrinaire spirit or love of philosophical speculation that leads us to study theoretical-general problems, but simply our striving after a truly scientific experience (*Erfahrung*). . . . If the economist chooses only the theoretical-general approach or only the historical-individual approach, the real world remains foreign to him (*wirklichkeitsfremd*). (Eucken 1940b, 40–41)

The pursuit of a theoretical analysis requires the use of "conceptual models" (*gedankliche Modelle*), even allowing the ceteris paribus clause to formulate questions from a general perspective. However, the theoretical method alone would lure economic science into sectarianism and a lack of realism. Paradoxically, Eucken (1940b, 53) called such a procedure "non-historical and non-theoretical" because it would break the link with concrete facts and problems in favor of a logical and metaphysical approach.

At this step, Eucken's "great antinomy" appears as a major ontological obstacle in the way of fully grasping an economic phenomenon.[8] To overcome this, it is necessary to simultaneously reconcile the specific and, therefore, historical particularity of economic phenomena with their relationship to the whole system, as revealed by general and theoretical analysis. "Simultaneously" is the key word because it is neither a sequence from one to the other nor two parallel—separate— approaches. However, Eucken was fully aware of the intrinsic difficulty of the method he was proposing because the historical and theoretical approaches required different and complementary qualities in the scientific investigation:

> A superficial compromise between theoretical and historical investigation or merely methodological reflections about their cooperation are pointless. . . . The historical-individual aspect of the problem requires perception, intuition, synthesis, understanding (*Verstehen*), and empathy (*Einfühlung*) for living

8. Eucken had formulated the expression "*Große Antinomie*" in a short introductory text published two years before *Foundations* and titled *Political Economy—What For?* (*Nationalökonomie—wozu?*) (Eucken 1938b). The word "antinomy" recalled Kant's vocabulary: a necessary contradictory statement faced by reason when it aims at grasping the world.

> individual experience. The theoretical-general aspect requires rational thinking, analysis, and the elaboration of models. (Eucken 1940b, 43)

In this passage, Eucken gave us the singularity of political economy as a science. It is not strictly historical because it is subject to rules of universal scope. However, it is detached from the natural sciences by the plurality of forms that the economic system can take in a given place and at a given time. We can then understand Eucken's (1940b, 295) frustration in qualifying political economy as a science: it was all at once a historical (or empirical) science, an experimental (or natural) science, and a social (or moral) science. In short, political economy was "truly a 'border science,'" even if this accurate definition was, in fact, later given by Röpke (1956, 122). In Eucken's view, the great antinomy was what precisely "determines the place of political economy in the cosmos of science" (1940b, 311). This situation directly implies that political economy cannot import methods from other sciences and vice versa.

However, until Eucken's time, economists would not have been able to solve this great antinomy.[9] Accordingly, Eucken (1950a, 9) claimed that political economy had not yet reached the "full understanding of the modern economic world [which had] new types of social problems, cyclical fluctuations, and contemporary struggles for economic power. The more pressing these current problems become, the more intolerable is the gap between economics and the real world." The social structure of the economy is increasingly complex, thus making this effort in bringing the two approaches—historical and theoretical—together crucial. Therefore, political economy requires a new method if it is to achieve its fundamental task; namely, the "scientific knowledge of the effective real economy" (Eucken 1940b, 221) or, in other words, knowledge having overcome the great antinomy. In the following paragraphs, I show that Eucken had less resolved to close the *Methodenstreit* per se than to set the conditions for overcoming it on an entirely different basis.

9. Eucken (1940b, 47–63) outlined four types of political economy based on the method used by economists: (1) classical, (2) conceptual or formal (Walras and Pareto), (3) dualist (Menger), and (4) empiricist (Historical Schools). Eucken also talked about modern theorists (such as Marshall, Pigou, and Keynes), admitting having trouble identifying where to put them.

### 2.2.2 The Deadlock of the *Methodenstreit*

In 1883, the publication of the *Untersuchungen über die Methode* by Carl Menger, followed by a ruthless book review by Gustav Schmoller in his *Jahrbuch*, inaugurated the famous German dispute over methods. This conflict of methods has often been reduced to a "simplistic and false formula, history without theory versus theory without history" (Bruhns 2004, 4) or to a sterile opposition between data collection, on the one hand, and abstraction, on the other (Campagnolo 2011, 472). The protagonists, especially Schmoller (Louzek 2011, 449), were partly responsible for the caricatural aspect of the debate by polarizing blunt oppositions (such as deduction vs. induction, individualism vs. holism, and theory vs. facts). While these categories are parts of the debate (see Fusfeld 2008), they are not fully relevant since, in the end, both Menger and Schmoller were trying to find the right articulation between each of these pairs. More prominently, the "process of abstraction" of reality and the relationship between political economy and social complexity were at the heart of the dispute (Campagnolo 2011, 475; Labrousse 2009, 147). In short, both sides developed a theoretical approach of inquiry to provide a causal scientific explanation for the required methodology.[10]

The two authors' opposition was quite explicit in the use of concepts, particularly that of political economy. Menger's definition of it was instrumental and formal, centered on individual (rational) behavior. On the contrary, for Schmoller, political economy was substantive and defined a certain geographical and historical field of the social. The concept of the community (*Gemeinschaft*) was at the heart of his research. Schmoller's national—people's—economy (*Volkwirtschaft*) endorsed an organic outlook, where every kind of economic system forms a coherent group "that can and should be considered as real as the family, the community, or the State" (1902, 329–330). In his case, the very association of individual elements conveys emerging properties that require an analysis of compound products or collective concepts: the whole cannot be reduced to the sum of the parts. The object of historical science was, therefore, to precisely apprehend the particular in what is accidental and singular.

On the contrary, Menger conceptualized a human economy through which he aimed at isolating pure elements—in their individuality—by an essentialist and analytical extraction. By explaining the particular and

10. Note that there is no real consensus on Schmoller's program, one characterized by a lack of theoretical unification (Gioia 2000, 63; Peukert 2001, 96).

evacuating accidental factors to grasp the essence, the economist could reconstruct the complexity of the real world. Menger offered a logical definition of abstract concepts without tangible counterpart in the world. Menger (1883) also rejected "collective concepts" (*Kollektiv-begriffe*) because this category abandons or "neglects the only economic behaviour that can be known for good, individual action" (Campagnolo 2011, 454). Hence, Menger founded two guiding ideas from the different Austrian schools and beyond: subjectivism and methodological individualism.

Although only appearing as an endnote in the *Foundations*, Eucken's assessment of the dispute over methods was final: the two positions are inconsistent because they raise methodological questions inappropriately. For Eucken, it was clear that

> in the unfortunate quarrel between Menger and Schmoller, both parties were wrong, nor was the truth somewhere in the middle between the two. Neither Menger's dualism, of which Schmoller perceived the danger, nor Schmoller's pure empiricism, the failure of which Menger foresaw, does justice to economic reality. A new start is necessary. (Eucken 1940b, 324, n. 11)

Eucken agreed that Menger and Schmoller were both correct in acknowledging some of the weaknesses of each other's approach. In Eucken's view, Menger provided theoretically sound answers to questions that have little relevance in reality. However, Schmoller offered theoretically weak answers while asking essential questions. What Eucken (1940b, 55) called Menger's "dualist" approach distinguishes theoretical analysis from historical analysis under different methods and objectives in two separate types of science (although Menger recognizes the intrinsic value of each). The main weakness of this "cooperative" approach between the sciences lies in its inability to account for actual problems, as each of the two sciences remains sterile in this field: "to the extent that the divide between theoretical and historical political economy is maintained, the real problems remain unresolved" (Eucken 1940b, 56).

It is on the strength of his theory conception that Eucken intended to distinguish himself from the Menger–Schmoller couple:

> True theory is not upstream of the examination of the real economy, as conceptualist economists assume, nor downstream, as empiricists believe, nor separately from the examination of facts, as extreme "Dualists" want, but true theory is at the centre of the knowledge process; it is a tool that is created to make scientific experience possible. (Eucken 1940b, 301)

Like Schmoller, Eucken (1940b, 59) stressed the unity of political economy. Nevertheless, the empirical method would remain faulty because it abandons the idea of starting with the formulation of a problem to question reality while striving to compile and assemble exhaustive evidence. It is at this price that a theoretical formulation will then be possible, and yet the essential (or theoretical-general) connections between the facts would remain inaccessible to the historicists.

Clearly, for Eucken, Menger and Schmoller left unsolved the ontological problem of the complex articulation between theory and history. However, Eucken's dissatisfaction regarding the *Methodenstreit* was not limited to this aspect. The protagonists of the battle of methods did not even explicitly perceive the epistemological problem emanating from vested interests. Eucken (1940b, 57) illustrated this with the example of cartels, claiming that the "scientific treatment" of actual cartel problems—and the struggle for power that came with it—was highly "unsatisfactory." On the one hand, theoretical economists like Menger would apply the monopoly theory to cartels and overlook the very specificity of the formation and strategies of cartels in contrast to pure monopolies. On the other hand, historicists like Schmoller would provide hundred-page long descriptive accounts of the formation and running of an individual cartel in Germany, thus missing the decisive explanation of the interdependency of every single economic unit within the whole economic process.

Eucken saw Menger's a priori conceptual definitions as "scientifically unfounded notions," divorced from factual analysis and, accordingly, as a path by which "interests-based views and confused ideologies creep into political economy" (Eucken 1940b, 303). As noted in the ordo manifesto of 1936, "all conceptual speculation" would have deleterious effects to "lure us into becoming doctrinaire and unrealistic" (Böhm et al. 1936, 24). Theoretical economists would disregard the "vital problems" of economic life in general and the key issue of power.[11] According to Eucken, Schmoller committed the reverse of Menger's mistake. Historicists did start from the facts and thus identified the crucial question of economic life. However, their lack of appropriate theoretical tools was bound to leave

11. As Pierre Dockès (1999) noted, theoretical economists like Menger (and Walras) pushed power issues into the background of an accessory situation, outside the core of marginalist economic theory. Eucken (1940b, 17) rejected what he called the "senseless conceptual systems" erected by the general equilibrium paradigm. Although Walras and Eucken shared the opinion that state intervention in favor of a competitive order was a central element for a rational economic policy, their respective philosophies of science and history indicated very different ways of seeing the state's role regarding the market economy (see Baranzini and Fèvre 2019).

the epistemological obstacle unsolved and political economy under the sway of interest ideologies:

> This [empirical] method has no way of advancing beyond a collection of unanalysed facts. Its vision and thinking is *pointilliste* and unrealistic, for it misses the significance of the interdependence of all economic activities. Because it cannot provide reliable answers to the questions posed, it has to fall back again and again on attempted explanation at the level of everyday experience. The result is the insecurity and inconsistency of many empiricist economists in dealing with interested opinions and ideologies. (Eucken 1940b, 63, emphasis in original)

Eucken provided a clear insight into the articulation behind the resolution of the two identified obstacles. The economists' failure to overcome the "great antinomy" (i.e., to solve the problem of the ontological obstacle) makes the epistemological obstacle more challenging to address. Thus, the ontological obstacle logically precedes (and in a sense gives momentum to) the epistemological obstacle. Given the sectarianism of conceptual theory and, above all, its permeability to the interests of the Historical School in particular and empiricism in general, the Euckenian project appears as an attempt to place political economy in a methodological approach that must protect science from any bias.

### 2.2.3 Opposing Schmoller's Optimist Outlook

Eucken distanced himself from both Menger's and Schmoller's views. However, Eucken's charge against Schmoller was much more documented than that against Menger, for a few reasons. First, the Historical School was the "straw man" to any dissident program of political economy in interwar Germany (Grimmer-Solem and Romani 1998, 275). Although Schmoller died in 1917, he continued to exert a strong influence on German social sciences despite a pluralism that was then greater than at the beginning of the century. Moreover, historicism—though severely in decline in the interwar period—marked a limited but genuine revival under National Socialism (Hagemann 2016, 228; Ptak 2009, 113). These contextual arguments motivated Eucken's tenacious critique.

A supplementary explanation can be found in Eucken's formative years as an economist. Indeed, the historicist tradition informed his early works. Eucken completed his doctoral thesis (in 1914) and his habilitation (in 1921) under the supervision of Hermann Schumacher (1868–1952), an economist intellectually close to both Schmoller and Wagner (Hagemann 2004, 408–409). The German Historical School's inability to satisfactorily explain—and therefore cure—the German hyperinflation of 1923–1924 pushed Eucken to gradually reject it (Klump 2003, 152; Abelshauser 2004, 25). Hence, Eucken embarked on a path from the endorsement of the quantitative theory of money (Eucken 1923) to the construction of an Austrian-like theory of capital (Eucken 1934). He finally called for "the overcoming of historicism" (*Die Überwindung der Historismus*) in an article published in Schmoller's *Jahrbuch* (Eucken 1938a). What has been hitherto neglected in the literature is that Eucken's rejection of Schmoller's methodology was comprehensive enough to embrace its ethical-anthropological bases. Schmoller's postulates on human nature and faith in progress were, according to Eucken, responsible for historicists' failure to address the epistemological obstacle of political economy.

In the same year Eucken published *Foundations* (1940b), he also authored a lengthy piece entitled "Science in Schmoller's Style" ("*Wissenschaft im Stile Schmollers*"). In this article, Eucken (1940c) leveled his critical fire at the ethical-anthropological postulate on which Schmoller's work rested. Eucken (1940c, 475) felt at odds with Schmoller's naïve optimism in the process of continual progress steered by the "inexorable ethicization" (*Ethisierung*) of "civilised men" (*Kulturmenschen*), a view broadly infused within the Historical School as a whole (Schefold 1996). According to Eucken, Schmoller's "ideology of progress" (*Fortschrittsideologie*) drove him to consider humans today as "more civilised" than before in a process characterized by the progressive disappearance of "selfish motives" from daily economic behavior.

Schmoller's anthropological postulate, Eucken claimed, was not only contrary to the actual historical trend (he saw the turmoil of the first half of the twentieth century as undeniable evidence of his point of view) but prevented any objective analysis of economic reality. Schmoller had neglected the central issue of rising power groups and their attendant ideologies within modern Germany:

> Schmoller was moving away from economic reality; like many other economists. Everyday economic life has always been and still is full of power struggles. And these struggles are not led by people who are infinitely civilized, but by individuals who have developed a sophisticated and brutal art of the struggle for power. (Eucken 1940c, 479)

To Eucken, Schmoller made a fundamental error with his optimistic assessment of the exponential growth of cartels in the newly and suddenly industrialized Germany.[12] Eucken (1940b, 264) accounted for this fault by pointing to Schmoller's lack of "direct and personal experience" of the exercise of economic power in economic life. He not only deprecated Schmoller's use of second-hand knowledge of cartels acquired through academic studies but also argued more critically that Schmoller's methodology of "interviews with industrialists and senior officials" (1940b, 264) was what precisely disqualified him from a sound scientific inquiry into power issues.

Eucken (1940b, 105) aspired to "break completely" with historicism. His dissatisfaction was rooted in two main shortcomings. First, historicists were leaving "knowledge about contemporary economic facts to practitioners or business managers." Second, they were leaving "knowledge about the past to historians." By contrast, Eucken claimed that these two tasks belonged to the economists' imperatives. Lacking an adequate method to "penetrate safely into economic reality," historicist economists were "often dependent on knowledgeable practitioners." On monetary issues such as devaluations, for instance, historicist economists depended on "the comments of—mostly interested—bank practitioners" (Eucken 1940b, 305).

According to Eucken, scientists alone can provide an objective analysis of the world and thus constitute the only medium for interest-free advice on economic policy debates. Eucken and the ordoliberals supported the scientists' privileged position with two arguments (Böhm et al. 1936, 15). The first one was linked to ethics regarding the scientist's "vocation (*Beruf*) and position, being independent of economic interests." The second argument concerned Eucken's perception of economic theory properly understood: scientists could overcome the interested and fragmented viewpoint "on the strength of their intimate knowledge of the intricate interrelationships of economic activity" as a whole (Böhm et al. 1936, 16). Ordoliberals contrasted the scientific expertise of independent academic economists seeking scientific truth with interested experts specialized in the "technical details of their professional field" (Böhm et al. 1936, 16). Thus, these experts would be biased advisers for the conduct of economic policy.

12. The historicists' attention to the institutional changes of capitalist economies led them to focus on the rise of new market structures alternative to pure competition (like cartels and trusts). In the first half of the twentieth century, these new structures were increasingly perceived as adjustment tools necessary for the stability of the economic cycle (Pribram 1986, 239; Schneider 1993, 367).

As we show in Chapter 1, the ordoliberals' act of faith in favor of scientific reasoning was, to them, utterly imperative to remedy the widespread political irrationality of the interwar period, which was inspired by ideologies. For Eucken, these ideologies were deceptive guides to action since "they affirm and promote movements that achieve exactly the opposite of that which ideologists hope from them" (Eucken 1932b, 69; see also Röpke 1935, 94).

Eucken's rationale against Schmoller's ideology of progress was a slippery slope. Although Eucken condemned naïve optimism about the human nature, he did not want to fall into pessimism and fatalism embodied, in his view, by authors like Friedrich Nietzsche and, closer to his time, Oswald Spengler. Eucken (1940c, 479) recognized that the pessimistic and fatalistic vision of human nature was to some extent "closer to the effective reality" than Schmoller's optimism. As Eucken stressed in many passages of *Foundations*, daily economic life was indeed "full of power struggles." However, Eucken refused to fully embrace what he termed the "predator-anthropology" (*Raubtier-Anthropologie*). Even if humans "act frequently as a predator," Eucken was convinced that men and women were always capable of responsible behavior by following "legal or moral obligations" before their instinctive will to power. In other words, the vast majority of individuals were bounded by "the rules of the game in the struggle for life" (Eucken 1940c, 478).[13] In Eucken's ordoliberal perspective, individuals' ethics of responsibility enforced by legal norms was essential to reconcile selfish economic interests with the common good (Vanberg 2014; Wörsdörfer 2010).

In the last analysis, Eucken argued that Schmoller (because of his progressive stance), as well as Nietzsche and Spengler (will to power), maintained the same anthropological-ethical confusion. And this flawed point of view would have "penetrated the German intellectual life under various forms" (Eucken 1940c, 478). Specifically, it would be characterized, according to Eucken (1940c, 478), by the equivalence of "the strongest" and "the best" of individuals in the "struggle for life" (*Lebenskampf*).[14]

13. Eucken (1940c, 479) also deplored the fact that so many "efficient actions in history" were also "successful crimes." Some of the arguments Eucken developed in his 1940 article tend toward a veiled criticism of the Nazi regime, which his unpublished diary further demonstrated (see Klinckowstroem 2000).

14. "Schmoller once said," stressed Eucken (1940c, 478), "that it is the privilege of the strongest and best individual to win." Schmoller's outlook was clearly informed by Wilhelm Dilthey's descriptive psychology and Herbert Spencer's evolutionism (Nau 2000, 515). In fact, social Darwinism was widely accepted in Germany (Weikart 1993, 478).

However, the "strong man" in the ordoliberal lexicon is not the person who abandons herself to a nihilist "lust for power" since that person would be "intrinsically weak." On the contrary, individuals are "strong" because they use their reason to "illuminate the darkness surrounding the acting agent" (Böhm et al. 1936, 23).

Thus, Eucken (1940c, 484, 489) invoked the skepticism of science as a contrary remedy both to Schmoller's optimism and to the Nietzsche-Spengler fatalism. Eucken, in affinity with Weber's ambition to consider "what is conventionally evident a problem" (Weber 1904), aimed at questioning conventions or political agreements. Eucken (1940c, 484) endorsed a "sceptical thesis" characterized by the initial condition of the scientist on the path to the "realm of truth" (*Reich der Wahrheit*), an expression borrowed from Husserl (Eucken 1940b, 304; see Goldschmidt 2013). According to Eucken, political economy as a science suffered from the relativism of truth introduced by romanticism, historicism, pragmatism, and even positivism, which thereby makes it susceptible to the influence of interests. Thus, to become a useful science in guiding political decisions, political economy would have to swerve away from interest opinions to embrace universal values.

Accordingly, in *Foundations*, Eucken asserted that the scientist must imperatively grasp and rationally explain power relations in the economy. Against the idea that reflecting about power was divorced from genuine scientific investigation, Eucken (1940b, 272) claimed that economic power was "not something irrational or mystical." On the contrary, it was "comprehensible and accessible by reason." Schmoller's optimistic outlook went hand in hand with an inadequate methodology, given the epistemological obstacle highlighted by Eucken. In his views, this was additional to Schmoller's inability to perceive the fundamentally theoretical nature of the economy, namely the ontological obstacle. This pushed Eucken to develop a competing methodology in its own right.

## 2.3 THINKING IN ECONOMIC ORDERS

### 2.3.1 The Morphological Analysis to Overcome the "Great Antinomy"

Let us summarize the ontological problem (the "great antinomy") that Eucken posed. On the one hand, the theoretical approach focused on the object in its general aspect: its criterion is truth, and its method is rationalist. On the other hand, the historical approach seeks to understand the object in its individuality: its criterion is actuality, and it uses empirical methods. However, Eucken stressed that the economic reality was made up of both historical contingencies and valid general principles. Could this great antinomy be overcome? If so, on what conditions?

Eucken claimed that articulating theoretical and historical analysis was possible only thanks to the existence of a certain invariance of the forms that govern the course of the economic activity throughout history. In other words, Eucken suggested that there was "a limited number of pure forms" from which all "economic systems present and past have been, and are, composed" (Eucken 1940b, 109). Furthermore, if economists succeed in isolating these pure elements, then they could "apprehend economic life as a whole" despite "the changing forms of economic reality" (Eucken 1950a, 10–11).

In practice, Eucken provided a historical account of various actual economic systems, starting from the economy of the Inca Empire through the ancient period (Rome, Egypt), the Middle Ages (guilds of Florence or Rotterdam), the European Enlightenment, to the contemporary (interwar) period. On deeper consideration, Eucken saw economic history as a laboratory where a series of experiments had already been conducted on a vast geographical and temporal range—experiments that were awaiting the economist's systematization. Eucken proceeded by variation and comparison, showing that actual economic systems manifested themselves to our perception (i.e., in effective reality) only as real types or, in fact, as a combination of various ideal types.

Eucken (1940b, 107) used an "isolating abstraction mechanism" in building his ideal types from recurrent and coherent individual facts by isolating and generalizing core features of the phenomenon to the detriment of less significant aspects. Thus, Eucken aimed at obtaining the truth and achieving a universal and exact knowledge of political economy, what he called, following Husserl, "evident truth of reason" (cited and translated by Goldschmidt 2013, 137). Eucken's method was clearly informed by Husserl's approach (eidetic reduction).[15] Consequently, Eucken's theory of science cannot be understood as an empirical induction, but instead as an essentializing process from the raw materials of reality. Eucken ended up

15. Again, Eucken aimed to make political economy a science of essences in its own right, following Husserl's idea that "apodictic truth and universal validity" (Oksala 2016, 7–8) could be achieved through invariance within the plurality of given historical experiences. However, according to Husserl, the essences of social science necessarily remain inaccurate (he called them *morphologies*) because it would be impossible to determine exactly all the characteristics of a social object, as in the case of a triangle (Moinat 2005, 44).

with a typology of standard ideal types from which the explanatory scheme of an economy can be (re)constructed. He called it a "comprehensive morphological device of economic systems" (1940b, 173), meaning a classification system considered exhaustive and based on the historical analysis conducted.

Thanks to his singular methodology, Eucken was confident of having solved both the ontological and epistemological obstacles. On the one hand, Eucken believed he overcame the great antinomy of political economy because the ideal types obtained would constitute "elements of lasting connection" (1940b, 174) between the historical-individual and theoretical-general aspects of the economic life. On the other hand, this kind of morphological analysis would allow the economists to extract themselves from the biased opinions of a given society. Indeed, they could account for historical events disconnected from their immediate surroundings and revealed by theoretical necessities.

The morphological analysis was an integral—crucial—part of Eucken's economic analysis. The construction of this morphology of pure forms has, for Eucken (1940b, 240), "two functions in the process of knowledge." First, its plasticity can account for any economic system, past or present. The result of his morphological work is reflected in an essential duality within economic systems (*Wirtschaftssystem*); that is, between "administered economy" (*Zentralgeleitete Wirtschaft*) on the one hand, and "exchange economy" (*Verkehrswirtschaft*) on the other. At the end of his historical work, Eucken concluded that "traces of other economic systems other than these two cannot be found in the economic reality of the present as well as the past." As a result, it seemed to him particularly "difficult to imagine" that other (pure) forms exist or may one day exist (Eucken 1940b, 118).

The opposition between the two systems was less binary than it seems. Each ideal type has subcategories that offer nuances. Moreover, an actual economic system was never comparable to either, as it was rather a combination of these elements, which tend toward one of these ideal types. To judge this, Eucken provided five partial economic orders corresponding to the five aspects of the economic problem: (1) the type of direction of the economy (decentralized/centralized), (2) the mechanism of price formation (e.g., competition, oligopoly, monopoly, etc.), (3) the type of ownership, (4) the type of coordination between households or enterprises, and (5) the type of monetary system (see also Weisz 2001, 190). Picturing any real type of an actual economic system would require picturing each of these five aspects as a distinctive combination of ideal types.

Second, each pure form (ideal type) constitutes the basis for proper theoretical work, which is the only one capable of grasping the causal relations of the economy. Eucken's morphological analysis was, therefore, logically prior to what we might call "standard" or "canonical" economic theory such as monopoly theory, oligopoly theory, and monetary theory (see also Chapter 3). Without morphological analysis, canonical economic theory would be blind. Otherwise, a deductive and theoretical analysis must be selected and applied. Epistemologically speaking, Eucken insisted on the relative validity (time and place) of standard economic theories. In the same manner an ideal type remains "true," economic theories are still logically correct in general. However, a theory is not always relevant to be mobilized depending on the given historical-individual conditions. Hence in Eucken's view, an economic theory gains less in truth than in "actuality" (1940b, 234). For example, when a particular market approaches a situation of a monopolistic type, then the monopoly theory can be used.

### 2.3.2 Eucken's Theory of Order: Ruptures and Continuities

Eucken's article, "Science in Schmoller's Style" (1940c), was part of a series of publications honoring the 100th anniversary of Schmoller's birth (with important pieces by Carl Brinkmann and Arthur Spiethoff). However, in discussing Schmoller, Eucken was taking a stand regarding his contemporaries: the "youngest" exponents of the German Historical School. Eucken (1940b, 66) highlighted that, before him, some historical studies tried to resolve the "great antinomy." More precisely, a whole section of German thought starting with Friedrich List followed a similar agenda. However, the attempt at a genuine articulation between history and theory was truly central for the youngest Historical School with the work of Max Weber, Werner Sombart, and Arthur Spiethoff. The growing influence of neo-Kantism on the development of the rational method in social sciences encouraged the process of zoning in on the problematic articulation between history and theory (Hédoin 2013, 44–46). For instance, Sombart (1929, 3) claimed that theory was "the prerequisite for any scientific study of history" in an article timely entitled "Economic Theory and Economic History."

Sombart and Spiethoff aimed at bridging the gap between theory and history through the study of economic "stages" (*Wirtschaftsstufen*) and "styles" (*Wirtschaftsstile*).[16] The latest generation of historicists engaged in a return to Marx in the specific theme of the development of

16. Eucken's theory of development provided a critical account of competing German theories (see Goldschmidt 2016; Schefold 1995).

capitalism, on the one hand, and the strengthening of analytical tools, on the other (Backhaus 1989, 602; Grimmer-Solem and Romani 1998, 272). Paradoxically, this search for a more theoretical orientation also resulted in the incorporation of a whole range of contemporary economic sciences and their marginalist accents, in particular, by Weber.[17]

Weber wanted to free his conceptual analysis from any metaphysics, in the sense that he aimed at reaching scientific objectivity without an underlying ethical or political agenda. Thus, Weber embodied the younger generation of the Historical School that explicitly distanced itself from what he called the "logical problems of historicism" (see Weber 1906), as evidenced differently by the works of Roscher, Knies, and by Schmoller himself. In this context, Eucken's project appeared as an attempt to break with the historicism of Sombart and Spiethoff through a return—and a new use—of the Weberian ideal type.

Shedding light on Eucken's discussion of Weber's ideal type will help us grasp the scope of the economic theory models of ordoliberal thought in more depth. Eucken (1940b, 348) claimed that he was "not trying to develop a new concept . . . but simply to define precisely what Weber has treated in an obscure and incomplete way." Weber's approach, he pointed out, was not only "fragmentary (*Torso*), but also contains serious flaws" (1940b). In Eucken's view, Weber mistook the ideal type for the real type and the different processes of abstraction to which they are subjected. For Eucken, the fundamental contrast between the two types was based on the purely logical nature of the ideal type. For instance, the isolated state (*isolierte Staat*) of Johann H. von Thünen embodied the ideal type par excellence in Eucken's view (see Goldschmidt 2013, 133).[18]

Eucken's harsh judgment regarding Weber can be partly explained by the latter's great diversity of uses of the notion of ideal type (see Schweitzer 1970). Weber (1904) himself stressed the need to multiply the creation of concepts that remain historically determined, relating to certain problems or angles of analysis. It can also be explained by the fact that Eucken (1940b, 348, n. 66) considered that "Weber's views on the construction of types are still influential today" as the remaining seminal reference in German social sciences. Thus, Eucken sometimes magnified the line and marks oppositions more clearly than they really are. For example, for Eucken, the

17. Weber endorsed Menger's marginalist value theory (Campagnolo 2005, 799) and was, for instance, extremely critical of the use of psychological (or biological) factors to explain individuals' social and economic behavior (Maas 2009, 507).

18. The German economist Thünen (1783–1850) is considered one of the forerunners of marginalist theory, with important contributions to the field of economic geography. For an overview of his work, see Hans Frambach (2012).

ideal type would have no normative or ethical basis whatsoever. In truth, Weber (1904) knew very well that his ideal type has nothing to do with an ideal image in the sense of perfection to be achieved. Similarly, the construction of "rational utopias," although it is "only one of the various possible figures of the 'ideal type'" (Weber 1917a, 470), was, in fact, compatible with the use proposed by Eucken.

However, a fundamental opposition remains between Eucken's and Weber's perspectives. From Weber's nominalist view, the ideal type was a pure heuristic principle that makes research advance, although it holds no ontological link with the real world (Goldschmidt 2013, 130). In Weber's words (1904, 180), the ideal type "is not itself a 'hypothesis' but seeks to guide the elaboration of hypotheses." It "has the character of a utopia arrived at by the conceptual accentuation of particular elements of reality." For his part, Eucken explicitly rejected Weber's nominalist approach:

> Such utopias are opposed to the concrete reality. These ideal types (*Idealtypen*) are obtained from concrete reality and serve in turn to understand it. To this end, they are even totally essential. These ideal types constitute, therefore, a firm link between the empirical view of individual historical events and the general theoretical analysis necessary for understanding interrelationships. (Eucken 1940b, 173–174)

The ideal type was a "limit concept" (*Grenzbegriff*) for Weber (1904, 185). To Eucken, however, the ideal type was the basis of all the logical "conceptual models" (*gedanklichen Modelle*). Indeed, it worked as a foundational concept that has no heuristic but origin value. It is not utopian, but rather exact in an almost geometric sense. Thus, Eucken firmly linked the actual problem of power and interest within economic facts but arrived at the dispassionate and objective morphology of ideal types.

What role do these methodological refinements play in the relationship between ordoliberals and praxis? The following section shows that this difference in the conception of the ideal type between Weber and Eucken confirmed an antagonistic meaning of the relationship to values.

### 2.3.3 From a Positive "Economic Order" to the Normative "Order of the Economy"

By the beginning of the twentieth century, Weber, Sombart, and Spiethoff had tried to distance themselves from the normative-orientated works of their predecessors, which were, at first, critically labeled the "socialism of the lectern" (*Kathedersozialismus*). This new generation insisted on making a clear-cut distinction between scientific studies, on the one hand, and pragmatic-political conclusions and advice, on the other (Gioia 2000, 65; Nau 2000, 519; Schefold 1996, 190). Eucken followed up this trend toward greater scientific neutrality while formulating his own combination between theory and policy. He saw his *Foundations* as a rational and positive study of the real world. Removing opinions and ideologies within science was, therefore, a fundamental task to satisfy this effort. Nevertheless, Eucken—like other ordoliberals—saw his scientific work as a tool to transform society and embrace explicitly guiding values and normative ends. In short, one could say that Eucken aimed at an "interest-free" rather than a "value-free" economic science, which implied several departures from the Weberian approach.

The 1909 meeting of the *Verein für Socialpolitik* in Vienna marked the climax of another famous battle in German-speaking countries: the *Werturteilsstreit*, the battle over value judgment (see Ciaffa 1998; Hagemann 2001). Weber emphasized the need for a social science free from value judgments (*Wertfrei*). He famously separated the inevitable "relation to values" (*Wertbeziehung*) from "value judgments" (*Werturteil*) within scientific works. While the scientist is intrinsically bound to a specific relation to values (science is value-laden), he must avoid taking a stand on the desirability of agents' goals and ultimate social ends.[19] Weber defined this aspect, especially in his famous Munich conference, *Science as a Vocation*: "There is no science that is absolutely devoid of presuppositions, nor is there any science that can establish its own value once these presuppositions are denied" (Weber 1917b, 20).

Holding to this dichotomy, Weber refused to hierarchize values or seek universal beliefs, which led him to a form of radical relativism (Hédoin 2013, 123). For his part, Eucken (1940b, 264) stated that political economy was to be a "very sober science." This statement is noteworthy: Eucken could have written "objective" (*Objektivität*); however, he preferred the term "sober" (*nüchterne*). In a sense, Eucken played the young Weber off against the older one (the Weber of *Science as a Vocation*) and especially against Weber's followers. Before conceptualizing the notion of "objectivity" and "value freedom," the young Weber spoke of the "pitiless sobriety (*Nüchternheit*) of judgment" (Hennis 1991). Thus, Weber outlined a scientific ethic rooted in the separation of the function of the scientist and that

19. The objectivity thesis received close examination in the literature and is still presented as a cornerstone of scientific methodology in social sciences, particularly in economics (Hammersley 2017; Mongin 2006; Reiss 2014).

of the politician rather than a methodological claim regarding scientific objectivity.

In line with Weber, Eucken was convinced that scientific economic analysis had to be free from any political or ideological agenda. In the context of Eucken's writing, it specifically implied opposing the invasion of the scientific realm by National Socialist dogma (see Nientiedt 2019a, 11–12). However, contrary to Weber, Eucken accepted the idea of universal values and, in particular, truth. Thus, Eucken paved the way for political recommendations based on what he considered permanent scientific knowledge. Much like his friend Röpke and other ordoliberals, Eucken maintained that Weber's objectivity thesis was essentially beneficial against the old historicists as they often distorted scientific analysis with personal, political, or theological opinions. Taken to its ultimate expression, however, the objectivity thesis would lead to a deleterious cultural subjectivism, standing in the way of any scientifically based policy.[20] Röpke provided a clear exposition of this argument:

> It was against this indiscriminate use of value judgement that men like Max Weber raised their voice, but then the reaction went much further until it reached the opposite extreme of stigmatizing as "unscientific" to express any definite views on values, ends and "oughts." (Röpke 1942a, 2–3)

This quotation comes from Röpke's article "A Value Judgement on Value Judgements" (1942a), published in the *Revue de la Faculté des Sciences Économiques d'Istanbul*.[21] In this text, Röpke (1942a, 10) aimed at shedding light on "what types of judgments are scientifically legitimate and on what basis." Röpke endorsed Weber's objectivity thesis as a necessary step in distancing the scientific outlook from the ideology of vested interest.[22] Nevertheless, Röpke believed that the Weberian thesis was pushed by its supporters to its opposite extreme, leading to a positivist attitude of

20. As Stefan Kolev (2018b, 13) noted, both Eucken and Röpke misinterpreted Weber's claim as a restraint from practical engagement, whereas Weber was actively involved in "the shaping of the economic, political, legal, and academic reality" of his time.

21. The birth of this journal in October 1939 was linked to the arrival of German professors (like Röpke and Rüstow) who were forced to leave Nazi Germany and find refuge in Atatürk's Turkey (see Ege and Hagemann 2012, 96–65; Masala and Kama 2018).

22. Although there was no direct mention of Eucken, Röpke did pick his reference within the same intellectual horizon (Kant, Descartes, Weber, and Rickert in particular). For detailed discussions of Röpke's article, see Samuel Gregg (2015) and Kevin Christ (2018).

bringing the discussion about values and ultimate ends away from the legitimacy of science. Röpke (1942a, 5) denounced a certain confusion. The fact that "monopolistic ideologies" were convoking fundamental Western values such as "common interest," "justice," or "patriotism" did not necessarily imply that those values were ideological statements themselves (see also Eucken 1952, 17).

Worse than mere confusion, Röpke considered that anti-axiologism was based on a logical contradiction since the refusal of value judgments and the sacredness of the principle of truth would precisely imply a value judgment. He concluded that "science, on its very foundations, is based on value judgments" (1942a, 8). Röpke argued further that certain value judgments were even necessary to economics. He gave the following example in the medical field to illustrate his argument more clearly: "medicine begins with the value judgment that life is better than death and health better than disease" (1942a, 8). Röpke then took an example from the field of economics regarding the question of the optimum and the interpersonal comparisons of utility or variation in the price index. By doing this, he claimed that "terms like "inflation" or "deflation" can hardly be used without an implicit reference to a value judgment about what should be regarded as "normal" in the monetary sphere" (1942a, 9).

However, medicine is not a science, but an art. Did Röpke purposely used the example of medicine in this sense? Probably not. However, Röpke did embrace a conception of economic science as a form of societal medicine, as discussed in Chapter 4 of this book. For Röpke (1942a, 2), any "attempt at restating the problem of value judgments seems tantamount to struggling with the solution of the spiritual crisis of the Western world." The reintroduction of value judgments into political economy was decisive from the moment that social and political prescriptions were the final objective of science. Thus, Röpke differed from Weber (1904) in that he sought in the scientific facts certain normative characteristics of universal value.

Röpke outlined a criterion to discern certain statements based on the universality of their acceptance to decide in which of the two subcategories—science or ideology—a statement should be placed. The use of certain values in scientific reflection was legitimate and can be seen as charged with a "degree of objectivity" when they would be "approved by all normal men" (Röpke 1942a, 5).[23] The line that Röpke draws may seem loose or even artificial. However, in the last analysis, Röpke's argument

23. In the same years, Gunnar Myrdal came to a similar conclusion, ensuring that the choice of certain values to guide a scientific study did not question its objectivity

concerned a small group of elementary principles, such as truth, justice, peace, community (Wörsdörfer 2012a, 12). He saw these value as "*anthropological constants* which, after careful examination, we are bound to accept as facts" (Röpke 1942a, 14, emphasis in original).

Like Röpke, Eucken claimed that (meta-) value judgments were among the core conditions leading to a scientific approach to reality. If universal values like truth were "becoming relative concepts," they would be "adapted readily to changing facts and opinions" by power groups that "are able to pursue their interests with ever-increasing success" (Böhm et al. 1936, 22). To decide whether any given claim made by interested individuals or groups was right, Eucken (1940b, 32) insisted that political economy needed a "strict criterion" and a "scientific method," both working hand in hand. Eucken (1940b, 305) argued that a "strict adherence to the idea of truth" (i.e., the "strict criterion") and the morphological apparatus to reconcile the historical and theoretical character of economic knowledge (i.e., the "scientific method") were required to overcome the epistemological obstacle raised by opinions and ideologies. Eucken (1940b, 272) claimed that only a combination of both the theoretical and morphological apparatus would equip economists to investigate "the sources and effects of the different positions of economic power."

In Chapter 3, we will see that the theoretical analysis of power operates at the macro level of the economic order (whether within centrally administrated or exchange economies) and at the micro level of market structures. It has been argued that the ordoliberal theoretical approach—and Eucken's in particular—maintained an "ambiguous relationship to the normative" (Broyer 2007, 239). Another way of looking at it is as a necessary but complex articulation between the positive and normative levels. Both Eucken and Röpke were not concerned with strictly demarcating the line between positive and normative science. They instead aimed at outlining a source of mutual reinforcement that does not weaken the scientific nature of the economy but is, on the contrary, a necessary step toward policy prescriptions.

Eucken's reflection on the core concept of "order" (*Ordnung*) can illustrate this continuum from a positive to a normative analysis. In *Foundations*, Eucken used two terms to conceptualize the economic system. Eucken spoke of "economic order" (*Wirtschaftsordnung*) to refer to a study of the pure abstract forms that can be taken by effective and, therefore, positive

as long as they "reflected *the values shared by a significant part of the society under study*, rather than those of the economist" (Cherrier 2009, 34, emphasis in original).

economic systems. At times, however, Eucken used the expression "order of the economy" (*Ordnung der Wirtschaft*) in the particular context of an economic order satisfying his normative view.[24]

For Eucken (1940a, 238), the "economic order" appeared as an "individual fact, positively given" to the scientific approach. Thus, the economic order can be defined as "the totality of the forms through which the running of the daily economic process—here and there, yesterday and today—took place in practice" (Eucken 1940a, 227). Nevertheless, this does not mean that any economic order would satisfactorily achieve economic efficiency and social justice. Indeed, many economic orders "can be inhuman" (1940a, 239), although science must study them as "forms of economic organisation."[25] However, Eucken did not end his reflection at this stage since "order" has yet another meaning: order also corresponds to "the nature of man . . . being based on the notion of moderation and balance" (1940a, 238). Thus, this "order of the economy," or *Ordo*, is also *Naturordnung*—Eucken referred to François Quesnay and spoke of an "*ordre de nature*"—in the sense that it would be faithful to the nature of man. *Ordo* was, therefore, an imperative necessity according to which the economic system must be organized:

> Today, this idea is being revived again, because of the urgent need to find a functional and humane order, and therefore to find the order of the economy, of society, law and State that are missing in our industrialized world. While versions of this order may change over the course of European history, the intention of the formation of this concept remains constant. (Eucken 1940a, 239)

However, the order of the economy can only be indicated after, and from, an overview of possible economic systems. Therefore, Eucken outlined a historical plurality of the types of organization and a theoretical plurality of possible orders. This multiplicity was embodied by a morphological "alphabet" of standard ideals that can be assembled differently while providing a variety of possible worlds (Eucken 1940b, 109). Thus, Eucken's approach was not teleological or deterministic but historically—and comparatively—orientated because it envisaged a plurality of feasible systems (or forms). It also envisages a specific completion of the economic order according to institutional conditions in a broad sense—that is,

24. The lawyer Franz Böhm used the same kind of dichotomy between positive (*Seinordnung*) and normative (*Sollenordnung*), though with a different terminology than Eucken's (see Mongouachon 2012, 205).

25. Here I follow the English translation by Lutz (1940a, 587).

according to the "geographical, intellectual, political, and social environment" (Eucken 1949, 228–229). Hence, ordoliberals envisaged the economic order in general and economic behavior in particular as "embedded in the cultural sphere" (Schefold 1995, 227), reflecting a specific form without altering its fundamental theoretical mechanisms. Although the political feature was still in its infancy in *Foundations*, the conclusions Eucken (1940b, 314) drew in his book were quite explicit: one must "consciously shape" (*Gestaltung*) the economic order if one wants to move toward the order of the economy.

## 2.4 CONCLUSION: POWER, METHODOLOGICALLY CONTEMPLATED

One of the specificities of Eucken's discourse was the way it articulated different traditions of the German philosophy of science. Eucken drew inspiration from Kant, Schopenhauer, and particularly from Husserl and Weber to underpin his thesis of the contamination of scientific knowledge by vested interests (see in particular Eucken 1940b, 321–322, n. 4). In *Foundations*, Eucken adopted a phenomenological outlook and tried to build a scientific investigation from everyday experience. However, Eucken was aware of the formidable challenge lying in the necessity to detach scientific production from any ideological hold. In addition to this epistemological obstacle, Eucken faced an ontological obstacle, what he termed the "great antinomy" between history and theory. To overcome this twofold—ontological and epistemological—obstacle, Eucken erected a morphological analysis of economic orders based on a typology of multiple ideal types. In doing so, Eucken's epistemology did not endorse a firm separation between positive analysis and normative recommendations. On the contrary, he saw the progression from theoretical analysis to policy prescription as a continuum: the epistemological conception of competition obliges intervention to achieve it in practice.

Eucken's epistemology aimed to penetrate effective reality, an objective that can only be achieved through theoretical analysis. However, Eucken rejected both historicism and positivism because they appeared permeable to pressure from interest groups. Based on these observations, Eucken seemed to have lost on both counts. On the one hand, Eucken tried to build typical ideals through a historical study and obtain essences that would lead to theoretical tools, which are themselves out of history. In this respect, Geoffrey Hodgson (2001, 133) claimed that Eucken's search for perennial truths was undertaken at the expense of "a clear focus on the key problem of historical specificity" and thus contributed to a forgetfulness of history in economics tantamount to that of the neoclassical approach (see also Tribe 1995, chap. 8).

On the other hand, Eucken's phenomenological approach cannot satisfy the critical rationalism in Karl Popper's falsificationist version (see also Broyer 2007). Eucken remained rigorously foreign to the scientific conception of the world as formulated by the Vienna Circle, where only directly observable (and testable) facts are objects of science. In trying to transcribe philosophy into the language of science, empiricism and logical positivism were going down a completely opposite path to that of Eucken. Increasingly, neo-positivism became the central philosophical reference for social sciences from its birth in the interwar period to its affirmation in the second half of the twentieth century. Economics followed an analogous path, illustrated by contributions as diverse as those of Lionel Robbins, Milton Friedman, and Paul Samuelson (see Caldwell 1982). Nevertheless, as we will see in Chapter 3, by building on the microeconomic theory of the interwar period, especially Stackelberg's, the ordoliberals cultivated points of compatibility, if not convergence, with the formal type of economics that would gradually prevail internationally in the aftermath of the Second World War.

# CHAPTER 3
# Economy Through Orders

We are now at the point where we can map the theoretical foundations of the ordoliberal political economy. This, in turn, requires us to deal with the substantial and contextual elements of Eucken's analysis of economics orders and market structures. One of the lessons that emerges is that the analysis conducted in Eucken's *Foundations* should be seen less as an economic theory in the canonical sense of the term, as suggested by Gerrit Meijer (1994, 2007) for instance, than as a *theory of the application* of economic theories.

Typically, applied economics might be defined as a method of "reductions of generality" that is exercised on "a previously existing body of theory or set of principles"; in this sense, pure theory and applied theory would be "almost completely independent" (Backhouse and Biddle 2000, 5, 7). By contrast, Eucken approached the question of application as an increase in generality, making it possible to organize theories or principles (usually already available) in order to grasp their empirical relevance in a given situation. Relatively independent in their construction, economic theory and applied theory only make sense to Eucken when combined together to understand how the actual economy works in general and how power manifests itself in particular.

Actually, for Eucken (1940b, 157), applying economic theory meant conducting "the theoretical analysis [of the economic process] in spite of the historical diversity," which led him to elaborate a "morphological apparatus." As a result, Eucken (1948c, 193) stressed that "an analysis of the forms of economic reality should precede theoretical analysis." Eucken aimed at casting a net over the various structures of the economy as a whole, what he called the "economic order" (*Wirtschaftsordnung*), in order to

*A Political Economy of Power.* Raphaël Fèvre, Oxford University Press. © Oxford University Press 2021.
DOI: 10.1093/oso/9780197607800.003.0004

understand the functioning of the "economic process" (*Wirtschaftsablauf*), of the interaction of daily economic events within this order. Hence, contrary to the standard approach in economics, Eucken's applied economics did not arise *downstream* of economic theory, but *upstream*. Thus, morphological analysis would be logically prior to economic theory which, without this morphological prerequisite, would be blind. Indeed, morphological analysis aimed at determining the relevance of the available economic theories.

In *Foundations*, Eucken conducted a reflection on the nature, bases, and limits of application in economics. However, this applied theory was often pursued to the detriment of (pure) economic theory itself. How are we to explain this unbalanced state of affairs? As a matter of fact, some ordoliberals, like Röpke (1940, 15), took a rather more ecumenical approach to economic theory, calling for a reasonable synthesis because "putting new doctrines in the place of old ones is neither a need nor a necessity." Similarly Eucken even went as far as emphasizing the "substantial unity" among modern economic theories going "well beyond an inconsistent juxtaposition of points of view" (Eucken 1940b, 339; see also Röpke 1936a, vi; 1944a, 144). The ordoliberal reception of modern theories is both surprising and questionable. Still, it helps us understand that, from an ordoliberal point of view, the question that remains to be solved was not directly that of pure theoretical conceptualization, but rather that of knowing when and where to apply these—preexisting—theories; hence the need for morphological analysis, according to Eucken.

We saw in Chapter 2 that while Eucken gave economic theory an epistemologically robust status with regard to the criterion of "truth" (*Wahrheit*), the criterion of "actuality" (*Aktualität*) conditions the use of a theory in relation to prior knowledge of the economic order. The question of relevance leads us directly to the question of application:

> The application of theory . . . always requires that the structure of the historical economic order, and in particular its predominant forms, are already known. The limit of the application coincides with the limit of the knowledge of the actual economic reality. *Only if one knows what pure basic forms have been, or are, realized in any economic order, is it possible to decide what parts of the theoretical apparatus are to be used.* (Eucken 1940b, 239, emphasis in original)

Economic power—the struggle for economic power—falls primarily within the domain of the "application" (*Anwendung*) of economic theory (Eucken 1940b, 213). Ultimately, in Eucken's view, the question of application was essential to address the actual problem of economic power.

Eucken's conduct of a morphological analysis led him to take a stand regarding two of the most lively and sophisticated discussions in the discipline during the interwar period, in those "years of high theory" (Shackle 1967). On the one hand, debate on the possibility of a system of "socialist calculation" found the Austrian-orientated economists (Ludwig von Mises, Friedrich Hayek, and Lionel Robbins) opposed to the market socialists (like Abba Lerner and Oskar Lange). On the other hand, the "revolution" of competitive market structures came to the fore with contributions by Piero Sraffa, Joan Robinson, Edward H. Chamberlin, and Heinrich F. von Stackelberg. A key figure in this context is Stackelberg, a German economist whose work provided some of the theoretical bases of the ordoliberals' views. Remarkably enough, these two debates combined sophisticated theoretical discussions with broader political issues regarding the social desirability of the economic order.

As we will demonstrate, these two debates were far from being mutually exclusive to Eucken's eyes. Rather, they embodied two aspects of the same problem of power manifestations in the economy, but on two different scales. With his morphological system, a hierarchical typology of ideal types, Eucken moved from the analysis of systems (administered economy vs. exchange economy) to the analysis of market structures (within the exchange economy):

> The centrally administered economy embodies the maximum possible concentration of economic power. The opposite is a system of complete competition in all markets, where the individual has virtually no power, apart from each man's infinitesimal influence on the economic process. An exchange economy, with monopolies, partial monopolies, or oligopolies, stands with regard to the distribution of economic power between these two extremes. (Eucken 1948c, 190)

In sum, the issue of economic power functioned as a pivot in the transition from one scale of analysis to the other. Eucken questioned each of the two debates from a power perspective, based on his morphological analysis, with a view to the issue of the application of economic theory.

## 3.1 THE ECONOMIC PLAN

Eucken conceptualized both economic orders and market structures on the basis of individual behavior. Thus, the concept of "economic plan" (*Wirtschaftsplan*) was the central tool in the construction of Eucken's morphologies. For each agent, the plan can be defined as the ex ante representation of economic action shaped by a set of constraints—six (historical) data subject to three (theoretical) rules of experience— whose ex post realization is subject to hazard (i.e., risk).

### 3.1.1 The Individual Plan: Data, Rules, and Risk

#### 3.1.1.1 *The "Data Wreath"*

The economic plan is essentially based on the articulation of six historical data: what Eucken (1940b, 213) called the "data wreath" (*Datenkranz*). These data should be understood as parameters, as a set of constraints on the basis of which the economic agent's action is carried on. For Eucken (1940b, 180), the "satisfaction of needs" (*Bedürfnisbefriedigung*) was the primary objective of economic activity. Accordingly, needs—their classification among themselves and over time—were the first in the set of data shaping the economic plan. Human needs reflected the purpose intended by each of the agents (whether they were heads of households or heads of large structures).

In the exchange economy, individuals use their purchasing power to satisfy their own needs. In this case, consumers are assumed to have a "decisive influence on the production process" (Eucken 1940b, 181). In contrast, in the administered economy, the director decides on the objective to be achieved, which may be contrary to individual satisfaction. This type of leadership is nevertheless appropriate for the achievement of certain specific needs—for example, to equip the nation with infrastructure or military supplies. Each economic plan includes some means to satisfy needs (a) at its disposal. Eucken distinguishes four types of means: the stock of goods already produced (b), land and natural resources (c), work (d), and the technical knowledge at a given time (e).

The stock of available goods (b) must be analyzed from a time-based perspective and, in fact, Eucken separated production decisions on a temporal basis. In the short run (within the same period of production), goods that can be allocated to final consumption are directly dependent on available stocks. However, in the long run (succession of periods of production), intermediate consumer goods, semi-finished products, and raw materials must be taken into consideration. It is necessary to decide on the quantity to be used in the production process, but also to be produced for future production cycles (in fact, consumer goods are both present means and ends to be satisfied in the future). Eucken (1940b, 182) thus defined capital as the "power to dispose (*Verfügungsmacht*) of consumer goods." This power was in the hands of the central director in the administered economy and in the hands of each of the entrepreneurs in an exchange economy, although under pressure from consumers.

Eucken saw natural resources (c) and the workforce (d) available to the director of an economic unit as an integral part of the economic plan. Nevertheless, he judiciously pointed out that the "services" (*Leistungen*) provided by these two factors of production should not be understood as data given in the shaping of individual plans, but as problems, meaning the subject of an allocation decision, which can therefore be subject to economic analysis (Eucken 1940b, 184–185). Technical knowledge (e), of which commercial knowledge is an integral part (accounting, financial statistics), constitutes the fifth element of the economic plan. Here again, Eucken (1940b, 186) introduced an important distinction between technical knowledge per se and the use of a particular method: "the former is a given," he claimed, "the latter an economic problem."

Finally, in addition to needs (a) and means (b), (c), (d), and (e) in the economic plan, the social and legal organization (f) also occupied a central position in the economic plan's data set. This last element is probably the most original and crucial aspect of Eucken's conceptualization. He famously interpreted it as the "rules of the game" (*Spielregeln*) of economic activity (1940b, 186). Social and legal organization should be understood broadly, for it includes traditional practices as well as the "intellectual and spiritual characteristics" of a country (1940b, 292–294). This last and sixth data brings to light an essential distinction between an exchange economy and an administrated economy. In the exchange economy in particular, social and legal organization specifically include the type of "monetary system and the monetary policy actually being applied, as well as the existing forms of markets, which it cannot do in a centrally directed economy" (1940b, 203).

As such, social and legal organization is the preferential medium for economic policy since the very essence of economic policy is precisely the capacity "to transform data" according to Eucken (1940b, 216). In this respect, the ordoliberals aimed at integrating into their analysis of power the ability of politicians to formulate the rules of the economic game. The role of scientists was precisely to inform politicians so that they could use their power to shape data to improve the structure of the economic order: political power was therefore a condition sine qua non for achieving the competitive economic order.

### 3.1.1.2 Three Economic Laws

Eucken (1940b, 187) then outlined three "rules of experience" (*Erfahrungsregeln*) for the economic plan: Gossen's first law, the law of diminishing marginal returns, and the prolongation of the production time structure linked to investment. These rules, Eucken held, emerged from daily experience and would be taken for granted by all those involved; the scientist's task was merely to state them clearly. These rules of experience apply to all the elements of the economic plan (whether in the exchange economy or in the administered economy). While, given the general and therefore theoretical aspect of the economy, it is possible to speak of "laws" (*Gesetze*) being "perfectly valid at all times and in all places," Eucken (1940b, 187) preferred to speak of "factual truths" (*Tatsachenwahrheiten*). He probably made this point to mark his distance from a formal, or abstract, axiomatic approach.

Each economic plan was therefore based on six data, assembled as "building blocks" (*Baustein*)—as Eucken (1940b, 186) called them—by the economic unit, conditioning its decisions and actions. While the six data constitute the core of the economic plan, the rules of experience should not be neglected as they are *theoretical* laws that are imposed on the *historical* nature of the data. According to Eucken (1940b, 202), the six data and three rules of experience were at the root of all "decisions to produce, repair and invest in production techniques and in the location of activities."

Gossen's first law is tantamount to the law of diminishing marginal utility (Eucken explicitly adopted Friedrich von Wieser's formulation). This law concerns mainly household economic plans for "everyone knows that his daily needs of meat, bread, and other consumer goods decrease as they are increasingly satisfied" (1940b, 187). While Eucken acknowledged that substitutable and complementary goods played a chief role in the way satisfaction decreases, there could be no calling into question the core principle of this law.

The law of diminishing marginal returns was the second rule of experience applied to the formulation of economic plans. Unlike Gossen's law, the justification for it did not come from individuals' "*inner* experience" but rather from "*external* observation of facts" (1940b, 188, emphasis in original). While Eucken did not offer graphical representation of it—albeit providing a numerical example (1940b, 18)—he implicitly endorsed the Marshallian formulation of the firm's equilibrium since returns are first increasing (decreasing costs) and then decreasing (increasing costs). The "U-shaped" cost curve is a formal condition for determining the optimal size of the firm.

Finally, the third rule of experience stated the time lag in investment or adoption of new technical processes. Choices in employing available resources involved in investment decisions raise the issue of taking time into account in economics, particularly in terms of the question of present versus future tradeoffs in resource allocation. In this perspective, Eucken investigated the role of time in the formation of capital along the lines of Böhm-Bawerk's roundabout methods of production.[1] Heads of economic units go through an "average period of gestation" (1940b, 191) in formulating their economic plans to increase productivity by means of capital investments. Therefore, the third rule of experience is binding for a firm's decisions, whether taken by an entrepreneur in an exchange economy or by the director of a central office.

### *3.1.1.3 Risk*

Risk was a fundamental element in Eucken's economic plan, although it was neither a factor of production, nor a data, nor indeed a rule of experience. Risk can be defined as the difference between the initial (ex ante) formulation of the "plan data" and the actual implementation (ex post) of the "factual data" (Eucken 1940b, 194–195). Thus risk lies in the imperfection of agents' expectations in the initial plan, regarding the course of future events.

Risk has three major consequences in the formulation of economic plans. First, short-term plans require constant adaptation to unforeseen circumstances. Eucken took as examples the case of unpredictable weather for agriculture or possible absences of workers from the factory. In these cases, the long-run plan of a firm was not fundamentally altered and could be restored to its original features as soon as these passing constraints disappeared. Second, risk could lead to long-lasting changes in agents' behaviors. In this case, risk merits ample consideration in the formulation of economic plans since it contributes to reshaping agents' long-run plans with lasting effect. Finally, the degree of risk could also change the time horizon envisaged by an individual unit. Confidence in political stability, and therefore in the uniformity over time of the social and legal rules of the game and in price stability, were two of the most important factors for

1. In early contributions, Eucken (1934) developed an analysis of capital and the real interest rate in his *Kapitaltheoretische Untersuchungen* (*Investigations in the Theory of Capital*). His students Friedrich Lutz and Fritz W. Meyer later claimed that Eucken planned to amend his contributions in the postwar period in light of more recent analyses. For a discussion of Eucken's theory of capital and interest, see Leland B. Yeager (1994).

the drafting of long-run and perennial economic plans in general and for investment decisions in particular.

### 3.1.2 From Individual Behavior to Global Structures

#### *3.1.2.1 The "Economic Principle" of Behavior*

The use of the term "plan" by liberal-orientated authors such as Eucken, Röpke, and other ordoliberals may come as a surprise. However, most of the neoliberal economists of the interwar period aimed to rehabilitate the term, anxious to separate the organized market economy from the chaotic system of laissez-faire (Burgin 2012, chap. 3). Like Lionel Robbins (1938, 21), for instance, the ordoliberals rejected the dichotomy "between a plan or an absence of a plan" in favor of an approach centered on "different kinds of plans." The liberal economic order was also based on plans, but these were individual in nature (consumer-orientated) and in sharp contrast to planning by a central authority.

Eucken assumed that each agent, each economic unit, shaped its action on the basis of an economic plan, on the basis of individual planning. The plan was the basic, universal, and irreducible element of economic rationality that Eucken (1940b, 117–118) outlined from the point of view of the agent himself: "The head of any economic structure always acts on the basis of an economic plan . . . human economic activity has always consisted in creating and implementing economic plans." Every individual action was based on an economic plan, being conditioned by the same economic objective to obtain more while sacrificing less. So that beyond the "*variable*" nature of human economic action, there would in fact be a "*constant*," a relationship of calculation between means and needs, of achieving "a certain end with as small an expenditure of means as possible" (1940b, 281, emphasis in original). Eucken called it the "economic principle" (*Wirtschaftlichen Prinzip*) of behavior. It served as a basis for him to justify the systematic analysis of the economic plans he undertook. And yet Eucken was careful to point out that this economic principle had nothing to do with "the objectives and purposes of human action," which were themselves subject to variation (1940b, 345, n. 61). Similarly, the agents' ability to carry out this calculation consistently or effectively in action also varies over time and space.[2]

2. According to Eucken (1940b, 283), the gradual refinement of instrumental rationality did not fundamentally alter the veracity of the economic principle but simply led to a more effective exercise of it in terms of actual satisfaction of needs.

Eucken's approach seemed to show familiarity with Robbins's well-known definition of economics as the "science which studies human behavior as a relationship between ends and scarce means which have alternative uses" (Robbins 1932, 16). Röpke (1940, 46) adopted almost exactly the same definition as Robbins (whom he knew personally), observing that "economy is nothing more than the constant choice between different possibilities, and political economy is basically only the science of the alternative." It should be emphasized, however, that Eucken was not defining the purpose of economics in general, but only of individual behavior. Furthermore, the implications that the ordoliberals drew from Robbins's definition cannot be taken to reflect the way it was later received by the profession. Indeed, the specification of economics as a purely analytical discipline focused on rational behavior and taking precedence over other fields of knowledge (Backhouse and Medema 2009, 805) was foreign to the ordoliberals. Rather, Eucken's approach was closer to the continental tradition embodied, for instance, in Max Weber's understanding of economic rationality.

### *3.1.2.2 Individual Plan and Morphological Analysis*

Eucken drew his morphological system from individual economic plans. It led him to an ideal subdivision between the exchange economy (*Verkehrswirtschaft*) on the one hand, and the administered economy (*zentralgeleitete Wirtschaft*) on the other. Power relations within each of these two systems was a central characteristic to differentiate them. One of the significant features of the administered economy was the powerlessness of consumers and entrepreneurs to shape their own economic plans since this power was in the hands of a central management. In contrast, Eucken characterized the economy of exchange as the abdication of the central powers and thus the ability of agents to form and carry out plans. However, even in this context the problem of economic power was not overcome, with obvious power struggles among producers within concentrated market forms (oligopoly, monopoly, etc.) exercised to the detriment of consumers.

Remarkably, it was also in terms of power that Röpke (1949b, 159) viewed the opposition between exchange and administered economic systems, referring to the "neutralization of power through its diffusion and decentralization" in the case of the former and to "a creative power and ideology as history has never produced" in the case of the latter. Regarding principles of the economic organization as a whole, the exchange economy and the administered economy show a clear-cut dichotomy:

> There is a simple "either-or" alternative. *Either* the control is through prices, and therefore on the basis of the plans of household and firm, *or* it is based on the plans and valuations of the central authority. The two methods of control exclude one another. (Eucken 1948c, 192)

Only the director of an administered economy addresses all the data—and the risk factor—of the global economic system with his economic plan. Thus, in the framework of the administered economy, the "overall plan (*Gesamtplan*) forms a complete unit," because it is imposed on all economic actions and on "short-term subordinate plans" (Eucken 1940b, 192).

By contrast, the exchange economy is characterized by individual plans (*Einzelpläne*), incomplete in their construction. Indeed, these individual plans only partially concern the overall economic process, although "only at certain points are they concerned with the data from the point of view of the whole economy" (1940b, 198). For instance, the technical knowledge available to an entrepreneur (e) and the social and legal organization (f) concern the economy as a whole. But the specificity of the exchange economy lies in the fact that each individual economic unit is "surrounded by prices" (*Preisen umgeben*), as Eucken (1940b, 199–201) put it on several occasions. Competitive prices imply simultaneous relations with all markets and the monetary system, as Eucken explained, directly quoting some expressions formulated by his student Karl Friedrich Maier:

> Prices can also be regarded "as representing the frontier line between the exchange economy as a whole and the individual economic unit." At those points "the firm is not *directly* concerned" with the overall economic data, but indirectly affected by it so far as the price system "takes account of the actions of all other individual units." (Eucken 1940b, 199)

Eucken considered that there was a direct relationship since the entrepreneur addresses the data from the point of view of his firm. But prices are also indirect data because they relate to the relationship of a firm with the rest of the market or economy; Eucken extended this analysis to apply equally to households. He further pointed out that analysis of a household or individual firm was only a starting point, "the first stage of theoretical investigation" (1940b, 201). Ultimately, he aimed not so much at partial market analysis as a global understanding of how the economy works as a whole. Indeed, according to Eucken (1940b, 197) "the analysis of single firms or households, or of the relationships between particular individual quantities, scarcely constitutes a theoretical analysis. It is impossible to understand particular economic events without understanding how they fit in the overall context."

Nonetheless, ordoliberals made only extremely allusive and "literary" (i.e., nontechnical) references to the theory of general economic equilibrium, based more on Cassel's and Stackelberg's formulations of it than on first-hand perusal of Walras and Pareto (Broyer 2003a, 97). It is therefore hard to see which analytical and formal tools ordoliberals actually intended to rely on to achieve their ambition to describe the overall functioning of the economic process.

## 3.2 MAPPING ECONOMIC ORDERS

When Eucken outlined his morphology of economic orders, he was far from being the first economist to offer a comparative analysis of economic systems. To understand Eucken's ambition, it should be contextualized within the lively debates on the possibility of socialist calculation that gained momentum in the interwar period. As I will suggest, Eucken's outlook did not sit well with the demarcation lines of the debate for he approached it through the lens of his particular views on power. Thus, Eucken conducted a singular analysis of the forms of the administered economy and the exchange economy.

### 3.2.1 The Socialist Calculation Debate

#### *3.2.1.1 Ludwig von Mises on the Impossibly of a Socialist Calculus*

The work of Ludwig von Mises (1920, 1922) marked the starting point of the debate on the possibility for a socialist economy to carry out proper economic calculation (*Wirtschaftsrechnung*). Mises defined the socialist economy as a society where the distribution of consumer goods must be independent of production conditions. In the absence of private ownership, economic calculation that unifies and objectifies the subjective use values of the various agents in an exchange ratio is impossible. In short, without free markets there would be no price system per se.

Mises developed his argument by focusing on the market for capital goods. Only private ownership would provide the necessary incentive for production, which makes it possible to develop market relationships whose final indicator is the price, as both source and result of the calculation. Accordingly, "the calculation in terms of money will here be impossible"

(Mises 1920, 4; see also Hayek 1935). In a competitive market economy, consumers classify their baskets of goods and producers arrive at investment decisions according to expected returns. Mises (1920, 20) saw this as a procedure that leads to economic efficiency everywhere. This economic efficiency coming from exchanges cannot be achieved with the "technical" or "statistical" calculation performed by a centralized bureaucracy (Mises 1920, 45–46). It would be possible to treat the "economic problem" as a "technological problem" only if "the order of importance of the different needs of the community were fixed in such a definite and absolute way that the provision for one could always be made irrespective of cost" (Hayek 1935, 5). On the contrary, the socialist solution could not be applied to the economic problem arising once competition for the available resources arose for various different purposes.

Mises's seminal criticism took root in the immediate aftermath of the First World War, marked by the political programs close to socialism and Marxism dominating the German-speaking governmental scene (notably driven by the Soviet experience in the East).[3] Inspired by the functioning of the war economy (*Kriegswirtschaft*), Otto Neurath (1919) advocated an economy of calculation in kind (*Naturalwirtschaft*), from which currency would be excluded (see Uebel 2008). In the same vein, although retaining the monetary apparatus, Otto Bauer (1919) proposed socialization of the banking system. Both Neurath's and Bauer's proposals were totally rejected by Mises (see Chaloupek 1990). Karl Polanyi, who had been introduced into the same Viennese circles, answered Mises with a federal socialism where economic calculation could be envisaged following the practical model of guilds.[4]

However, the theoretical answer to Mises's challenge to socialism came from the English-speaking world a few years later. Fred M. Taylor (1929) introduced the mathematical solution into the debate during his presidential address to the annual meeting of the American Economic Association, an idea that was then further developed by Henry D. Dickinson (1930, 1933). The two American economists insisted on the possibility—provided

3. In Germany, politicians sought to reorganize industry in the form of cartels and trade unions through a socialization commission, of which the socialist economist Emil Lederer (1882–1939) was a leading figure. The ordoliberals were well acquainted with Lederer, having encountered him in various scholarly and political circles (see Commun 2016, 29).

4. The interactions between Viennese scholarly circles in the interwar period received special attention from Dekker (2016) and Wright (2016). On the "first socialization debate," see the collective book edited by Jürgen Backhaus, Günther Chaloupek, and Hans A. Frambach (2019).

the relevant data be collected—of calculating equilibrium conditions from an equal number of equations and unknowns. In the same vein, European socialist economists challenged Mises's argument on the strength of Vilfredo Pareto's work on general equilibrium (through Gustav Cassel's reformulation) and especially Enrico Barone's article "The Ministry of Production in the Collectivist State" (1908).

The mathematical solution introduced by socialist economists implied a significant number of transitions from their usual positions. Perhaps the most striking of these was the shift from labor value theory to marginalist price theory, as well as the acceptance of consumer sovereignty as a guiding principle of the economic process. These transitions were judged very harshly by the Marxist economist Maurice Dobb (1933, 591), who saw it as a bourgeois compromise. In response to Dobb, Abba Lerner (1934, 51) argued that economic calculation and the existence of market prices "should no longer be considered antisocialist tricks or bourgeois illusions," but should be at the heart of the theoretical project of socialist economists, with respect for consumer preferences as the foremost criterion of economic efficiency. The conversion of some of the socialist economists to the market was by then (almost) a reality.

On the basis of this new socialist paradigm, economic calculation was plausible, at least theoretically. Hayek recognized this in 1935, publishing a book that brought together critical contributions on socialism (including Mises's 1920 article). And yet Hayek (1935, 218) wondered whether the socialist solution "still deserves the designation of planning. It certainly does not involve much more planning than the construction of a rational legal framework for capitalism." Similarly, Röpke (1949b, 146) stressed that "revisionism has already gone so far that it is difficult to recognize the socialist character" of recent contributions in a brief overview of the literature entitled "On the Theory of Collectivism" ("*Zur Theorie des Kollektivismus*"). This line, aiming at undermining the credibility of the socialist economists' approach, certainly reflects an unease on the liberal side.

However, Mises, Hayek, and Robbins were not short of arguments to oppose the socialist economists' approach. According to them, the amount of information that the central authority should collect and process involved solving "millions" (Robbins 1934, 151) or "hundreds of thousands" (Hayek 1935, 212) of equations (production units, technical properties of goods, consumer goods in continuous change). Mises, Hayek and Robbins were in fact repeating Pareto's argument about the technical feasibility of determining economic equilibrium by calculation. Indeed in the *Manual*, Pareto (1906, 234) considered that "if all these equations could really be known, the only way for human forces to solve it would be to observe the practical solution provided by the market." And Oskar Lange precisely addressed this challenge with a procedure that would accurately reproduce the market functioning.

#### 3.2.1.2 Oskar Lange's Market Socialism

The market socialist solution that took shape in the thirties completely altered the terms of the debate. This was due to a dual diagnosis—hitherto contradictory—made by socialist economists. On the one hand, the development of the economy as a science would be closely linked to the development of the market, while, on the other hand, the market economies of the interwar period proved unable to safeguard coordination between agents. The Polish economist Oskar Lange (1945, 26) was an exponent of this ambivalent position, showing an unwavering confidence in marginalist economics coupled with a bitter assessment of an unprecedented crisis of market capitalism.

In a two-part article published in *The Review of Economic Studies*, Lange (1936, 1937) offered a new formulation of "the economic theory of socialism." Based on the above-mentioned work of Pareto, Barone, Taylor, Dickinson, and Lerner, Lange (1936, 64) argued that in a socialist economy the pricing process would be in fact "quite analogous to that in a competitive market," provided that "the Central Planning Board performs the functions of the market." In particular, the central planning board must ensure that the managers-entrepreneurs, no longer driven by profit, follow two rules (or subjective conditions of equilibrium). The first rule stipulated that each firm should choose a combination of factors of production and a scale of production such that it minimized the average cost of production, leading to "each commodity being produced with a minimum sacrifice of alternatives," which is based on the technical condition that the marginal cost and the price of the product are equal (Lange 1936, 62). The second rule "replaces the free entry of firms into an industry or their exodus from it" with the aim of bringing the average cost equal to the market price of the product, thus ensuring respect of consumer sovereignty according to Lange (1936, 62).[5]

5. Abba Lerner (1937, 255) then noted that compliance with these two rules (subjective conditions) does not ensure the achievement of an economic equilibrium comparable to a competitive situation (objective conditions); i.e., that the "*most economical use of resources*" is achieved. Here Lerner built on Joan Robinson's work on imperfect competition. Lerner was one of the few economists to draw explicit connections between the two theoretical debates that are at the center of this chapter.

In Lange's model, the Central Planning Board would simply announce prices "chosen *at random*" or "*historically given*" on the basis of which economic agents would be able to conduct their own economic calculation (1936, 66, emphasis in original). The central board must rely on the results of the "*accounting period*," since "any price different from the equilibrium price would show a surplus or a shortage of the commodity in question" (1936, 64, emphasis in original). The board would respond with an accompanying increase or decrease in this price for the next period (indeed resulting in short-term waste). In the end, when it comes to determining the equilibrium, everything would end up as in the competitive economy.[6] Individuals would act on the basis of the "*parametric function of prices*" which would gradually lead them, through a process of "trial and error," to an equilibrium solution; just like Walras' *tâtonnement*, which Lange (1936, 59, emphasis in original) captured in the—centralized—figure of the auctioneer.[7]

Lange's result turned out to be a real tour de force. Not only because it provided a solid theoretical basis for market socialism via the model of general economic equilibrium—a model that was usually seen as the theoretical justification for a decentralized market economy—but more pointedly because Lange's model responded to the practical objections set out by Mises and refined by Hayek and Robbins. Lange, with the same irony that runs through his entire 1936 article, emphasized that the planned economy he envisaged would not require any particular mathematical skill whatsoever on the part of the planning authorities:

> The only "equations" which would have to be "solved" would be those of the consumers and the managers of productions plants. There are exactly the same "equations" which are solved in the present economic system and the people who do the "solving" are the same also. Consumers "solve" them by spending their income so as to get out of it the maximum total utility; and the managers of the production plan "solve" them by finding the combination of factors and the scale of output which minimizes average cost. They "solve" them by a method of trial and error, making (or imagining) small variations *at the margins*. (Lange 1936, 67, emphasis in original)

6. Lange left open the question of stability (convergence) of the general economic equilibrium (Arrous 1990, 71).

7. Without knowing it, Lange embodied the experience of a "unique entrepreneur" responsible for maximizing the social utility envisaged by Walras (1898, X: 251) himself. Nevertheless, the affinity between Lange's and Walras's projects is less obvious than it may seem, because "trial and error is the algorithm for calculating absolute free competition" and therefore does not correspond to "the functioning of concrete markets and is not a price adjustment process either" (Baranzini 2011, 165).

According to Lange, this system should "work *much better*" than the competitive market because the central board had a "broader knowledge" of the economic process as a whole, in contrast to the myopia of individualistic capitalism (Lange 1936, 67, emphasis in original). From this perspective, the debate was not only about whether socialism can do as well as the competitive market economy, but whether it can outperform it in terms of efficiency (Levy and Peart 2008).

Faced with these new arguments, the Austrians' objections followed two main lines (Vaughn 1980). While Mises insisted on the irreplaceable role of the capitalist entrepreneur and therefore on the incentives inherent in the market economy under private ownership (Mises 1949, 704), Hayek brought to the fore the informational role of the market. On the basis of his work on knowledge, Hayek (1937, 1945) outlined the theoretical argument that would become central to his subsequent work on competition as a "discovery procedure." What market socialists would have neglected, he claimed, was that the "cheapest" method of production, under given conditions, is something that "has to be discovered, and to be discovered anew sometimes almost from day to day, by the entrepreneur" (Hayek 1940, 139). In doing so, Hayek shifted the vision of the market institution and price system from the allocation of scarce resources to the issue of the formation, dissemination, and acquisition of information.[8]

### 3.2.1.3 *The Incommensurability of Economic Orders*

On March 12, 1946, Eucken wrote a letter to Friedrich Hayek with an informal review of *The Road to Serfdom* (Hayek 1944) in which Eucken drew critical attention to the socialist calculation debate:

> Your book had encouraged me to describe systematically the German experiences that I have observed very closely. This relates to the problem of economic calculation in a planned economy. The difficulties identified in theory have now appeared in reality and have critically compromised the functioning of central planning. (Eucken 1946b, 138)

The result of Eucken's ambition appeared two years later in the form of a long article, published in two parts in *Economica* (then edited by Robbins and Hayek). "On the Theory of the Centrally Administrated Economy: An Analysis

8. On Hayek's position on socialism in general, and on the socialist calculus debate in particular, see Caldwell (1997).

of the German Experiment" (Eucken 1948c) examined the functioning of the German planned economic order from 1936 onward. Over and above this particular case, Eucken raised more general issues: Did the exchange economy and the administered economy follow the same process, did they share the same goals? Is a single theory sufficient to account for the economic process of these two systems? In short, are these two systems commensurable worlds? Eucken's article gave a clearly negative answer to these questions. It could not be otherwise because the exchange economy and the administrated economy embodied two different exercises of economic power, preventing ordoliberals from considering them under one single model.

Historians of economic thought now consider that the core of the debate on socialist calculation was entangled in a epistemological problem (Lavoie 1985; Cubeddu and Vannucci 1993), much as Eucken had pictured it at the time. In short, the debate on calculation was apparently seen "by Market Socialists as well as by mainstream neo-classical economists as a contest *within* the same theoretical paradigm; the Austrian tradition considers this debate as a contest of mutually excluding theoretical models" (Bridel 1993, 6). And yet incommensurability was not only characteristic of Austrians, and the demarcation was indeed more complex than it may seem. For instance, Dobb (1933, 589) criticized both Dickinson and Mises, although in principle opposed to each other, for considering "that the categories of economic theory are equally valid in a socialist as in an individualist order." Dickinson (1933), Lerner (1934), Durbin (1936), and later Lange (1945) argued that the same economic bases could account for the two systems and, more surprisingly, the Chicago economist Frank Knight (1936, 265) made much the same observation.

By contrast, Eucken emphasized the need for different morphological frameworks to analyze the exchange economy, on the one hand, and the administered economy on the other. Fundamentally, they belong to profoundly alien realities, indeed to incommensurable worlds. Remarkably, the positions between "monists" (one model) and "dualists" (two models), to use Eucken's categorization, did not coincided with the classical positions (socialist vs. liberal) regarding the possibility of socialist calculation. Clearly, Eucken (1948c, 80) placed himself among the dualists, under the patronage of John Stuart Mill and Heinrich Dietzel.[9] He ranked among the monists Pareto and Barone, followed by Taylor, Lange, and Lerner, but

9. Heinrich Dietzel (1857–1935), professor in the University of Bonn, was a liberal socioeconomist who tried to modernize classical economics. Eucken had been his student during his study time in Bonn (Goldschmidt and Hesse 2013, 128).

also by some of the Austrians like Wieser and Schumpeter.[10] Eucken's categorization did not date back to his 1948 article because it had already been outlined in the first edition of his *Foundations*, where he defined the antinomic features of both models very clearly. Once again, the question of the exercise of power was paramount in his ambitious attempt to delineate a comprehensive picture:

> The course taken by the economic process in the two extreme forms—the totally centralized economy and the perfect competitive economy—show certain similarities. Indeed, the controller of the totally centralized economy *can*, in some circumstances, direct the economic process in a way similar to that in which it proceeds under complete competition. However, this should not mislead one into believing that in both cases the economic process *must* follow the same path, nor that the analysis of one model can be substituted for that of another. Great differences remain. . . . The distribution of power is quite different in the two cases. . . . People live in two quite different economic worlds. (Eucken 1940b, 212, emphasis in original)

Eucken's typology of orders integrated contradictory systems into the same explanatory scheme, precisely by adopting the plan criterion mentioned earlier. In the background, the subject of analysis common to both systems is the issue of the power of agents within the economic process.

### 3.2.2 The Administered Economy

Eucken arrived at an apparently paradoxical position on the antithetical positions of the debate. While denying Barone and his successors the unity they claim between the two economic systems, Eucken was willing to recognize that the theoretical solution through market socialism could, in a very specific case, be equivalent to the competitive market order and that therefore the two systems could be examined as one. Yet, ultimately, Eucken rejected the Barone-Lange solution because even if it was conceivable in theory, it would be unfeasible in practice for this market socialism would be tantamount to a central authority abandoning one of its constitutive elements: control over economic plans.

10. There was no unanimity among the so-called Austrian economists: neither in the nature of their arguments (Mises, Hayek), nor indeed in their positioning within the debate since Schumpeter (Lakomski 1999), like Wieser before him (Bostaph 2003), recognized the effective possibility of socialist economic calculation.

### 3.2.2.1 A "World of Values"

According to Eucken (1940b, 192), every form of administered economy had in common the fact that it was a "world of values" (*Welt von Werten*) for it was based on a "system of valuations" (*Bewertungen*). "Values" have an important role in that the administrated economy entails evaluations between physical quantities of a disparate nature, as opposed to the price homogeneity of the exchange economy. Behind Eucken's concept of a "world of values" we find two kinds of arguments relating to the incommensurability between the administered economy and the economy of exchange: technical, on the one hand, and epistemological, on the other.

To some extent taking a Misean perspective, Eucken stressed that the administered economy lacked an adequate method for assessing the relative scarcity of goods and means of production. The administered economy on the domestic scale is unable to carry out effective management of capital and investment since production decisions are based on calculations of physical quantities. Indeed, the planner can only rely on "rounded global assessments" and statistics. Thus, it cannot lead to an economic calculation per se without the "compelling force" of marginal prices and costs (Eucken 1948c, 89). Eucken therefore argued that only a *statistical* equilibrium was achievable in an administered economy and not an *economic* equilibrium, as in the exchange economy.

Eucken based this technical argument on his analysis of the actual functioning of the National Socialist planned economy from 1936 onward. He argued that this system and an exchange economy could not be assessed with the same criteria because their objectives were fundamentally unlike. Indeed, the success of an administered economy relied less on consumer satisfaction than on the success of the central plan; that is, on reaching the objectives set by and for the central authority (usually oriented toward investment and production in heavy industries). Similarly, Röpke (1936b, 321) had emphasized in his article "Socialism, Planning, and the Business Cycle" that, with planning, "people will suffer as consumers rather than as producers."

However, it was not so much the (in)ability to carry out a rational economic calculation that concerned Eucken as, rather, the picture of two worlds with fundamentally alien determinations. From there Eucken developed his argument on the dichotomy between the two systems on an epistemological level. Admittedly, the exchange economy and the administered economy shared the three "rules of experience," but the ways of carrying out plans and acting economically were radically opposed. Eucken (1948c, 189) pointedly noted that "scarcity," or the approach of "saving," had different meanings depending on the economic system. For example, in the administered economy prices play only a subsidiary role as wages no longer remunerate participation in production but take the form of subsistence wages (1948c, 181). Eucken stressed that the very terms—"money" in the first place (see also Röpke 1947e, 244), but also "exchange," "prices," "markets" and so on and so forth—masked the difference in nature between two types of economic reality:

> With exchange replaced by allocations, all other economic institutions and procedures change their character, even though they do not change their names. . . . In economic orders of society in which the methods of control are those of a central administration, in contrast with the views of Barone and his followers, the same terminology may be in use as in the exchange economy ("price," "interest," etc.), *but these words mean something entirely different.* (Eucken 1948c, 190–191, emphasis in original)

Eucken (1948c, 191) then developed his argument by observing that there were still "bankers, farmers, traders," but that "their economic significance is fundamentally different" depending on whether the "centre of gravity" of the economic order is based either on consumer and producer decisions or on central direction. For Eucken, any approach that failed to recognize this plurality and its consequences in the functioning of the economic process would fail to analyze the effective reality and therefore fail in attempting an applied study of power. But speaking of the administered economy in general was still too indeterminate for Eucken, as he unfolded a morphology composed of several subcategories.

#### 3.2.2.2 *The Forms of the Administered Economy*

In *Foundations*, Eucken began by analyzing the forms of the administered economy (rather than the forms of the exchange economy) because it would historically be the elementary form of economic relations. The morphology of Eucken's economic systems outlined two forms of centrally directed economy (*zentralgeleitete Wirtschaft*): the simple economy (*Eigenwirtschaft*) and the administered economy (*Zentralverwaltungswirtschaft*). As such, the problem of "the impossibility of an economic calculation" did not arise for all forms of administered economy, but only in those that required the development of a bureaucratic apparatus (Eucken 1940b, 119).

In fact, the basic and daily supervision of a family economy offers a simple solution to the allocation problem. This consideration is central in Eucken's construction, first because the family (or household) is an integral part of the exchange economy, yet without needing external intervention to ensure coordination. Eucken put it very clearly: "the central direction of the economy is present at every period and among all societies" (1940b, 337, n. 40). Elements of central control are therefore always present in any actual economic order, even if it is an exchange economy. Second, study of the family economy shows, in negative, the difficulties caused by the increasing size of centralized structures typical of modern nation states.

Finally, each of these two forms can appear in three mutually exclusive patterns: (1) the *totally centralized economy*, the *centrally directed economy* (2) *with free exchange of consumer goods* or (3) *with freedom of consumers' choice*. Surprisingly enough, Eucken's morphology did not include the type of ownership (private or collective) as a decisive factor. As Eucken experienced first-hand, private ownership was a necessary condition for an exchange economy but by no means a sufficient condition to preclude an administrated economy.

In the first case, the *totally centralized economy,* all economic decisions (production, consumption, labor, etc.) are made with the economic plan of a single director. Accordingly, no exchange—in the sense of free, reciprocal, and mutually beneficial transfer of ownership—would be allowed after the initial allocation provided by the central director. Eucken claimed that he had shaped this ideal type on historical examples of past family economies as well as the large-scale economy of ancient Egypt, but also the modern functioning of a household. This form embodied an "extreme case" (*Grenzfall*) where the individual dependency on the administered economy "finds its perfect expression," insofar as there are "no exchange, no prices and no exchange values for goods . . . there is no economic process" (Eucken 1940b, 122, 127). In the second case—that of the *centrally directed economy with free exchange*—despite the distribution of goods and services set by the central planner, consumers can reallocate them through exchange as a second step. To Eucken's eyes, this was the typical form of the war economy that European countries set up during the two World Wars. The last, third variant offers a special case, a borderline case. In fact, in the centrally directed economy *with freedom of consumers' choice*, the central planner completely detaches the "individual consumption" data from his plan. As a result, choices are freely made by each consumer within the limits of their income (which does not imply that the central authority abandons all means of influencing household final consumption, as will be discussed in the next section).

What characterizes the transition from one variant of the administered economy to the other is therefore a gradual loosening of the constraints of the central economic plan in favor of individual economic plans and, in particular, consumers'. Again, it is the notion of economic power that is crucial to understanding what clearly distinguishes the different forms of the administered economy. Indeed, both forms of administered economy, as well as their variants, incorporate a significant concentration of economic power. But in the totally centralized economy, Eucken (1940b, 128) pointed out that economic power would be "economically unlimited" (*wirtschaftlich unbeschränkt*). In total, Eucken outlines six ideal types of centrally directed economy, a number not affected by Eucken's later specification. Indeed, in the case of the central administrator following the preferences expressed in the consumer plans—a very particular situation—we obtain a borderline ideal type that switches to the form of the exchange economy. Based on this borderline case, Eucken developed his own criticism of market socialism à la Barone-Lange.

#### 3.2.2.3 The Paradox of the Barone-Lange Solution

The Barone-Lange model was, according to Eucken, not only unsuited for *descriptive* analysis of a planned economy, but also inappropriate in the *prescriptive* logic of a new form of socialist or collectivist economy. From Eucken's point of view, satisfying consumer sovereignty by duplicating a competitive procedure (trial and error) was tantamount to forgoing central direction of the economy. Therefore, the Barone-Lange model would be built on a contradiction undermining both its theoretical and empirical relevance.

In the case of the *centrally directed economy with freedom of consumers' choice*—the order leaving the greatest scope for individual action—Eucken underlined a particular difficulty from the point of view of the central authority: consumer demands may run counter to the authority's initial production plans. Indeed, as a result of abandonment of control by the administration, the individual plans and market interactions between consumers and producers could enter into "contradiction" or even into "conflict" with the central plan (Eucken 1940b, 94). In the event of overproduction (demand deficit) or underproduction (demand excess), the central authority can implement two strategies.

On the one hand, the central authority may contemplate overriding consumer decisions. As the only producer (by ownership or hierarchy), the authority has a wide range of strategies at its disposal. The most obvious is to try to contain high demand for a good by increasing its price (and vice-versa), although the success of pricing policy depends on price elasticity (Eucken 1940b, 126–127). Other solutions compatible with freedom of consumers' choice may be production of substitutable goods, standardization of goods, introduction of rationing coupons, or propaganda. However, in the endeavor to influence demand trends, the central planner excludes "*any* influence on the part of consumers," implying that the consumer is "dethroned" from the leading role of guiding production (the level of investment in particular) through the variety of individual preferences (Eucken 1948c, 176, emphasis in original).

On the other hand, the authority may attempt to adjust its central economic plan in light of the needs actually expressed by consumers. A central plan responding to impulses provided by individual plans is tantamount to the market socialism indicated by Barone and developed by Lange. This socialist formula could be regarded as "democratic" insofar as it prevented fixing of the scale of needs by the bureaucracy (Lange 1936, 68).[11] In this very specific case, Eucken claimed that the directed economy would follow a logic similar to that of the exchange economy. Indeed, everything would proceed as if individuals actually had an impact on the course of the economic process, as is precisely the case in the exchange economy:

> This is where the limits of the central direction of the economy are reached or crossed. This second case of our third variant of the centrally directed economy is really to be classified as an "exchange" economy. A monopoly administration in control of all markets is trying to supply consumers according to the principle of "optimum output" (*bestmögliche Versorgung*). (Eucken 1940b, 126)

Eucken's morphology of economic orders led him to consider the Barone-Lange socialist model from a paradoxical viewpoint. On the one hand, Eucken accepted the validity of this solution from the point of view of economic efficiency (general economic equilibrium) since the principle of "optimum output" is satisfied. In this sense, "the balancing of satisfactions or marginal utilities [would be] in accordance with Gossen's second law" (Eucken 1948c, 97), implying that at equilibrium agents are in a situation equalizing the marginal utilities (relative to the price) of all goods and services.

On the other hand, however, Eucken ruled out the possibility of a type of abstract solution belonging to the morphology of a centrally directed economy and ranked it as a particular form of the exchange economy.

11. Like Eucken, Lange (1945) outlined a binary (ideal type) typology of coordination (planning vs. market). Yet contrary to Eucken, he noted that "planism and market do not exclude each other" but "coexist" in a form of "*mixed economy*" (1945, 26–29). Accordingly, the socialist state must be able to leave economic coordination to the entity best able to ensure community satisfaction depending on actual conditions.

Consequently, the market socialist model "cannot legitimately be used in dealing with contemporary problems of 'collectivist' economic systems" such as the distribution of economic power, the problem of economic calculation, or the fluctuations in investment and savings (Eucken 1940b, 334, n. 32).

In his 1948 article, Eucken underpinned an argument he had already developed in *Foundations*. Eucken compared German planning experience with the trial-and-error procedure theoretically indicated by Lange. Eucken aimed to underline the absurdity of implementing such a procedure from the point of view of the central power:

> By this adjustment of prices would not demand and supply have been brought into equilibrium and would not thus exact cost calculation have been possible? In this way, the German authorities would have been proceeding in accordance with the proposals outlined by, for example, by O. Lange. Wouldn't it have been possible to follow out this proposal? . . . This method of control was out of question for the central administration, for it would have meant letting the control of the means of production out of its hands. (Eucken 1948c, 93)

Eucken's argument was clearly speculative since, as he acknowledged himself, no attempts à la Barone-Lange had been envisaged in Germany. In any case, Eucken was convinced that the theoretical solution was indeed impossible in practice because it would amount to leaving the planned economy form and moving toward the exchange economy. From Eucken's viewpoint (1948c, 191), the argument that a Ministry or a Board of Production could direct the economic process "as though perfect competition ruled"—and derogate from the competitive system only in the distribution of the social product—was truly absurd. In radical opposition to the competitive solution put forward by the socialists, Eucken once again insisted on the dichotomy between the exchange economy and the administered economy through the existence of a competitive price system: "Competition can be used to improve efficiency, but as a mechanism of direction for an important section of the economy it cannot be applied without the abdication of the central authority" (Eucken 1948c, 94).

Therefore, Eucken (1948c, 192) pointed out that any attempt to use the price mechanism to control the economic process will de facto "set a limit to the power of the central administration." Ultimately, for Eucken, the Barone-Lange solution lay in the attraction of building a priori intellectual models without empirical foundations. This competition-like procedure would be tantamount to an utterly "unrealistic" proposal, which Eucken (1948c, 192) considered to be based on "interest in political and economic controversy" rather than scientific and historical analysis. But, on deeper consideration, Eucken could not accept this solution, for this procedure consists in ignoring the matter of power, its manifestation, and its demands, which contravenes the vision of economic power in the hands of the central state, which would, however, at the same time forego its use.

Moreover, Eucken (1940b, 334) claimed that he had found no trace of it in his historical study, on the basis of which his morphological system was built: that a state owning the means of production could "transfer the control of the economic process from the officials to consumers" was a historically unrealistic assumption. How could planning officials abandon the guidance the economy to consumers? How could they be encouraged to do so when, according to Eucken (1940b, 337–338, n. 40), they themselves were in the grip of the power struggle for the allocation of resources between the different subgroups of the central board? The strength—and in some ways also the weakness—of Eucken's analysis was that it was rooted in the particular experience of German economic planning:

> The concentration of economic power, its association with political power, uncertainty and inadequacy in the supply of consumer goods, the increase in social dependence, the threat to the rule of law and freedom. We do not need to learn it from books, because we have lived and experienced it every day. (Eucken 1949, 225)

Over and above analytical arguments, the ordoliberals' conceptions in terms of anthropology and political philosophy conditioned the institutional solutions that they could accept as realistic and legitimate. Eucken thus combines theoretical and historical arguments, which is essential to address the issue of power. Eucken accepted the theoretical compatibility of a certain type of economic control with the exchange economy while rejecting the Barone-Lange model as a practical solution.

### 3.2.3 The Exchange Economy: An Introduction

Eucken (1940b, 129) defined the exchange economy (*Verkehrswirtschaft*) as "a pure form" where companies and households are in exchange with one another. Just like the administered economy, the exchange economy has to solve the economic problem of scarcity. But it faces an additional difficulty, that of "coordinating individual actions and plans" (1940b, 196)—in short, answering the question of how individual actions are linked to each other. In a monetary economy, coordination is achieved through the price system. Therefore, price formation is decisive from a theoretical point of view in grasping the economic issue of the exchange economy. According to Eucken (1940b, 131), both a "calculation scale" (*Rechnungsskala*) and the coincidence of supply and demand on a market determine the two categories of forms of exchange economy, decisive in the overall conduct of the economic process.

Eucken (1940b, 160) defined money as "a universally recognized means of exchange" and did not explicitly consider its function as a store of value (unlike the medium of exchange and unit of account functions) without advancing further justification. This lack is all the more surprising as the accumulation of money can be an important source of economic power. Nevertheless, the question of the articulation between wealth and power was marginally present in ordoliberal considerations on economic policy (as will be discussed in the next chapter).

Eucken (1940b, 163–172) outlined a morphological analysis of monetary systems (*Geldsysteme*) based on two mains forms. In the first form (I) of monetary systems, Eucken distinguished between a currency that fulfils the function of a medium of exchange and a unit of account at the same time (Ia) and a second form where the currency as a medium of exchange and a unit of account are separated (Ib). In the second form (II), Eucken draws our attention to the problem of money creation, which can take three typical ideal forms. Money has its source in a particular commodity (IIa). This would be characteristic of traditional economies, but also relevant to analysis of a barter economy: in a subsequent edition of his *Foundations*, Eucken mentioned the use of cigarettes in postwar Germany, for instance. Second, currency may come from the provision of goods/services or work (IIb). In this context, private banks and the central bank create a large part of the currency in the commercial circuit. Finally, money can be created mainly by credit (IIc). Hence, the form and functioning of the banking system plays a predominant role in the overall economic process.

According to Eucken, the latter case is the most typical of contemporary economies. The great facility of monetary creation (credit) has been particularly favorable to investment, but it has also had the effect of significantly amplifying fluctuations in the money supply. In Eucken's view, increased industrial development was accompanied by chronic monetary and financial instability because the amount of credit granted to finance investment is increasing, but the sustainability of the activity is uncertain. Unlike the form of administered economy, where money is subsidiary, credit is fundamental to the proper functioning of the economic process of the exchange economy.

In addition to monetary systems, Eucken devoted a significant part of his *Foundations* to analysis of the market forms within the exchange economy. Market forms uncover agents' economic power, which is very varied: "the *form of market* will affect the position of the individual economic unit, which has a decisive influence on the whole process of the exchange economy" (1940b, 133, emphasis in original). Just as with the debate on socialist calculation, it was analysis of economic power that led Eucken to focus on the debate on market forms. Indeed, Eucken approached the two debates as investigation into analogous manifestations of economic power but on different scales. This discussion on market structures is subordinated to the analysis of the broader context of the main forms of economic orders since these market structures only make sense within the ideal type of the exchange economy.

## 3.3 MAPPING MARKET STRUCTURES

To capture the specificity of power relations within the exchange economy, Eucken developed a morphological analysis centered on the variety of market forms. By doing so, he offered a definition of competition based on his concept of economic plan, leading him to a position in the discussion of markets structures led by Joan Robinson, Edward Chamberlin, and, in particular, Heinrich von Stackelberg.

### 3.3.1 The Market Structures Revolution

#### *3.3.1.1 Piero Sraffa's Charge Against Marshallian Economics*

The publication of the article "The Laws of Returns under Competitive Conditions" by Piero Sraffa (1926) marked the beginning of controversies over the analysis of market structures. In this article, Sraffa (1926, 536) argued that the supply curve "based upon the laws of increasing and diminishing returns" constituted a "dark spot" of Marshallian price theory. Indeed, Sraffa suggested that the assumptions necessary for nonproportional returns (U-shaped cost curves) contradict the partial equilibrium analysis of a competitive market. The logical coherence of Marshall's theory was only safeguarded in extremely specific cases, not in the general one. For instance, Sraffa (1926, 540) stressed that increasing scales of returns—reducing the unit cost of production as the quantity produced increases—were possible within a specific branch of production;

that is, external to the firm (to avoid monopoly), but internal to the production sector (to avoid a partial equilibrium analysis).[12]

Sraffa (1926, 542) claimed that the logical outcome of his demonstration would be "to abandon the path of free competition and turn in the opposite direction, namely, towards monopoly," outlining this path in the second part of the article. In doing so, Sraffa (1926, 544) introduced some of the elements that were at the heart of the developments of imperfect competition, focusing, for instance, on "long custom, personal acquaintance, confidence in the quality of the product, proximity," but also ease of access to credit, advertising, and reputation effects. With imperfect competition, Sraffa was able to "reformulate the symmetric theory of value while freeing himself from Marshallian constraints on returns" (Lallement 2004, 1561). Sraffa's path-breaking article exerted a remarkable influence among Cambridge (UK) economists, and particularly on the work of Joan Robinson, although the international impact was much more limited. As a matter of fact, Chamberlin and Stackelberg conducted their work taking no account of Sraffa.

#### 3.3.1.2 *Imperfect, Monopolistic, and Oligopolistic Competition*

Almost simultaneously, in the early thirties, Joan Robinson (1933), Edward Chamberlin (1933), and Heinrich Stackelberg (1934b) laid the foundations for a new approach to market structures and price theory. This "revolution" of monopolistic (Chamberlin), imperfect (Robinson), or oligopolistic (Stackelberg) competition broke with the old paradigm that recognized in pure monopoly versus pure competition a fundamental dichotomy in the analysis of market price formation (Bettendorf and Heijdra 2003, 7).

In *Economics of Imperfect Competition*, Robinson (1933) generalized Sraffa's insight to analysis of all forms of markets, pure competition being only one marginal case in the analysis of all market structures. Her book benefitted from continuous discussions and seminars held in Cambridge, where, alongside Sraffa, Richard Kahn was the other leading figure in this discussion on market structures (Marcuzzo 2008). Robinson developed new conceptual tools, such as partial static equilibrium and the Marshallian notion of branch.

In the same year, Chamberlin published his *Theory of Monopolistic Competition*, the result of his doctoral work under the supervision of Allyn

12. As stressed earlier, Eucken (1940b, 189) implicitly fits into the Marshallian formulation of the firm's equilibrium since his scale returns are first increasing (decreasing costs) before being decreasing (increasing costs).

A. Young at Harvard. Using a "hybrid" theory, Chamberlin (1933, xi) aimed to address "the whole of value theory." The fundamental situation underlying Chamberlin's work is that of competitive behavior: for instance, a policy of increasing the selling price does not necessarily lead a company to lose all its customers (as would be the case in conditions of pure competition). Every company has a certain degree of monopoly power. Yet, as cases favoring natural monopolies remain exceptional, profits will attract firms within the sectors so the degree of competition is maintained (Screpanti and Zamagni 2005, 273). Consequently, the degree of monopoly power will vary according to the intensity of substitute products available to consumers; thus Chamberlin considered the rivalry between sellers of a nonhomogeneous quality of goods or services.

For Chamberlin, study of monopolistic competition takes as its starting point the theory of pure monopoly but differs from it in analyzing the "competitive relationships of groups of sellers" rather than conducting isolated analysis. Thus, rather than assuming a given demand curve for a good, Chamberlin aimed at showing that the "curve depends on the nature and price of substitutes that are in close competition with the product under consideration" (1933, 74–75). In moving from pure monopoly theory to imperfect competition theory, Chamberlin (1933, 75) actually refocused from analysis of "*individual* equilibrium" to analysis of "*group* equilibrium (the adjustment of economic forces within a group of competing monopolists, ordinarily regarded as merely a group of competitors)." Sales are therefore affected by new factors; not only price, but also product quality and marketing expenditure, primarily on advertising. Unlike Robinson, Chamberlin did not take preferences as data, but focused on the commercial practices that are designed to forge these preferences, a perspective similar to Sraffa's (Marcuzzo 2008, 302). In analyzing interactions within large groups, however, Chamberlin faced difficulty in defining rival monopolists, but also in explaining the type of adjustments that occur between them. By contrast, it was precisely this aspect that lay at the heart of Stackelberg's book which, by insisting on the problem of "interdependence between firms," positions itself as "the exact complement to the work of Robinson and Chamberlin" (Triffin 1940, 49).

*Market Form and Equilibrium* (*Marktform und Gleichgewicht*) was Stackelberg's habilitation thesis (1934b). Despite a more modest international reception than was accorded to Robinson's and Chamberlin's books (due in particular to the fact that it was in German), John Hicks (1935), Nicholas Kaldor (1936), and Wassily Leontief (1936) praised its analytical subtlety and technical sophistication. In contrast to what Stackelberg (1934b, 85–86) called the "ideal picture" of the "classic model of the economy for a general equilibrium," he showed that by taking into account the market forms present in a real economy (oligopolies, bilateral monopolies, etc.), theoretical analysis offered "a completely unstable picture that is fundamentally chaotic and forever undergoing shocks" generated by the capitalist market economy. Stackelberg was conducting an economic analysis focused on the question of the indeterminacy of the (partial) equilibrium that informed the ordoliberals' theoretical perspective.

#### 3.3.1.3 *The Empirical Relevance of Economic Theory*

The discussion on competitive market structures emerged less as a pure product of analytical sophistication than as "a quest for an empirically relevant competition theory," as Jan H. Keppler (2004) termed it. This critical approach to abstract conceptualization in economics in fact predated Sraffa's internal criticism of the Marshallian paradigm. For instance, the economic historian John H. Clapham (1922) regretted seeing economics working on the construction of theoretical objects that were inapplicable to the actual economy and lacking in empirical content: what Clapham famously termed the "empty boxes." Although Robinson, Chamberlain, or even Stackelberg embodied this trend toward greater empirical relevance of economic theory, Eucken considered that it was precisely from this point of view that their approach had failed.

Generally speaking, Robinson (1933, 1) intended to work toward greater realism in economic theory. However, by referring to her conceptual work as a "toolbox," to some extent she contributed to perpetuating the debate on the technique of analysis rather than its adequacy to reality. In the preface to the first edition of his *Theory of Monopolistic Competition*, Chamberlin claimed that, despite confidence in the usual analytical method (partial equilibria), it is the assumptions necessary for modeling that are at fault by their distance from actual circumstances:

> A comparison of the conclusions with those of pure competition indicates that economic theory is often remote and unreal, *not because the method is wrong*, but because the underlying *assumptions are not as closely in accord with the facts* as they might be. (Chamberlin 1933, xi, emphasis added)

Whether Chamberlin had successfully completed the project of endowing competition theory with greater empirical relevance remains an open question. One to which Hicks (1935) answered negatively, as for him the controversy fueled by Sraffa, Chamberlin, and Robinson was logical and theoretical only, disconnected from the issue of empirical relevance or from the actual problem of economic concentration.[13] By contrast, Edward S. Mason (1939, 61) clearly acknowledged "a trend towards the inclusion in price analysis of an increasing number of institutional considerations" underlying the attention given to the empirical relevance of the theory of market structures.

In any case, one of Eucken's singularities regarding the market structures debate lay in the fact that he raised the question of empirical relevance in terms of his own notion of applied economic theory. In the following pages, I will show that Eucken adopted the opposite seminal statement to that of Chamberlin (quoted earlier). According to Eucken, forging a useful concept of competition would require a different scientific method—informed by morphological analysis—rather than merely less restrictive assumptions. In doing so, Eucken aspired to show the possible articulation of this concept with the actual economic life by means of its market morphology.

## 3.3.2 The Morphology of Markets

### *3.3.2.1 Measuring Market Power*

Eucken separated the exchange economy from the centrally directed economy by means of his plan criterion. In particular, he focused on the location of decision-making capacity guiding the economic process: the consumers versus the central board. However, one should not conclude too quickly that economic power was, therefore, absent from the exchange economy. On the contrary, the whole morphology of markets that Eucken built was precisely about mapping the exercise of private power within the exchange economy:

> Wherever the system is fundamentally that of an exchange economy, where, that is, individual economic units depend on the market and adjust their plans and actions accordingly, economic power asserts itself in another way. Very powerful economic positions can be built up here as well. (Eucken 1940b, 266)

In the exchange economy, in contrast to the administered economy, the place of power analysis has shifted: it is among producers as well as between

13. Hicks's reading was far from being unanimously shared (see Galbraith 1948, 102; Stackelberg 1935, 338). Later, Karl Pribram (1986, 453) followed Hicks in deciding against Chamberlin: by "willing to find more or less defined solutions," the latter "formulates his hypotheses according to their convenience for analysis rather than their conformity with reality."

consumers and producers that the power struggle must be identified. Eucken cautiously noted that each of the possible market forms were "always a combination of different forms of supply and demand" (1940b, 156). Consequently, talking about *the* market would inevitably lead to talking about very specific markets. Eucken also introduced two levels of supply and demand analysis.

The first specification introduced by Eucken concerned the guiding forms of supply and demand: each would be either "open" or "closed." A market is said to be open when "any individual or group has access to the market as a supplier or demander, and each individual or group can offer or demand as much as it deems appropriate" (1940b, 134). Otherwise, the market is said to be closed. For example, a market is closed when a small group of contractors is allowed to sell, when there are investment vetoes, or when only certain individuals are allowed to work. This first aspect of the market (open vs. closed), which can switch from one to the other quickly, is of decisive influence in the formation of economic plans.

Second, Eucken considered market forms in terms of structures such as competition, monopoly, oligopoly, and so forth. Analyzing the ex ante representation of economic action on the basis of a set of constraints—the economic plan—led Eucken to a morphology of five ideal types: monopoly, partial monopoly, oligopoly, partial oligopoly, and complete competition. For each one of these specific cases, it should be specified whether the form (e.g., monopoly) applies to supply, demand, or both (bilateral monopoly). Therefore, five market forms, each specified in the case of supply and demand, generate twenty-five possible cases. Eucken provided systematic representation in the form of a double-entry table.

Eucken's approach was actually a refinement of Stackelberg's analysis of market structures, which was also summarized in table form. Stackelberg (1934b, 3) had identified nine cases in total, to which Eucken added what he termed the "partial" (*Teil-*) cases.[14] In fact, to the forms "competition," "oligopoly," and "monopoly" (of supply and demand), Eucken added as essential forms "partial oligopoly" and "partial monopoly" which, according to his criterion of the individual plan, cannot be reduced to the other three forms.

Eucken's meticulous typology may seem excessive, especially in comparison to past representations of market structures first historically

14. By adding the "open" or "closed" character either of supply or demand, or both at the same time, Eucken obtained a hundred possible cases. The fact that on each market the official authority could fix market prices even brings the total to two hundred types of virtually possible cases.

dominated by a duality between competition and monopoly, then refined in the interwar period to intermediate forms (monopolistic competition, oligopoly).[15] Eucken to some extent anticipated this criticism by comparing his morphological table to Mendeleyev's periodic table of elements, stressing that "no one blames chemists for taking into account the many existing elements, and that the same should be true for the economist" (1940b, 156). By providing an overview of the infinitesimal variations in market power, this classification attests to his great interest in an analysis placing strong emphasis on the issue of power: "Our classification of market forms enables us not only to describe the historical facts more precisely," Eucken (1940b, 268) pointed out, "but also to appreciate better the concentration of power on the one side and the loss of power and independence on the other." Excluding monopoly, the remaining four market structures allow a degree of freedom for consumers or other entrepreneurs with regard to the economic power that a particular agent, or group of agents, can exercise.

#### *3.3.2.2 Defining Competition: From Homogeneity to Substitutability*

Based on his morphological analysis derived from economic plans, Eucken claimed that it was possible to systematically distinguish between when a firm was actually in a competitive or monopoly situation. Eucken thus justified the fact that "monopolistic" or "imperfect" competition does not belong to one of his pure morphological forms. Ultimately, Eucken considered that Chamberlin's and Robinson's approaches were part of the same perspective. Indeed, from Eucken's viewpoint, Robinson's and Chamberlin's competition analyses went almost blind to the fundamental forces of an exchange economy by blurring the line between the various pure market forms. Eucken believed that these approaches led to the disappearance of the distinction—which he considered essential—between monopoly and competition. For him, the erosion of this clear scientific distinction would be advantageous for the interested power groups who would exploit it to demand a greater socialization of the economy and support their market positions by invoking arguments in terms of stabilizing the economic process.

15. However, Edward S. Mason can be cited as an exception. In the same years, Mason (1939, 66) also saw a systematic classification of market structures as a tool to provide "realistic treatment of the question necessary for the use of the analytical apparatus." Mason began to formulate what would later be called the *Harvard approach*, based on the explanatory pattern: structure-behavior-performance (Phillips and Stevenson 1974, 336–337).

Eucken (1940b, 289) did not separate the theoretical outlook from the political one, as the "distinction between competition and monopoly is important both theoretically as well as for economic policy." Consequently, failing to identify the actual cases of competition and monopoly was tantamount, from Eucken's point of view, to failing to prescribe a rational economic policy. Röpke (1942d, 229), while welcoming the future developments that may result from the research programme initiated by Robinson and Chamberlin, shared Eucken's concerns:

> The fact that free competition hardly exists in reality in a chemically pure state and that most prices contain a monopoly element should not give rise to the erroneous view that our economic system is no longer based on competition, but on monopoly. (Röpke 1940, 203)

By stressing the lack of homogeneity of goods, Chamberlin had pointed out that each supplier was selling its own good on its own market, as a monopolist. Therefore, monopolistic competition designated a "network of interrelated markets (Chamberlin)" (quoted by Eucken 1940b, 141). Because Robinson approached competition as a borderline case of monopoly, Eucken believed that she was guilty of the same error when stating that "the analysis of monopoly 'swallows up the analysis of competition' (J. Robinson)" (Eucken 1940b, 141). According to Eucken, both Chamberlin and Robinson used the inadequate criterion of homogeneity, popularized by Sraffa, to assess effective competition in a market.

While Eucken justified Chamberlin's and Robinson's attempts from the perspective of the dynamics of the history of ideas—the economic analysis had long been devoted almost exclusively to competition[16]—he nevertheless challenged their analysis. In doing so, Eucken (1940b, 142–143) invoked three main criteria that allowed him, precisely in borderline cases, to distinguish between competition and monopoly: (a) the availability of a substitute for the product sold on the market, (b) the firm's area of influence, and (c) sales techniques. The first point was clearly Eucken's favorite argument, which would be assiduously invoked by the ordoliberals as a whole (Röpke 1940, 193; Lutz 1956, 161; Hensel 1966, 132). Eucken claimed that the lack of homogeneity of goods—leading each producer to a monopolistic position—was largely offset by the increase in substitutability between goods from different markets. In this sense, the existence

16. With the notable exception of Cournot, whom Eucken (1940b, 290, 332, 334) mentioned on several occasions.

of a monopolistic firm (for a given good) was no longer a problem insofar as competition also takes place outside its own sphere of activity. The ordoliberal approach to market relations was decompartmentalized and insisted on the development of substitutes:

> The resulting elasticity of demand for individual commodities brings the market nearer to complete competition, even if the seller of any particular type of commodity is a monopolist, since monopolies are forced to behave as though they were in competition. (Eucken 1951, 42)

According to Eucken, the price elasticity of demand and supply was decisive in working against market power. Indeed, the greater the price elasticity of a good, the weaker the position of power, for infinitesimal variations in price will lead to greater variations in the demand for that good (Eucken 1940b, 271).[17] The existence of substitutable products often caused negative price elasticity of the good (i.e., a positive cross-elasticity in relation to the substitute).

All these explanations led Eucken to forge an external critique of the competition analyses based on a priori formal models developed by Sraffa, Robinson, Chamberlin, and Stackelberg. Eucken nurtured an epistemological outlook focused on the tangible characteristics of individuals' behavior and certain historical-institutional features:

> The old customary procedure must be amended. It approaches the reality by making formal assumptions about it "from above," as when the criterion of homogeneity of goods is adopted. . . . To start from units homogeneous in size is to fail to do justice to the actual economic reality. This postulate is in fact almost never achieved. Thus with such definitions, competition or oligopoly are only intellectual constructions, having scarcely any contact with reality, and the theoretical propositions arrived at on such a basis can almost never be applied. (Eucken 1940b, 150–151)

In the following, I will show that Eucken proposed to define what he called "complete competition" (*vollständige Konkurrenz*) on the basis of its economic plan category and in accordance with a "bottom-up" approach on the part of the actual behavior of economic agents.

17. The same argument about the correlation between increasing elasticity and increasing competition was already to be found in Sraffa (1926, 545).

### 3.3.2.3 *Defining Competition: Against Formal Hypotheses*

Frank Knight (1921) is generally credited with the first formulation of the assumptions of pure competition. He set out four conditions: (1) perfect knowledge (the rationality of agents), (2) perfect mobility, (3) perfect communication (absence of transaction costs), and (4) individual independence, which excludes any form of agreement and collusion or degrees of and tendencies toward monopolies (Stigler 1957, 12; Rainelli 2000, 138). With this approach he outlined the hypotheses of pure and perfect competition, particularly those essential for mathematical formulation and resolution. From the set of hypotheses, Stackelberg selected the hypothesis of homogeneity of goods and of agents (i.e., equal size and wealth). Chamberlin (1933) also opted for the hypothesis of homogeneity of goods, but preferred that of a large number of agents. Although she denounced "the tyranny of the hypotheses of perfect competition," Robinson (1933, 105) followed a rather similar approach.

By contrast, Eucken aimed at defining complete competition on the basis of his category of economic plan. Complete competition would be achieved in a given market when not only "there is competition on the supply side, as well as on the demand side," but also "if individual economic planning is based, on both sides, on such competition" (Eucken 1949, 230). Röpke also rejected employing analysis based on monopoly to characterize the mechanics of the market economy. Hence, he relied no more than Eucken on the formal and a priori definition of competition:

> Concepts of "pure" or "perfect" competition based on abstract mathematical models, whose assumptions must necessarily remain unrealized in the dynamic reality of economic life, should be replaced by the concept of "active" or "workable"[18] competition in which the continuous striving of the producers for the favour of the consumers is emphasised as the essential note of competition. (Röpke 1963, 162)

Eucken (1949, 229) spoke of complete competition using the metaphor of a "race run in parallel," which is nothing like "impediment or injurious competition" but rather what he termed "performance competition" (*Leistungswettbewerb*). Eucken countered technical discussions on the hypotheses of pure and perfect competition with his economic plan

18. An obvious reference to John M. Clark's article "Toward a Concept of Workable Competition" (1940).

criterion as the only relevant tool to understand, in tangible terms, whether a firm was in a competitive situation or not. He was well aware that in real cases it was easy to switch from a monopoly position to a competitive one, and vice-versa. Although the practical situation was not modified with regard to theoretical hypotheses (number of actors, homogeneity, etc.), the relationships between subjective plans within the market process can nevertheless indicate an entirely different dynamic:

> Whenever monopoly and competition are adjacent it is possible to draw the frontier precisely by a consequential application of our criterion of the nature of the data in economic plans. . . . From the formal mathematical point of view monopoly is a limiting case of competition, or competition a limiting case of monopoly. *In the effective economic reality monopoly is something quite different from competition.* (Eucken 1940b, 144–145, emphasis in original)

Eucken used the same argument to distinguish between oligopoly and monopoly, or between oligopoly and partial monopoly. In fact, Eucken insisted on the irreducibility of each of his five forms of markets. In the case of monopoly (supply or demand), it is the reaction on the other side of the market which becomes a given in the economic plan; the monopoly can decide the price more or less freely. In this respect, from the monopoly's point of view, price is no longer "*given* in the plan but *results from* the economic plan of the monopolist," and thus appears as "a *problem*" to be solved (Eucken 1940b, 141, emphasis in original).[19]

By contrast, in the case of competition "price is a datum" in the economic plans of each of the actors (i.e., the actions of firms or households are based on a price that they consider given exogenously). Over and above any technical condition or hypothesis, what ultimately differentiates market structures is to be found in economic plans. Eucken's approach was undoubtedly less technical but also less restrictive than that of perfect competition (Lutz 1944, 213). Eucken's morphological analysis led him to highlight the sole criterion of the nature of the price (as planning data vs. object of a strategy) in the economic plans of firms and consumers to judge competitive situations. Competitive behavior occurs when prices are used as market-based planning data (*Plandaten*) in the economic plans

19. More precisely, Eucken defined supply monopoly as a market structure in which "the supplier may take the *expected reaction of his customer* as a datum in his economic plan" on the basis of which he "fixes either the price, which for him is not a datum, or the amount offered, letting the price adjust itself"; conversely for the demand monopoly (1940b, 136–137, emphasis in original).

of producers and consumers, never the conscious result of individual strategies. The agent cannot set the price or even anticipate the influence of his action on the price system. Eucken frequently expressed this idea and came up with one of its most telling formulations in the case of the agricultural market:

> A farmer's economic planning does not take account of how his wheat sales affect the wheat market since his supply is too small in relative terms. His plans are therefore based on wheat or pig or vegetable prices that he regards as fixed values—as data—and these are prices formed on the market. He may expect certain market prices, estimate the prices he believes he will be able to charge or assume that these prices will move within particular parameters. This is competition. (Eucken 1949, 229)

Eucken did not take the figure of the farmer randomly: the agrarian sector was often excluded from discussions on competition, being considered too specific (industry was generally preferred). Yet, with his criterion, Eucken underlined the importance of starting from the real behavior of agents and not from formal assumptions a priori.

Eucken refused to describe competition as a form of supply and demand in which variations in the quantities supplied or demanded by a person do not cause any alteration in the price in question; definitely "such a form of supply or demand does not really exist and is scarcely conceivable" (Eucken 1940b, 139). In the vast majority of competitive cases, there is indeed a real influence deriving from the strategies of individual firms (unlike neoclassical price-taking), and this is precisely the object of competition. What is significant for Eucken is not the disappearance of power (because this would lead to the disappearance of the economic process itself), but the distance from a conscious exercise of power within the economic plan.

However, the "phenomenon of economic power disappears under conditions of a single form of market, that is complete competition" (Eucken 1940b, 269). This clarification was fundamental in Eucken's conceptualization: while in the context of a centrally directed economy, the consumer has—subjectively as well as objectively—no influence whatsoever over the economic process, in the case of the exchange economy ordered according to the principles of complete competition, the exercise of power is far less obvious. The consumer formulates—subjectively—his economic plan as if he had no power, but in fact does contribute—objectively—to the formation of market prices. Hence, on deeper consideration, the consumer does exercise an effective influence on the global economic process. Accordingly, Eucken (1940b, 270) stressed that under a regime of "complete competition, the individual unit is disempowered (*entmachtet*), but not entirely so."

In some respects, Eucken came up against the ambiguities and circularity of reasoning of marginalist neoclassical economics: at the margin, the choice of no individual affects the process, yet the choice of all does affect the same process. Is it the price that determines demand, or does demand determine the market price? The mathematical solution arrived at through the theory of limits cannot be satisfactory from Eucken's point of view since this technical treatment eliminates the materiality and causality of power relations in the economy. In the same vein, Eucken emphasized that perfect elasticity was also subjectively essential for individual units (in their economic plan), although undeniably not achieved in actual markets. This subjective dimension of the plans formed by the agents was the cornerstone of the ordoliberal definition of complete competition, in contrast to the objective dimension of the factual and observable market data:

> What is decisive under competition is not the actual reactions resulting from an individual's conduct . . . but just the fact that, owing to the considerable size of the market and the negligible size of his supply or demand, the individual *does not reckon* with any such reaction in his economic plan. . . . Whether the price is *actually* influenced by an increase or decrease in the supply from this firm is not decisive for the action of the supplier, nor, therefore, for this form of supply. (Eucken 1940b, 139–140, emphasis in original)

Here, it is the number of participants that counts in Eucken's observation. But even if the company is alone in the market, the potential competition allowed by the opening of the market is vitally important. To Eucken's eyes, the issue of free market entry (open vs. closed market) was important to judge the degree of competition, but not decisive. In an open market, even if there are no real competitors, potential competition invites the monopoly to adopt competitive behavior. On the contrary, when the monopoly market is closed, "its position of power" is de facto "far stronger" (Eucken 1940b, 154). Power positions are obviously easier to consolidate when the market is closed and the degree of economic power of a company varies according to the size of the market in key sectors.

### 3.3.3 Applying Theory? The Stackelberg Hypothesis

Eucken criticized theoretical approaches based on unrealistic and formal hypotheses in the definition of market forms. However, his criticism should not lead us to conclude that he rejected the mathematical economic theory of his time altogether. In particular, Eucken endorsed some of Stackelberg's theoretical results. In our inquiry into the theoretical foundations of the ordoliberal political economy, Stackelberg's centrality is twofold. On the one hand, Stackelberg ordered the different market structures according to their economic efficiency (in terms of both price and quantity). More significantly, on the other hand, Stackelberg depicted problematic cases of market structures without equilibrium. While Stackelberg offered the theoretical basis for ordoliberals' microeconomic conceptions, the latter were no strangers to Stackelberg's political veer from the corporatist state to the competitive order.

#### 3.3.3.1 *Price Theory and Market Equilibria*

Eucken and the ordoliberals developed a rather instrumental use of Stackelberg's work, in the sense that they did not dwell on assessment of his hypotheses nor discussion of the mathematical demonstrations (technically advanced for the time). By developing a formal analysis of market structures, Stackelberg contributed to the rise of marginalism in Germany; in fact, neoclassical economics received scant attention in the first half of the twentieth century (Peacock 1950). Stackelberg discussed contributions by Cournot, Bertrand, and Bowley on partial equilibrium, but placed himself on Edgeworth's path, aligned with the so-called Lausanne School of Walras and Pareto. By providing broad access to the most advanced microeconomic analysis of that time, Stackelberg would provide ordoliberals with an unparalleled German-language exposition of competitive market behavior.

Based on the analysis of duopoly, Stackelberg had demonstrated the superiority of the pure competition equilibrium (where the price equals the marginal cost) in terms of a greater output and a lower price as compared with other solutions (Cournot, Stackelberg, and Bowley equilibria in particular). Cournot's solution to duopoly (the central case of the oligopolistic market) is to consider the two firms as mutually dependent. Each firm would maximize its profit based on the quantity produced by the other firm. Here Stackelberg (1935, 334) referred to Cournot's "theory of adaptation," a theory whose result "occupies an intermediate position between monopoly and free competition." Eucken adopted Stackleberg's results and formulations of monopolist and duopoly behavior:

> We saw that the monopolist in his plan takes as given the reactions to his policy he expects from the other side of the market. If he follows the principle of

> maximum net revenue (*höchstmöglichen Reineinnahme*), with given productive equipment he produces up to what has been called "Cournot's point." The actual market price enforced is always higher than marginal cost, and the supply to customers is always smaller than it could be without any violation of the economic principle. If the principle of optimum output (*bestmögliche Versorgung*) is followed, then the monopolist fixes the price so low that it equals marginal cost, and the supply to consumers is larger than if the other principle is followed. (Eucken 1940b, 289–290)

In addition to Cournot's solution, Stackelberg envisaged asymmetric solutions, where one of the two duopolies achieves a better result by letting its competitor behave in a strategic way (anticipate the reaction of the other in its maximization calculation without considering the other's supply) and only adjusting to it. In such cases, one firm is a leader (position of independence) and the other is a follower (position of dependence). Modern textbooks labeled this solution *Stackelberg's duopoly* (Senn 1996, 2012). Nevertheless, it must be noted that Stackelberg considered the leader–follower case very unlikely in practice. Indeed, the temptation for each of the two firms to establish itself as leader was a far more credible outcome (Keppler 1994, 87).

This last case leads to *Bowley's equilibrium*, which is relatively close to the pure competition solution and in some situations may even be superior. However, Stackelberg (1934b, 201) pointed to a fundamental difference between Bowley's case and that of pure competition: the latter is an equilibrium position, while the former is a "position of struggle" (*Kampfsituation*). Indeed, Bowley's solution implied that the two firms would behave as leaders, independently of one another. This attitude leads to an economically irrational result from the point of view of the suppliers, insofar as the profit actually made is lower than the expected profit. However, this may be explained by the fact that, for both firms, "victory in the Darwinian struggle for economic survival contains an intrinsic utility that exceeds the expected utility of monetary gain" (Keppler 2002, 557).

With this brief outline of Stackelberg's analytical results, we can understand why, from the point of view of consumer satisfaction, the ordoliberals supported the competitive order rather than any duopolistic equilibria. Moreover, Stackelberg considered that neither Bowley's nor Cournot's cases represent proper equilibria and that there exist a whole range of possible alternatives in duopolistic price formation. This is what led him to consider the duopoly as unstable, a market structure without equilibrium (*gleichgewichtslose Marktform*). This result of general instability was at the heart of Stackelberg's thought and was endorsed by the ordoliberals.

### 3.3.3.2 Market Structures Without Equilibrium

To shed light on Stackelberg's approach and findings in *Market Structure and Equilibrium* (1934b), one might start from his definition of a "free market capitalist economy." This definition outlined three principles: (1) maximum utility; (2) maximum net profit, or the "commercial principle"; and (3) freedom of pricing, in the sense that prices result from individual behavior on markets (1934b, 5). However, Stackelberg (1934b, 25) concluded his analyses by stressing that certain market structures were fundamentally "irreconcilable" with the capitalist economy thus defined. He noted in particular the incompatibility of supply oligopolies, demand oligopolies, oligopolies, and bilateral monopolies with two core principles of the market capitalist economy: (1) maximum utility and (3) freedom of price formation (1934b, 88–89).

The conclusion Stackelberg reached was decisive for shedding light on the theoretical foundations of the ordoliberal political economy, especially regarding its aversion to every kind of monopolistic structures. Just like the jurist Franz Böhm (1954, 154) who mentioned "states of equilibrium that can be analysed scientifically," the economist Leonhard Miksch (1937b, 1942) made some brief reference to Stackelberg's analysis. Eucken also gave direct evidence of the ordoliberal integration of Stackelberg's findings:

> It is true that there do exist "unstable orders" which tend to transform themselves. A market, for example, in which there is bilateral monopoly, or bilateral partial monopoly, or oligopoly on the supply side, frequently changes in form. The absence of equilibrium in these forms of market results in a deliberate effort to reach some more stable form, and often a supply oligopoly transforms itself into a collective monopoly. Cartels develop out of the oligopolistic struggles of a few firms. (Eucken 1940b, 249; see also 1948b, 273)

Therefore, Eucken incorporated Stackelberg's results within his own analysis of economic orders and used unstable market forms as a dynamic factor in accounting for the transition from one market form to another and, eventually, in the evolution of economic order as a whole. Eucken (1940b, 250) concluded the just cited reasoning by emphasizing that "the economic process, through the lack of equilibrium, shapes the economic order." Indeed, the absence of equilibrium, through strategies aiming to reach a more stable position, shaped the process toward a noncompetitive order. Bilateral monopolies and oligopolies threaten the stability of the economic order to the extent that they represent struggles for economic power. Eucken had first-hand experience of the problem of the cartelization of the German economy (discussed in Chapter 1).

However, the oligopoly was not a factor of economic instability by itself. As long as the dependency relationships between firms remain too complex to be directly perceived by the actors, strategical moves remain highly unlikely. And yet, according to Stackelberg (1934b, 86), the process of rationalization and concentration of the economy made it easier for firms to obtain strategic information, making the respective dependencies more visible. Intuitively, the empirical situation of a cartel might theoretically be seen as corresponding to an oligopoly, for a cartel is formed by a small group of actors. Actually, when several firms form a cartel, it is precisely with a view to "influencing the market through collective action with the aim of making monopolistic gains," so that they form what Eucken called in his morphology a "collective monopoly."[20]

Market relations between two cartels—or collective monopolies—are elements that particularly exacerbate all the difficulties of stability in economic equilibrium: hence the case of the bilateral monopoly. As, for instance, when wage determination involves negotiations between the employers' organization and the workers' union (Stackelberg 1934b, 90; 1948, 182). Beyond these paradigmatic cases, there are many possible relationships between cartels selling raw material and industrial cartels (chemicals, steel, metallurgy). The supply monopoly that faces a demand monopoly (or monopsony) on the market is therefore particularly instructive from an ordoliberal perspective because of the difficulties it raises.

Stackelberg outlined a whole series of theoretical solutions depending on the bilateral relations between the two monopolies. However, these solutions did not constitute equilibria per se, but only special cases. In the end, his fundamental finding lay in the demonstration of a "region of undetermined price formation in the case of bilateral monopoly" (Stackelberg 1948, 188). According to him, the ultimate determination of trade was eventually conditioned by the monopoly's ability to negotiate and dominate—in reality through a struggle—the monopsony, and vice-versa.[21] In response

20. From a theoretical perspective, Eucken analyzed cartels as a particular case of monopoly that he called "collective monopoly." In this case, the coordination difficulty comes from the harmonization of the different individual economic plans of the firms composing the cartel, whose conflicting interests generally lead to "the growth of internal conflicts" (Eucken 1940b, 149). Stackelberg (1948, 176–177) borrowed Eucken's expression in his last book.

21. With regard to the analysis of concrete cases, only empirical surveys that focus on highlighting "inertia factors" and "organizational factors" are able to complete the theoretical analysis of price formation (Stackelberg 1938).

to this observation, Stackelberg (1934b, 89) outlined three possible ways to settle this chronic instability of the capitalist market system: first, elimination of unstable market structures; second, elimination of free market price formation; or third, elimination of the principle of maximum utility (or profit). Nevertheless, Stackelberg (1934b, 89) pointed out from the outset that, in a capitalist regime, the latter solution is impracticable because profit represents "the essential characteristic of a capitalist system".

Finally, Stackelberg also addressed the solutions envisaged in the field of economic policy. What should the role of the state be? Would it be better to organize markets in such a way as to reflect the pattern of a form of competition? Or should prices be set to counter the unstructured tendencies of certain market forms? The following section will show that, over time, Stackelberg came up with different policy answers to these questions.

#### 3.3.3.3 *From Corporatism to Competition: Stackelberg Ordoliberal*

Having, in two steps, addressed the imprint of Stackelberg's work on Eucken and the ordoliberals, the reverse influence deserves a few words. This last section deals with Stackelberg's shift in the political interpretation of his economic theory from fascist corporatism to the ordoliberal competitive order. Stackelberg's conversion to ordoliberal principles is generally highlighted in the studies dedicated to his thought, but the secondary literature on ordoliberalism has hardly mentioned his name. Brief references are limited to competition analysis on the one hand (Broyer 2003a; Rieter and Schmolz 1993), or to his "active Nazism" (Ptak 2009, 119), in order to discredit ordoliberal authors as if by contagion.[22]

In 1934, Stackelberg ended his *Market Structure and Equilibrium* with a section entitled "The Theoretical Model of Fascist Corporate Markets," influenced by the work of the Italian economist Luigi Amoroso, whom he met during a nearly three-month stay in Italy (Konow 1994, 148). In this final section, Stackelberg outlined state corporatism as a means of limiting economically unstable market structures in favor of market structures with equilibrium. Nevertheless, the creation of monopolies, particularly in the case of the labor market, can lead to an economic war that threatens the stability of the equilibrium. The state may then intervene to replace

22. Stackelberg's career in the Nazi Party is well documented. He was a strong supporter of the National Socialist Party from 1931 and joined the SS troops in 1933 (he was then twenty-eight). Yet some commentators noted that he grew "disillusioned" with the Nazi movement as early as 1936, and his attempts to leave the SS for "reasons of conscience" were rejected twice (Kurz 2016, 213; see also Möller 1948; Senn 1996).

the lack of "'natural' equilibrium" with a "'conventional' equilibrium" that would "function in the manner desired by the state" (Stackelberg 1934b, 91). The state can ensure that the "'conventional' equilibrium from the bilateral monopolised corporative market . . . leads to the same outcome as with 'free competition'" (1934b, 94). This decision appears no longer to be a matter of economic theory, but rather of the author's political choices. For instance, Stackelberg (1934a, 4) had emphasized the "irreconcilable opposition" between the liberal conception of the state and that of "National Socialist science," taking a position in favor of the latter (quoted by Düppe 2015, 26).

In stark contrast with his 1934 book, Stackelberg concluded his *Grundlagen der theoretischen Volkswirtschaftslehre*, translated as *The Theory of the Market Economy* (1948), with a section entitled "The Competitive Economy and Consumer Satisfaction."[23] In the ten years separating the redaction of the two books, he converted from what John Hicks (1935, 336) scornfully termed "a pæan to the corporatist state," to an economic model where "the competitive system is the best way" to allocate resources and promote the development of productive forces (Stackelberg 1948, 318). Stackelberg also developed certain arguments relating to the technical difficulties faced by a central board contemplating performance of the market calculation procedure. From one book to another, the theoretical demonstrations and results concerning price formation in the different market structures remained analogous.

Stackelberg's veer on economic policy was explained by Eucken in the obituary the latter wrote to the memory of the former. Eucken insisted on Stackelberg's technical abilities, while stressing his interest in the question of the empirical relevance of mathematical models. In an effort to avoid "unnecessary abstractions," Stackelberg increasingly turned to "practical problems" which, according to Eucken (1948e, 133), would have "considerably affected his attitude towards economic policy problems."

Remarkably enough, Stackelberg's last book contained many direct references to Eucken (one of the most quoted authors). Stackelberg referred to Eucken not only to support and take up certain ideas, but also in directly endorsing Eucken's conceptual vocabulary. In particular, Stackelberg (1948, 4, 11) borrowed the analysis in terms of economic plans and the definition

23. Written in 1943, in Germany, the book was first published under the title *Grundzüge der theoretischen Volkswirtschaftslehre*. Stackelberg largely completed this work in the following years during his tenure as visiting professor at the Complutense University of Madrid. The amplified version of the book first appeared in Spanish and then in a posthumous German version (Peacock 1952, xiv).

of the data. It is therefore far from surprising to see him thinking through Eucken's central dichotomy between an exchange economy and a centrally administered economy (1948, 14–15).

These remarks, which attest to the importance of Eucken's reflections for Stackelberg from 1940 onward, raise questions about the strengthening of personal ties between the two German economists. True, Stackelberg had published a long and enthusiastic book review of Eucken's *Foundations* (see Stackelberg 1940). But these links are based on more than just cross-reading. Indeed, in his article in memory of Stackelberg, Eucken gave some indications of this while highlighting Stackelberg's political transition:

> In his *Marktform und Gleichgewicht* [1934b] he had shown certain sympathies for the corporative state. This, however, was a temporary phase. As he became more familiar with the facts of economic life he became a determined critic of every form of planned economy. In a paper which he read to a small circle in 1943 and which is soon to be published he elaborated this criticism from a mathematical point of view.[24] He had come to the conclusion that the competitive order is the only principle by which the economic problems of our time can be solved, but he drew a sharp distinction between the competitive order and a system of *laissez-faire*, and he was fully aware of the importance of the task of elaborating a suitable legal framework for such a competitive order. It has been his hope to contribute to this task. (Eucken 1948e, 133–134)

In the course of 1943, Stackelberg attended the clandestine seminar of the *Freiburger Kreise* working groups. These circles of intellectual resistance, with ethical and Catholic orientations, aimed to anticipate the requisite of a postwar economic and social order (see Rieter and Schmolz 1993; Goldschmidt 2005a; Maier 2014). A good example of the type of reflections that were conducted there can be found in "*Wirtschafts- und Sozialordnung*," signed by Constantin von Dietze, Walter Eucken, and Adolf Lampe (1943). This short text focused on post-war priority measures, including the ambition to establish a competitive order and restrict the money supply (an issue at the heart of Chapter 5).

More precisely, Stackelberg participated in the *Arbeitsgemeinschaft*.[25] This working group was led by his former thesis director, Erwin von Beckerath,

24. The article "Possibilities and Limitations of Economic Planning" ("*Möglichkeiten und Grenzen der Wirtschaftslenkung*") was published posthumously in the second issue of the journal *Ordo* (Stackelberg 1949).

25. The summaries and protocols of the seminars were edited by Christine Blumenberg-Lampe (1986).

a historicist who took to a "literary" form of marginalism (Niehans 1992, 190). The participants included ordoliberals like Eucken, Böhm, and Lampe, but also Dietze, Erich Preiser, Gerhard Ritter, Günter Schmölders, and, more surprisingly, Jens Jessen, Stackelberg's colleague at the University of Berlin. Jessen, although a former member and prominent economist of the Nazi Party, eventually joined resistance groups and was executed at the end of 1944 because of contacts with the organizers of the failed assassination of Hitler (in July of the same year). Eucken himself was interrogated twice by the Gestapo, but released. His friends Lampe, Ritter, and von Dietze did not share the same fortune and were imprisoned by the regime, to be eventually liberated by Soviet forces.

All in all, Stackelberg probably did not attend more than a couple of seminars in Freiburg because he was already on his way to Spain. Yet, in this context, Stackelberg completed his conversion to ordoliberal theses. These links established in 1943 with the Freiburg circles played a major role in Stackelberg's rehabilitation after his death from Hodgkin's disease in October 1946 in Madrid (at the age of 41). Although Stackelberg spent less than three years in Franco's Spain, he exerted a lasting influence on Iberian economists (Fuertes 1996; Ban 2012), contributing to the spread of ordoliberal ideas in postwar Europe beyond the German borders.

## 3.4 CONCLUSION: THE MORPHOLOGY OF POWER

A we saw, the concept of economic plan lay at the basis of the ordoliberal approach to economic theory. Indeed, Eucken used the economic plan to build both his morphologies of economic orders and of market structures. On deeper consideration, the morphological analysis Eucken tailored in his *Foundations* (1940b, 128) can be seen as the necessary way to approach "one of the greatest of historical problems, that of economic power." In doing so, Eucken questioned the relationship between theory and reality from the point of view of the application of economic theories.[26]

26. Obviously, one could have found other ordoliberal contributions to economic theory than those I discussed here, but none that would have fitted within a framework embracing all the authors. One possibility would have been to analyze early ordoliberal writings on the theory of economic fluctuations (Eucken 1929; Lutz 1932; Röpke 1932; 1936a). However, Eucken (1940b, 244–246) abandoned the ambition to provide a proper theory of cycles insofar as there would be "no inevitable law inherent in cyclical fluctuations," and consequently "no normal business cycle." Eventually, Eucken (1940b, 262) claimed that his morphological analysis could also be applied to investigate the issue of fluctuations. Another possibility would have been to focus on the work of Friedrich Lutz (1938, 1940, 1945) on the theory of money, interest,

In conclusion, we have brought to the fore two major internal tensions in Eucken's approach to economic theory. The first tension lies in the articulation between Eucken's morphology of markets and the available economic analysis of competition. Eucken stressed the complementarity of his morphological analysis with canonical economic theory while at the same time being critical of the models based on formal restrictive assumptions outlined by Robinson, Chamberlin, and Stackelberg. Thus, we may ask, was Eucken's endorsement of Stackelberg's theoretical results (demonstrating the superiority of the competitive solution) a sign of an ideological bias to the detriment of coherence? Clearly the debate on market structures was not politically neutral, and imperfect, monopolistic, or oligopolistic competition was often invoked to call for "a higher degree of state intervention in private markets" (Keppler 1994, 5).

However, Eucken's apparent inconsistency can be partially overcome. Indeed, his criticism of the hypotheses asserted by Chamberlin, Robinson, and Stackelberg was less a questioning of the theoretical validity of their models (and their results) than of their inability to be applicable to real cases. If one were to try to picture a real market situation fulfilling the hypotheses of pure competition, it might well end up with competition having disappeared from reality to the benefit of merely monopolistic situations everywhere. By contrast, Eucken aimed at capturing real cases of market forms following competitive behaviors through his model of complete competition. In short, according to formal hypotheses, a firm might be seen in a monopolistic situation while its actual behavior reflects a competitive attitude according to Eucken's criterion of economic plan.[27]

A second point of tension lies in the compatibility—granted by Eucken—between an exchange economy, on the one hand, and an economic order where the central authority would try to follow individuals' consumption decisions, on the other. Indeed, the special case of planning simulating the

and investment. Of all the ordoliberals, he was the only one to fully embrace the formal economic theory of his time. Still, to demonstrate the compatibility of Lutz's contributions with the ordoliberal political economy as a whole would be truly challenging, to say the least.

27. The fact remains that, to Eucken's eyes (1940b, 240), "complete competition" functioned as a borderline concept being—simultaneously—part of morphological analysis (allowing one to understand the economic order historically) and part of pure analysis (necessary for theoretical inquiry). Eucken did not specify whether the concept of competition must have the same definition in both one (*complete* in morphology) and the other (*pure* in theory) cases. But then, it is doubtful whether two distinct definitions of competition actually constitute a borderline concept, thus removing the great antinomy between history and theory (discussed in Chapter 2).

market mechanism could have led Eucken to a more nuanced position regarding the theoretical validity of economic planning. However, Eucken—like Mises and Hayek—claimed the impossibility of proper economic calculation in a socialist-like economic order. Indeed, Eucken considered that the Barone-Lange solution was not only unsuitable for positive analysis of an actual collectivist economy, but also inappropriate as a normative guide to the building of an efficient economic order. Unlike Mises or Hayek, though, Eucken accepted that an official (but independent) authority safeguarding competition could impose marginal cost pricing on a monopoly as a solution fully compatible with the exchange economy (as will be discussed in Chapter 4). Again, one might observe that Eucken's theoretical coherence would appear to be giving way to incoherence or ideological inclinations.

The key to Eucken's logic lays in an argument that brings together the two theoretical debates that were at the heart of this chapter. Indeed, when Eucken completed his analysis of market forms, he raised the following question: Are competitive prices and officially fixed prices equivalent regarding the functioning of the economic process? In each case, individuals would integrate prices as given data into their economic plans. However, the official fixing of certain prices is clearly an element belonging to the administered economy within the exchange economy. Yet, officially fixed prices could be equivalent to market prices if, and only if, "official regulation took place in a market in which complete competition on both sides had existed previously and followed the previously existing price" (Eucken 1940b, 149). Therefore, if an exchange economy is mainly ordered in accordance with the logic of complete competitiveness, then an authority can formally set certain prices without any harmful consequences for the system as a whole (since it satisfies the principle of consumer sovereignty).

In sum, the fixing of a monopoly price similar to the competitive price makes no sense as a policy generalized to the whole economy but is indeed valid in certain particular cases on the subscale of certain—limited—markets. From this perspective, it is possible to reconcile Eucken's apparently contradictory assertions: the Barone-Lange model was historically and institutionally unrealizable at the general level of the economic order, but, in some very specific (monopolistic) markets, the direction of the economic process in favor of consumers can be taken from above by an official authority. In the last analysis, it all follows through as if Eucken had transferred the argument from the debate on market socialism to that on market structures within the framework of his antitrust approach.

# CHAPTER 4
# Authority Taming Power

"The task of political economy is not only analytical, but also constructive" K. Paul Hensel (1951, 13) once wrote in an article published in the journal *Ordo*. An economist who produced his habilitation thesis under Eucken's supervision, Hensel was in a way voicing one of the ordoliberal mottos. At this point, we are interested in the constructive facet of ordoliberalism, reconstructing in particular the path from the objectives it set to the means of action advocated. The ordoliberal policy to shape the economic order was obviously rooted in analytical considerations. And yet it should also be analyzed in the light of the ordoliberals' historical doctrine and the epistemology set out in the preceding pages of this book.

Ordoliberal writing on economic policy, while clearly embedded in the debates of the interwar period, came thick and fast to take on definitive form in the postwar years accompanying the birth of the Federal Republic of Germany (FRG). One of the main ordoliberal victories in the political and legislative arena was the adoption of a law against restrictions on competition in July 1957 (coming into effect in January 1958). It provided the FRG with a legislative arsenal of private law sanctions against companies showing anti-competitive behavior.[1] Final agreement on the actual content of the text was preceded by bitter and lengthy debate—with discussions involving certain ordoliberal views. With Eucken and Miksch gone (they both died in 1950), the jurist Franz Böhm, who had joined the Christian Democratic Union (CDU) as early as 1945, was the foremost advocate of

1. The keystones of the *Gesetz gegen Wettbewerbsbeschränkungen* (GWB) are prohibition of anti-competitive agreements and curbing abuse of dominant positions and concentrations. The GWB is currently in its eighth version, notably revised within the framework of the European Union (Möschel 2006; Demme 2013).

*A Political Economy of Power.* Raphaël Fèvre, Oxford University Press. © Oxford University Press 2021.
DOI: 10.1093/oso/9780197607800.003.0005

the ordoliberals' thesis (Nörr 1995). Promoting promulgation of the law, Ludwig Erhard, a member of the CDU and then Minister of the Economy, emphasized the central role of competition in the first pages of his programmatic book *Wohlstand für alle*, translated as *Prosperity Through Competition*:

> It is no exaggeration when I declare that a law against monopoly is an indispensable principle of the "economic constitution". Should the State fail here, there would be an early end to the "social market economy" . . . "Prosperity for all" and "Prosperity through Competition" are inseparable. The former marks the aim, the latter the path leading to it. (Erhard 1957, 2–3)

But what is the allegedly "social" character of the market economy Erhard refers to? Erhard claimed that the competitive order would lead to general enrichment of the population, or economic growth in contemporary terms (in his argument, the question of distribution is deemed secondary). Such was the promise of the social market economy that Erhard and Alfred Müller-Armack conceived and popularized.

While Erhard's reading does not basically contravene the ordoliberal analysis, it does not capture its central focus. Indeed, the ordoliberals saw resolution of the "social question" (*soziale Frage*) as the fundamental objective of economic policy. In retrospect, Böhm recognized that the social question was the ordoliberals' "major pre-scientific interest" (quoted by Wohlgemuth 2013, 162); an interest marked by a process of careful reformulation, which was an integral part of the ordoliberal political economy. The ordoliberals refused to endorse the established definition of the social question as poverty and inequality (the old social question), or indeed as insecurity and injustice (the new social question). They reformulated it as the collapse of human autonomy (in a moral, almost existential sense) in the face of rising private (cartels) and public (the economic state) economic powers. In doing so, the ordoliberals aimed at reappropriating the social question that had been abandoned to the socialist tradition in nineteenth-century Germany. The ordoliberals embarked upon a critical reading of Karl Marx and Gustav von Schmoller's *Sozialpolitik* in the light of the new modes of economic management—state planning, state interventionism, the welfare state—which gained traction in the aftermath of the First World War.

According to the ordoliberals, solving the social question requires establishment and perpetuation of the competitive order by a strong state in order to find an answer to the "vast problem of regulating economic and social power" (Eucken 1948b, 272; see also Röpke 1942c, 299). Clearly, for Eucken (1948b, 275), "social motives, in particular, indicate that there is no alternative to competition." Indeed, the ordoliberals saw competition as an incomparable tool for the disempowerment of the exchange economy. However, the establishment of competitive markets would require a significant number of preconditions and respect for normative principles. The legal fight against cartels was undoubtedly a key principle of ordoliberal policy. It symbolized the ultimate intervention within a broader set of legislative principles, which should preferably be underpinned by an "economic constitution" (*Wirtschaftsverfassung*). It was therefore the fight against the various illegitimate manifestations of economic power that drove the ordoliberals to formalize a broad economic policy agenda.

## 4.1 REFORMULATION OF THE SOCIAL QUESTION

### 4.1.1 The Social Question: Old and New

With the (second) Industrial Revolution of the nineteenth century, the German Confederation (*Deutscher Bund*) went through rapid modernization of its production structures. This late but abrupt industrialization prompted questioning of the consequences it held for society in general and for the labor force in particular. Max Weber (1904, 144) encapsulated these issues in the term "social question," which he defined in terms of investigation into the "relations between the modern class of employees and the existing social order."[2] Before Weber, Marx had embodied the main, and arguably most radical, expression of this questioning. However, German social sciences as a whole had not remained insensitive to the fate of the working classes. Indeed, the attempt to bring together "history, theory, financial science, economic politics," from Cameralism to the Historical Schools, can be seen as an "examination of the 'social question,' in all its legal, moral and economic aspects" (Priddat 2004, 53; see also Schmidt 2011, 106).

The Wilhelmian era (1890–1918) of the newly unified Germany was rich in reforms. Schmoller and his colleagues of the *Verein für Socialpolitik* had a decisive impact on Chancellor Otto von Bismarck's social measures, particularly with the introduction of a social security system in 1883, occupational accident insurance laws in 1884, and disability and old age insurance

2. The transformation of the German social and economic structures in the second half of the nineteenth century had disastrous effects on a significant segment of the population, particularly on the "social base" of the electorate of German liberal parties, which can partly account for the growing interest of liberal authors in the social question (Jarausch and Jones 1990, 20).

in 1889.[3] Röpke (1934a, 4) interpreted the rise of social policy as part of a "new era of protectionism" endorsed with Bismarck's 1879 revision of tariffs, and one which marked the end of free trade between Germany and the rest of the world, thus constituting a major historical turning point. An understanding of the way the economists and social reformers raised the social question is therefore essential to analyzing their policy recommendations since they are closely linked to one another. Indeed, Eucken (1951, 56) claimed that the social question had emerged as the fundamental problem of industrialized societies and, as a result, had become "a moving force in the history of our time. Addressing it has had a prior claim on thought and actions." The ordoliberal discourse was no exception, but it would attempt to redefine the contours of the social question.

To this end, Eucken explicitly looked to Marx and Schmoller. The former came in for ambivalent critical treatment by Eucken. On the one hand, Eucken emphasized Marx's penetrating historical observation regarding the old social question of unequal distribution while, on the other hand, he rejected the solutions Marx envisaged. Nevertheless, the Marxist current had clearly identified the influence of the oppressive economic power of capital resulting from the class struggle between workers and entrepreneurs, which extended into the social and political sphere. Eucken (1948b, 267) conceded that formal equality and freedom brought about by law had proved to be largely violated in practice. From this perspective, the ordoliberals joined Marx and Engels in recognizing that capitalist exploitation of industrial workers had left them in deplorable living conditions (Eucken 1949, 220; Röpke 1942c, 230; Rüstow 1951, 163). Nevertheless, by anchoring the social question on the issue of the ownership of the means of production, Marx made of the "disappearance of capitalist private property and the emergence of communal property" (Eucken 1948b, 268) the deus ex machina of the social question. Hence, despite Marx's "keen insight into the economic forces of his epoch," the fact that he saw common ownership of the means of production as a solution to the issue of private economic power led Eucken (1948b, 271) to call him "a dreamer."

Schmoller was less concerned than Marx with questioning the foundations of nineteenth-century society and advocated the introduction of social legislation to offset the negative consequences of capitalism. Yet, from the ordoliberal point of view, both Marx and Schmoller, in their

3. This aspect of German history is well researched (Grimmer-Solem 2003; Lindenfeld 2008). The reader interested in Schmoller's impact on social reforms can consult the works by Powers (1997) and vom Bruch (2004). For a historical account of the *Verein*, see Harald Hagemann (2001).

desire to resolve the old social question, directly contributed to the rise of the new social question of the twentieth century—a new social question that would be characterized by the shift of the monopoly of oppressive economic power from the private hands of capitalists to the public hands of the state.

While the turn of the nineteenth to the twentieth centuries marked an improvement in workers' living conditions, Eucken (1951, 57) claimed it was less due to German social policy than to "the general economic and technical progress." As early as 1914, though, Europe entered a period of spreading unemployment. Eucken (1951, 56) stressed that this change had led to a shift in the substance of the social question from the objective of a more egalitarian distribution of wealth to "social security and social justice" so as to address the issue of mass employment.

From an ordoliberal point of view, the disintegration of the nineteenth-century competitive order and its replacement by interventionism or planning confirmed a common trend among European countries in meeting the need for security and social justice. For planned economies, in fact, achieving full employment would not raise insurmountable difficulties. Eucken emphasized that security of employment was achieved precisely by abolishing a price system capable of taking into account relative scarcity (building his argument on the case of Nazi Germany). However, achieving full employment had a cost in terms of inefficiency in resource allocation. Therefore, achieving full employment would not necessarily imply addressing the central problem of the economy: namely, adequate satisfaction of consumers (Eucken 1948a, 44; Röpke 1949a, 15–16).

According to Eucken (1948b, 269), economic planning had not resolved the social question but had, on the contrary, made it more pressing than ever for "as soon as the steering mechanism in a modern economy fails to function, the social question assumes greater poignancy." In short, economic planning provided everyone with a job, but with scarce goods to consume. Röpke corroborated Eucken's analysis with some considerations on the planning system still in force in West Germany under Allied occupation:

> Full employment can be achieved, but combined with a tragic waste of productive forces and, consequently, with a terrible degree of general poverty, which is all the less bearable as it increases rather than decreases. (Röpke 1947e, 247; see also Eucken 1948a, 44)

Following the ordoliberal rationale, it can be said that the "old" and the "new" social questions came to overlap. Indeed, with its management of the economic process, the state decides on the content and location of work, which are not left to individual choices but are part of an overall plan established over several years. The old social question that continued to affect industrial workers would now be extended to all the other professions (farmers, craftsmen, merchants, liberal professions, etc.). To ordoliberals' eyes, state planning only aggravated the social question which the Marxist, socialist, and historicist thinkers were trying to resolve (Eucken 1951, 64; Miksch 1948, 319). As Eucken (1947, 408) put it, it was therefore clear that in such economic orders "social problems are thus not solved, but recreated in a new and harsher form."[4]

The ordoliberal reformulation of the social question is, in the end, simple, but operative. As pointed out in Chapter 1, economic liberalism in its *historical* form (i.e., laissez-faire) had opened the way for the private economic power of the capitalists to spread, essentially to the detriment of the workers. In order to respond to the degraded living conditions of the latter, the socialists and Marxists encouraged the state to take control of the production process, in particular through social policy and legislation, but also through the socialization of certain enterprises, together with investments and the allocation of resources and factors of production, such as labor. In response to the rise of mass unemployment after the First World War, governments sought to address the problem on two fronts: by encouraging the formation of social pressure groups (such as opposition unions) and by (pre-)Keynesian-type full employment policies (Eucken 1951, 56).

According to the ordoliberals, the three major doctrines—liberalism, socialism, interventionism—failed to recognize the essential task of shaping the framework of a market economy. Liberalism failed because of its "confidence in the spontaneous realization of the natural order," socialism because of its "confidence in an inevitable evolutionary process," and interventionism because of an "*ad hoc* approach to economic policies" (Eucken 1948a, 40). In short, the old social question, far from being resolved through public policy, had been joined by unemployment and insecurity (the new social question)—problems due precisely to mismatch interventions detrimental to economic stability. The ordoliberals aimed to break out of what they saw as a vicious circle between increased political intervention, on the one hand, and increased social distress, on the other.

4. On this issue, ordoliberal arguments were often built on a "perverse effect," to borrow the concept Albert O. Hirschman outlined in his essay *The Rhetoric of Reaction* (1991).

### 4.1.2 The Ordoliberal Social Question

From an ordoliberal perspective, behind the problem of lack of freedom lies the issue of the rise of economic powers, both private and public. As we have seen, Eucken pointed out that social security and social justice were, regrettably, "the great question of the hour." These demands came from both workers and entrepreneurs and were characteristic of the post-First World War period (Eucken 1932b). Demands for security and justice gradually found an answer in what the ordoliberals perceived as state ownership of the economic process, whether in a totalitarian version (the Bolshevik, fascist, or National Socialist regimes) or in a more moderate version (the interventionism associated with Keynesianism). In this respect, a liberal order based on the freedom of individuals in the economic sphere seemed outdated in view of the economic and political crises of the interwar period.

As Eucken saw it, governments had favored security over freedom in a sort of mutually exclusive choice—an otherwise artificial antithesis to his eyes, since "German experience has shown that the antithesis between security and freedom does not exist at all" (Eucken 1951, 63). Based once again on the case of Germany, Eucken (1951, 64) attempted to reverse the argument: "deprivation of freedom," whether through the allocation of consumer goods, housing, the location and content of work, would be precisely "what causes insecurity . . . for security presupposes the possession by the individual of liberty and choice of action" in contrast to a state of total dependence. The "planning" solution, which ended in assimilation between private and public powers, certainly solved the question of unemployment but aggravated the social question as reformulated by the ordoliberals: individuals went from dependence on the private power of firms to dependence on the public power of the state.

According to Eucken, the problem of adequate control of the economic order lay neither in pursuit of full employment nor in responding to individuals' demands for security and justice, but in the dispersion of private economic power. The presence of illegitimate private powers within society was the real social question to the ordoliberals' eyes:

> The structure designed to accommodate the sequence of economic events requires continuous government supervision and possibly organization in an age of industrialization. But in commodity and labor markets—in other words, in the everyday economic process—there must be freedom. That is the real goal. Without freedom, there can be no solution of the social question. (Eucken 1948b, 275)

The ordoliberal defense of freedom was not so much a matter of a strictly economic idea leading to greater efficiency as, rather, an issue of social regulation. Basically, the ordoliberal policy of order (*Ordnungspolitik*) aimed at suppressing the exercise of economic power in the market economy. Thus, purely negative action by the state—abdication from central management of the economy and recognition of liberal legislation—cannot be sufficient for the exercise of freedom. How can the ambiguity that "freedom has often been seen as an individual's right to violate the freedom of others" (Eucken 1948a, 35) be resolved? Such ambiguity is specific to the laissez-faire system but arises for every liberal system.

Through proper management of the economic framework, the ordoliberals sought to neutralize the exercise of economic power. The political issues of freedom and the liberal system would eventually be driven by a problem with economic foundations. Equal (free) market access would give every agent the measure of his effort or sacrifice (in the absence of monopolies that distort prices and ration quantities). Here we find the liberal credo according to which the market institution can be this anonymous, impersonal, and neutral economic process that will reveal the "true" contribution of each individual to social production. In short, solving the problem of (economic) freedom is already to a considerable degree a response to the social question of insecurity and injustice:

> Here our analysis of the German experience penetrates to the heart of the social question: freedom. It was lack of freedom that crushed individuals' conditions of existence (*Daseinsbedingungen*). The hegemony of private or public concentrations of power endangered the rule of justice, and lack of security arose from lack of freedom. (Eucken 1951, 64)

For the ordoliberals, achieving social justice therefore meant realizing economic freedom. The negative freedom of agents would consist in the absence of the exercise of market powers in terms of quantity rationing and fixing excessively high prices. Such a socioeconomic order would secure a meritocratic market structure, in the sense of justice in exchange (or commutative justice) and neutrality of exchange in terms of income effect.[5]

With the issue of private and public economic power, the ordoliberals sought a joint response to two issues that cut across the history of German political economy: freedom and justice. Focusing on the particular challenge

5. Negative freedom is a fundamental precondition, but the ordoliberal approach to liberty also incorporated a positive dimension of freedom coupled with distributive social justice (Bönker and Wagener 2001; Wörsdörfer 2013b).

of economic power, the substantial implications made of ordoliberal economic policies a line that was resolutely distinct from both socialism and traditional liberalism. By "linking together the theory of justice and conceptions of freedom and power" (Wörsdörfer 2013b, 313), the ordoliberals aimed at solving these issues simultaneously by highlighting their respective constitutions. In particular, rather than "refusing an arbitration between freedom and social justice" (Peukert 2000, 105), the ordoliberals claimed that the former was the instrument for resolution of the latter. Given that the ordoliberal resolution of the social question is ultimately conditioned by the primary objective of freedom, it can be difficult to grasp what remains of the *social* in the *question*. Indeed, it might be argued that the ordoliberal reformulation of the social question provided not so much a detailed account of how it could resolve the difficulties raised with the "traditional"—old and new—social question (poverty, inequality, unemployment, etc.) as apparently a way to, if not to clear away, at least to put these difficulties in the background.

In the following pages, we will see that the space of economic freedom must be built and safeguarded by public authority: the economic sphere does not have an existence of its own outside the pre-established institutional conditions, which are the responsibility of the political sphere. The pattern of the economy should emerge from a normative-legal and political framework. In the end, economic freedom was a conquest resulting from government action (Bonefeld 2012, 6). Yet the ordoliberals perceived this economic order, in all its institutional dimensions, as ultimately embedded in a moral and cultural order.

### 4.1.3 The Spiritual Question

The social crisis that spread through the West in the early twentieth century was marked by a general phenomenon that the ordoliberals—like many others—termed the "massification" (*Vermassung*) of modern society. This massification of the West, in its sociological, economic, political, and spiritual components, encompasses the social question as we defined it in the previous pages.

In the economic sphere, the massification took the form of "proletarization"; a phenomenon that Röpke (1942c, 14) defined as "a sociological and anthropological position which is characterized by economic and social dependence, a rootless life, where men are strangers to nature and overwhelmed by the dreariness of work." From the outset, laissez-faire liberalism was to remain blind not only to the material but also to the spiritual deterioration of the worker. An "average liberal of that time, Röpke (1942c, 53) pointed out, never thought of looking upon the social question also (or even in the first place) as a problem of vitality, i.e., as a non-economic, spiritual problem posed by the industrial form of life." Röpke (1942c, 52) formulated a question that is certainly linked to the social question, but one whose perspective embraces what classical liberals had "a supreme disregard for," that is, "the vital and anthropological conditions which must limit the development of capitalist industrialism."

Of the ordoliberals, it was clearly Röpke and Rüstow who dedicated most attention to a civilizational outlook in their work, although this is not to suggest that the rest of the ordoliberals neglected societal and spiritual issues. Indeed, both Eucken (1932a, 86) and Miksch (1948, 322) appeared equally concerned about the constant threat to "the human personality" posed by industrial society.[6] As they saw it, the phenomenon of proletarianization was largely dependent on the increasing concentration of firms combined with the division of labor and the mechanization of tasks (Eucken 1940b, 314; Röpke 1942d, 228). While the technological revolution had considerably increased the wealth produced in absolute terms, Miksch (1948, 338) also stressed that it had "wounded humanity in its soul" (*Seele*). All this appeared to be leading, in Eucken's strong terms, to the emergence of a "new type of human being . . . a mass product whose existence depends on the state" (1948b, 269).

According to Röpke, a major factor in the rise of massification was the deprivation of property for most individuals, which meant that peasants and craftsmen were less likely to be affected by this cultural condition. He insisted on the importance of maintaining an economic structure that met human needs, mainly through a sense of measure and balance: "the market, division of labor, competition and economic rationalism—they all have in common that there is an optimum in their use, after which their harmfulness increasingly exceeds their utility" (Röpke 1942c, 119). Röpke voiced an indisputable mistrust of technological progress, but even more of the mechanization, which he perceived as inherently damaging. Big businesses embodied this modern decadence as the driving force behind the desertification of the countryside and the rise of large cities, mass

6. In the interwar period, Eucken wrote several short pieces published in *Die Tatwelt*, a journal associated with Rudolf (Walter's father) Eucken and the family entourage. One of the central aim of this journal, for which Lutz (1933) also wrote, was to thwart the alleged cultural decline of German civilization (Gerken 2000, 133–166; Dathe and Goldschmidt 2003; Dathe 2009).

media, mass political parties, advertising, and shopping malls. The power that big business exercised was not only economic in nature, but also cultural and spiritual:

> Is it not the great factory that has transformed everything, man, his way of thinking, his way of life, his work, his faith, which has endowed us with the stone deserts that are the great cities with their nomads, which has weakened so many solid things, made so many essential things sick, deprived of soul so many living things? (Röpke 1947c, 29)

The ordoliberal view centered on the deracination of workers in capitalist societies was far from unique in mid-twentieth-century Europe. Concern over the articulation interrelation—and in particular propagation of harmful effects—between the economic and cultural spheres was a central theme for scholars close to the ordoliberals, such as the Spanish philosopher Ortega y Gasset, the Dutch historian Johan Huizinga, or even the Austrian economists as a whole (Dekker 2016).[7] Nonetheless, the same concern can be found among academics at the antipodes of the ordoliberals' political stance, as, for example, in the works of Theodor Adorno and Max Horkheimer, developed within the framework of the Frankfurt School (Arnsperger 2008).

Clearly, the ordoliberal discourse on societal issues sought reference more in socialist and Catholic thought than in the liberal sphere. Indeed, Röpke (1942c, 255) claimed the ordoliberal "third way" (*dritter Weg*) partly originated from the reflections of authors as disparate as Riehl or Le Play, but also Sismondi, Kropotkin, and Proudhon. The ordoliberals shared with socialist thought an undeniable distrust of massification, which is reflected in its political program. However, the ordoliberals were also anchored on the social doctrine of the Church. The elective affinity between Catholic thought and liberalism as understood by the ordoliberals was also explicitly claimed by Eucken (1952, 348) and Hensel (1949) and can be found in many ordoliberal writings (Rieter and Schmolz 1993, 104–105). In particular, the principle of "subsidiarity"—central to the Church's social doctrine (Delsol 1992; Barroche 2013)—is reflected in the ordoliberal discourse on the decentralization of decisions. Ultimately, subsidiarity appeared to Röpke as a solution to the *unsociable sociability* problematized by Kant. Röpke (1944b, 12) went a step further than his fellow ordoliberals by claiming that "a good

7. For detailed analysis of Ropke's cultural pessimism, see in particular Jean Solchany (2018) and Frans Willem Lantink (2018).

Christian is a liberal who doesn't know it," arguing that the 1931 encyclical *Quadragesimo Anno* actually enclosed a "social and economic philosophy" much like that of liberalism.[8] The crisis of liberalism, the crisis of the Church (secularization), and the overall societal crisis of the West is seen to originate from the same development of mass capitalism.

In the final analysis, industrialization and technological progress had been a formidable driving force, the ordoliberals recognized, increasing wealth and standards of living, but they had at the same time proved deadly for the spiritual conditions of peoples. How can the economic system be adapted to these new conditions so as to maintain its benefits in terms of living standards while removing its socially and spiritually harmful consequences? This was precisely the conundrum ordoliberals were trying to answer.

## 4.2 COMPETITION AS AN "INSTRUMENT OF DISEMPOWERMENT"

How did the ordoliberals approach a response to the social question of their time? They were fully convinced that the competitive order would take care of the essential task of dissolving illegitimate economic powers. If the ordoliberal response was quite straightforward, the set of conditions and procedures for achieving and maintaining the competitive order were far less so. To begin with, the ordoliberals had to impose the competitive order on a German public opinion customarily in favor of further concentration and socialization of the economy.

### 4.2.1 Challenging the Standard Narrative on Monopoly

The idea of promoting competition and fighting against monopolies appears, in retrospect, a basic liberal policy to uphold in a market economy. Nevertheless, it should be stressed that, throughout the changing context examined in this book (1932–1950), this policy found few supporters but many staunch opponents. German opponents, in particular, mobilized various arguments to demonstrate that competition policy was "*neither*

8. The encyclical by Pope Pius XI marked a turning point in Catholic economic thought with the consideration that the capitalist system was not evil, but that its excesses had to be tamed, particularly in terms of concentration of wealth (Calvez 2000; Almodovar and Teixeira 2008).

*desirable nor attainable*," as Böhm recalled (1954, 155, emphasis in original) .

Böhm opened his article "Monopoly and Competition in Western Germany" by lining up the arguments against the competitive order, only to then proceed to knock them down.[9] The first argument of the opponents of the competitive system was that competition as empirically observed did not correspond to theoretical competition (invalidating the defense of empirical competition with theoretical arguments). Even when there was some form of competition on a market, it would always take on imperfect forms such as oligopolies, partial monopolies, etc., and it is often difficult to discern whether or not there are in fact elements of competition within these market structures. Here we find arguments in line with the "revolution" of theories on monopolistic competition (see Chapter 3). The second argument stated that, in general, few large production units are more efficient than countless small and dispersed ones. Furthermore, competition between many small firms would often lead to the domination of a few large firms whose technical advantages must be taken into account and which are based on legitimate economic power regarding economic progress and stability, particularly in the face of business cycles turbulence.

These arguments coincided with Schumpeter's position in *Capitalism, Socialism and Democracy* (1942), where he legitimized the existence of monopolies with three arguments. First, cartels could act as stabilizers of the overall level of production in times of crisis. Second, in the process of creative destruction, some dominant positions are legitimate as the driving force of entrepreneurial capitalism (in the long run, there is also a strong tendency for monopolies to disappear, or at least to replace old ones with new ones). Third, in some cases, a monopoly is actually technically superior to competitive firms in terms of the "long-run expansion of total output" (Schumpeter 1942, 106).

In sharp opposition to what was later termed the "Schumpeterian thesis" on large firms (Mayhew 1980), the ordoliberals saw monopolies as elements intrinsically harmful to the economic order in particular and to the social order in general. Although Röpke (1942c, 228) partially conceded the superiority of the monopoly in terms of innovation, he argued that this alone could not make up for its many defects: "not only are monopolies socially intolerable but they also interfere with the economic process and act as a brake on productivity as a whole." In a later edition of his manual

9. Böhm's article was published in a 1954 collection of essays edited by Edward H. Chamberlin but based on a 1951 conference.

(adapted for US readerships), Röpke lined up arguments with the explicit aim of exploding the Schumpeterian thesis:

> The decisive fact remains that monopolists have a degree of power over their markets and the economy, and that a well-ordered economic system based on a fair relationship between performance and reward cannot tolerate. (Röpke 1963, 161–162)

The ordoliberals disregarded the various advantages, particularly technical ones, that can result from a monopoly position.[10] Their position was only implicitly coherent with ultimate aims regarding economic efficiency and growth. Indeed, the question of productive efficiency in a market was secondary to the objective of regulating the economic and social process. If the objective is the disappearance of economic power, the monopoly was de facto an obstacle to the resolution of the social question. In short, any defense or encouragement of the development of monopolies was to be ruled out.

The ordoliberal campaign against monopolies was uncompromising, to say the least. Yet, even for those who were far from dismissing these arguments, monopolies were often perceived as necessary evils coming with the very functioning of market capitalism. So, what were the arguments advanced by the ordoliberals to prove that a successful economic policy toward competition was both *possible* and *necessary*? To answer this, Böhm (1954, 157) outlined several arguments which had been put forward, in his words, by a "minority consisting mainly of economists, lawyers and politicians"—indeed, by the ordoliberal collective.

Was competition policy even *possible* at all? Bohm (1954, 157) answered the question positively on two counts. First, securing competition would not be so much a matter of transposing the theoretical conditions of perfect competition to reality as, rather, of reaching "a reasonably satisfactory degree of competition." Such (complete) competition would rest less on technical data than on "political will" and "economic views" that must prevail in a "free society." In short, the degree of competition that can be achieved in a given market cannot be known by means of "theoretical discussion or historical speculation" alone, but can only be arrived at through "political

10. Eucken (1951, 39) noted—again explicitly against Schumpeter—that the admiration of the technical progress achieved through monopoly was in any case overestimated, since without a given monopoly "other branches of production would have had more means at their disposal and—most important of all—the supply of consumer goods in general would have been better" (see also Lutz 1956, 168–169).

experiment," albeit guided by scientific expertise (in line with the message of the ordoliberal manifesto of 1936). Second, Böhm argued that certain technical conditions for competition were indeed achievable in practice. The competitive state of a market should not be assessed solely through comparison with an ideal theoretical situation, but to the extent that there is potential to encourage any improvement, however small, in competitive conditions (see also Miksch 1948, 337). And indeed, the ordoliberal "complete competition" (*vollständige Konkurrenz*) aimed at reconciling theoretical and practical approaches.[11]

Why was competition policy not only *possible* but also *necessary* according to the ordoliberals? Their main argument, the one that summed up all the others and made sense of their entire economic policy, was the force that competition exerted in bringing the agents' exercise of power to a minimum, or to its maximum dispersion (Eucken 1940b, 269; 2001, 83; Eucken and Böhm 1948, xi). In other words, the essential advantage of a competitive order lay in the fact that power was "so fragmented (*zersplittert*) that it no longer had any harmful effect" (Eucken 1946b, 142). In stating the "anti-power" (*machtfeindlich*) aspect of the competitive order, Böhm (1947, 125) emphasized a key point: competition was not about leaving everyone with an equal share of power, but rather bringing "powerlessness" (*Machtlosigkeit*) to every single economic actor. With hindsight, Böhm (1961, 42) encapsulated the ordoliberal approach to competition by describing it as "the most efficient and ingenious instrument of disempowerment (*Entmachtungsinstrument*) in history."

According to the ordoliberals, competition drives firms to reach their optimal size (in contrast with oversized monopoly), thereby enhancing their ability to make short-term adjustments. In his 1932 article, Eucken (1932b, 52) had already observed that "the lash of competition" worked against the (German) process of "feudalization" (*Feudalisierung*) of the entrepreneur's role in the economy. Therefore, the enhanced short-run elasticity of firms granted by the competitive order would make the economy more stable and resilient to economic crisis in the long run. From this idea, Böhm (1954, 158) drew an even more important lesson regarding the interaction between the economic and political orders, stressing that "the minimization of power structures in the social foundations minimizes the need for concentration of power in the political superstructure." Hence competition

11. Thanks to conditions looser than perfect completion, the ordoliberal complete competition could be empirically assessed through the absence of market strategies and should serve as an instrument for analyzing real cases (Ahlborn and Grave 2006, 200).

was a central aim of ordoliberal economic policy but also a precondition to maintain a liberal state that is not driven toward concentration itself.

Consequently, the competitive price system was for the ordoliberals neither "simply a measure of scarcity or a calculation device" nor an incentive mechanism, but rather "a control mechanism of a binding nature" (Eucken 1948c, 88; see also Böhm 1966, 52). From the ordoliberal point of view, satisfying the requirement of economic freedom of individuals and, consequently, orienting production in favor of consumer choices, prevails over any argument based on performance. The greatest advantage of this control mechanism was that, in this way, the price system would be imposed on the will of all individuals while at the same time being the result of the exercise of their will. If Eucken held that "the aspiration for competitive order is closely linked to the desire for freedom" (1949, 231), it was because he perceived the competitive price as an instrument of social control and regulation, of the mechanics of a society freed from illegitimate economic power. Ultimately, the ordoliberals embraced competition as a cultural asset, at the same time condition and result of the open society.

### 4.2.2 Political Authority as "Liberal Interventionism"

The ordoliberals focused on the institutional—constitutional—conditions that were mandatory for establishment of the competitive order. This kind of economic policy can only be achieved by the highly visible hand of the state; what Rüstow (1932) and Röpke (1934a, 50) tellingly termed "liberal interventionism." As a promoter of the general interest, the state would be an essential actor in guaranteeing the functioning of the competitive order. Rüstow detailed this idea in a text published as an appendix to Röpke's 1942 book *International Economic Disintegration*:

> A strong and independent state is the prime condition in every case, but state intervention must be restricted to the indispensable minimum; it must not be in opposition to the functioning of the market mechanism or disturb the structure of the market; it must, on the contrary, maintain them. (Rüstow 1942, 281)

However, Rüstow's formulation could be misleading. Indeed, this minimum intervention happens, as Röpke (1944b, 65) emphasized, to be based on an extensive program of "positive economic policy" with an important list of tasks to perform. Like his friend Rüstow, Röpke (1942c, 299) stressed that state policy that would never be tempted to "exceed the limits assigned to it by conformable interventionism." So where was the line to be drawn between what is acceptable and what is not? How could the ordoliberals ensure that their positive economic policy would not lead to untimely and growing interventionism dictated by interested groups? In a number of writings, Röpke (1936a, 195; 1940, 268; 1942c, 206) formulated the opposition between "conformable" interventions (e.g., custom duties, monetary devaluation, a measured redistribution policy) and "non-conformable" interventions (e.g., foreign currency controls, quota or trade controls, price fixing). And again, Röpke (1944b, 68) warned the state against any tendency toward over-interventionism, for conformity was just a "necessary condition, not a sufficient one."

Later, Eucken formulated a more general principle for assessing whether an economic policy measure was in line with the principles of the competitive order:

> The realisation of a price system of complete competition is the essential criterion for any economic policy measure. *This is the fundamental principle of the economic constitution.* (Eucken 1949, 232, emphasis in original)

In this passage, Eucken formulated the fundamental principle of the ordoliberal desired order of the economy: the competitive price mechanism, stated in the economic constitution, must become the normative criterion for state action in economic policies. Similarly, interventions are therefore in line with Röpke's (1936a, 195) approach when they respect "the inner structure of our economic system, . . . leave intact the market mechanism itself and attain their objective not by contravening the rules of this mechanism but by making use of them" (Röpke 1936a, 195). Any intervention likely to divert (in the short and long run) the effective price system from the results of a theoretical competitive price system will be abandoned. Böhm (1966, 57) summarized the limits of the ordoliberal economic policy by stressing that the government must exert a "neutral" influence on the process.

This core ordoliberal principle must be enshrined in the "economic constitution," defined by Böhm, Eucken, and Großmann-Doerth (1936, 24) in their programmatic text *Our Task* as a "general political decision that shows how the economic life of nations should be structured." The economic constitution was conceived as the centerpiece of the broader legal framework of the political constitution. The economic constitution primarily brings together principles of private law with a view to regulating relations between persons (natural and legal), of which market relations are an integral part (Walther 2016, 110; Wakote 2016, 147). Miksch (1948, 315), emphasized the requirement that a "uniform and coherent economic constitution" should indicate the guidelines for every possible measure and prevent "internal contradictions" from arising in economic policy measures. Perhaps no other concept had embodied more clearly than the economic constitution the "mutual dependence" between the economic and the legal orders that Eucken (1952, 278) and other ordoliberals emphasized so firmly.[12]

Both a strong state and a comprehensive program of economic policy were mandatory to achieve the competitive order and thus resolve the social question. Therefore, securing the maximum dispersion of—private—economic power in society must be performed, in the final analysis, by another—public—form of power. Hence the question: How did the ordoliberals justify the use of a power considered legitimate (the economic policy pursued by the state) to discipline another form of power, considered illegitimate (e.g., the price strategy of a monopoly or a cartel)? Is there a difference in nature between these two expressions of power in the economy? Disempowerment of economic power through the competitive mechanism is at the heart of the ordoliberal political project. And yet the social order as a whole cannot exist without any form of power. Indeed, Eucken (1951, 38) made it quite clear that power plays a vital role in society: "without positions of power there can be no social life; for there *must* be authority for all community life, whether in the state or in the firm." And again, Eucken (1951) referred to a real "economic policy dilemma," power being both socially indispensable for the realization of a free society, but also the main threat to it (see also Eucken 1940c, 479; Hensel 1966, 131).

To some extent, Eucken bypassed this difficulty by moving on from the notion of "power" (*Macht*) to that of "authority" (*Autorität*). This semantic shift is crucial in understanding ordoliberal economic policy and, in particular, the institutions that can conduct it. Here, authority can be defined as the legitimate expression of power within the organizational framework of hierarchical structures.[13] Hence the ordoliberals did not question the authority of the state, central bank, office of monopoly control, nor indeed of the entrepreneur (within the firm) or the trade unions. On the contrary, legitimate power was a key condition in achieving the competitive order, and economic and political power should therefore only be tolerated "to the extent necessary to maintain the competitive order" (Eucken 1949, 238).

12. The ordoliberal economic constitution has come under scrutiny from the legal viewpoint in some recent collective volumes (Rabault 2016b; Hien and Joerges 2017).

13. Here Eucken departs from the classical Weberian vocabulary, although the meaning is nevertheless quite similar since Weber spoke of authority (*Herrschaft*) as "legitimate domination" (Dockès 1999, 83).

Eucken illustrated this argument regarding the institutions by taking the example of the monetary issue:

> A central bank which has the exclusive privilege to issue bank notes also exerts economic power, which gives rise to the difficult problem of its control. But this formation of power (*Machtbildung*) is created for the purpose of enabling the competitive order, by creating a sufficient monetary order. (Eucken 1949, 238)

Eucken outlined two forms of legitimate exercise of economic power: that of economic agents (heads of households or businesses), limited by the mechanism of competitive prices, and that of institutions in a logic external to the functioning of the market (here the central bank). If the consumer's freedom of choice is critical, it is not absolute. Individual freedom is always subject to the rules of application which are ultimately defined by the "*Ordnungspolitik*" (economic policy of the order). As a result, the consumer has the freedom to set neither "the rules of the game" (*Spielregeln*) nor "the forms of the economic process" (Eucken 1949, 227).

The limitation to the power of institutions appears much more difficult precisely because they are not regulated through the daily economic process of the competitive order. Moreover, the state (or any other institution) must exercise its authority to minimize the existence of illegitimate, or arbitrary, economic power while refraining from violating individuals' liberty. Of the institutions, the ordoliberals also saw economic policy itself as a form of power applied externally to coordination between agents. Again, both Miksch (1950a, 46) and Eucken (1951, 38) stressed that the issue of the legitimacy of economic policy rested on the fact that it should not be "arbitrary" (*Willkür*). The ordoliberals devoted much room to setting out what they saw legitimate economic policy as residing in.

## 4.3 SHAPING THE ECONOMIC ORDER

The ordoliberals' explicit formulation of a set of economic policies was a direct response to the various practices they witnessed in the interwar period (interventionism, planning, pricing, and rationing). The ordoliberals claimed that these disorganized and ad hoc policies gave rise to an ineffective price system that was clearly not resolving but aggravating the social question. Eucken, Böhm, Röpke, and various others called for the implementation of a competitive pricing system as the key goal in guiding policy measures.

### 4.3.1 Framework and Process

According to the ordoliberals, the state should be the central architect of the competitive order yet should perform its tasks without embracing planning. The ordoliberal set of economic policies was precisely an attempt to guide the state in the shaping of a particular social order, one based on the competitive order in the economic sphere. To this end, the ordoliberals highlighted what they perceived as a central duality in the functioning of an economy, separating its "framework" (or form) from its "process." While the framework embodies the perennial rules of the economic game, the process represents the daily "movements"—decisions, actions, etc.—of the economic agents within the limits set by the rules.

On the basis of this duality between framework and process, Eucken divided economic policies into two categories: the "constitutive principles" (*konstituierenden Prinzipien*) aimed at organizing the structural framework of the economy (or form), while the "regulative principles" (*regulierenden Prinzipien*) should deal with the internal process—and daily defects—of the economy, yet without deliberately taking on direction of it:

> What should be the nature of the state's activity? The answer lies in the fact that the State must influence the forms of the economy, but not itself direct the economic process. . . . *Planning* of forms by the State—yes; State planning and control of the economic process—no. The key point is to recognize the difference between form and process, and to act accordingly. (Eucken 1951, 95–96)

The constitutive principles are predominantly legal, while the regulative principles allow for economic actions per se.[14] The economic framework is based on a "careful conception of the constitutional foundations" (Miksch 1948, 334), a field specific to the state that encompasses all the rules necessary for the functioning of the competitive order (see also Röpke 1940, 124). By contrast, the process concerns the infra-constitutional level—it is the domain of individual initiative and activity, the domain of coordination between agents.

14. In formulating constitutive and regulative principles, Eucken stressed several contributions that inspired him by Böhm (1933), Miksch (1937b), Stackelberg (1934b, 1948), and Röpke (1942c, 1944b). He also mentioned the Chicago economist Henry C. Simons, in particular his *Economic Policy for a Free Society* (1948). On Simons and the ordoliberals, see Ekkehard A. Köhler and Stefan Kolev (2013).

#### *4.3.1.1 Constitutive Principles*

Eucken formulated the principles mandatory for implementing the competitive order in federal Germany. He outlined in particular seven "constitutive principles" (*konstituierenden Prinzipien*), which were to be reflected in his *Principles of Economic Policy* (Eucken 1952, 254–291). However, these seven principles can be divided in two groups, with a first group including two meta-principles that would organize and frame the other five principles that are more directly related to legislative principles:

K. 1. The realization of a price system of complete competition
K. 2. The constancy of economic policy
K. a. The primacy of monetary stability
K. b. Free access to markets
K. c. Private property
K. d. Contract law
K. e. Corporate liability

We already discussed the first meta-principle (K. 1) a couple of pages earlier, and the principle of "constancy" of the economic policy (K. 2) will be address later when dealing with ordoliberals' aversion for discretionary policy management. Taken in their generality, the other five basic principles actually seem quite classical within the liberal tradition. Indeed, Eucken (1952, 290) emphasized that "some of the principles such as freedom of contract, liability or private property have been developed by philosophers and lawyers as purely legal principles, practically as principles of natural law." But the meaning Eucken attributed to them merits detailed analysis, for he aimed at radically distancing himself from some of the core legal principles of liberalism:

> It is not a question of legal dogmatism or principles of natural law. The global order context (*Ordnungzusammenhang*) that interests us here does not emanate from natural law or from a higher plane of dogmatic axioms. For example, the requirement to establish private property is often deduced from the nature of man and is justified as an imperative of natural law. This is not the case here. Private property is—along with other principles—essential to shape the competitive order. (Eucken 1952, 290)

The perspective Eucken developed in this passage was certainly informed by the work of Böhm. Although the latter could be approached as a natural law theorist, for he insisted on the necessity of equating legal norms to the functioning of the economic order, he nevertheless opposed reference to any form of metaphysical arguments in law (Nientiedt 2019b). So it was that the ordoliberals considered the transcription from economics to law an essential task. Böhm (1937, 13), in particular, made it his leitmotif, for he intended to "use economic concepts to interpret and renew private law" and in particular property law, contract law, firm law, etc.[15] The various areas of law that directly concerned economic activity were to be oriented to satisfy the first principle since the fundamental aim was to translate the solutions arrived at in political economy into legal language. Some laws were, in fact, to affect the regulation of production, as is the case, for example, of real estate law, administrative law, and even family law (Böhm et al. 1936, 24).

On closer scrutiny it emerges that each constitutive principle can be misinterpreted and thus monopolized by power groups to promote industrial concentration and monopoly. It was, after all, also the possibility of concentration of economic power in the form of cartels or monopolies that worried the ordoliberals and guided discussion of these principles.

Controlling inflation was clearly an ordoliberal priority (K. a), although this did not mean arriving at any numerical inflation "target." An unstable currency upsets the competitive allocation mechanism, leads to a disproportionate number of productive structures, and disrupts the distribution of income. More seriously, from the point of view of state economic management, the destruction of an efficient price system by inflation calls for state intervention in the management of the economic process. It must start managing the supply of money, imposing certain quotas and commodity prices. Such interventions lead the liberal economy down a different path, that of interventionism and planning. Management of monetary policy is probably the most complex of all from this point of view: the difficulty of grasping the relevant factors at any given time and the pressure of particular opinions and interests are issues raised by Eucken (1952, 257).

To overcome these shortcomings, the ordoliberals sought an order ensuring a stable value for money. According to them, this can be achieved with a more automatic system (i.e., with rules). For instance, the gold standard system (*Goldwährung*)—of which Lutz (1935; 1949a) was the main proponent—seemed to them to be the surest way to secure a neutral currency from an international perspective. With regard to the balance of the national market, they held monopoly of money creation to be justified,

15. Later, Böhm (1966, 53) forged the concept of "private-law society" (*Privatgesellschaft*) to underline the need for a well-designed legal system to keep the market economy functioning well (see Streit 1992; Nörr 2000).

adding, however, that it was to be viewed in the light of historical development since "any economic monopoly can be misused" (Miksch 1948, 324). Miksch (1948) identified a particular case in the monetary system: that of the existence of a "monopoly that is not really a monopoly, i.e., the metric monopoly." Miksch distinguished between two types of money creation monopolies, endorsing the theoretical dichotomy of market forms set by Eucken:

> In the *economic monopoly of money creation*, the monopoly holder determines the money supply, which, however, if it is metal, is constrained by certain limits. In the *metric monopoly of monetary creation*, the holder of the monopoly only determines the modalities and certain elements of technical arrangements, while the money supply results from the resolutions of economic actors and is therefore subject to the law of large numbers. The *metric monopoly is therefore part of the form of a fully competitive market*. (Miksch 1948, 325, emphasis in original)

Miksch's metric monopoly was a means by which to protect monopoly of currency issue from ordoliberal criticism of the concentration of economic power of supply-and-demand monopolies. The question of the rules and monopoly of monetary issuance provoked a great deal of controversy among the various strands of economic liberalism, as clearly evidenced, for example, by the debate between the *Currency School* and *Banking School* at the beginning of the nineteenth century—a debate Eucken (1940b, 169) explicitly mentioned.

For Eucken, competition is imperative in the field of banking services and loans, although "on money creation, the state must exercise a crucial right of control" (Eucken 1946d, 46). This view implies the separation of private lending activities from monetary creation activities and the rejection of the granting of credit at all costs, which would promote concentration and positions of power, the spread of external controls, and, ultimately, planning (Miksch 1948, 337). The ordoliberal reflections are based on the Chicago Plan—itself inspired by Irving Fisher's *100% Money* (1935)—of which Henry C. Simons (1936, 4–5) was also one of the main promoters. This was seen by the ordoliberals as an update of Ricardo's analysis and the *Currency School* (Eucken 1946d, 54–55; Lutz 1936, 86).

Free market access (K. b), or the principle of open markets (*Offene Märkte*), is one of the ordoliberals' technical requirements in their theoretical definition of complete competition. In practice, augmenting market openness is not only a negative policy—of the state against itself—of removing barriers to international trade (embargoes, quotas, customs, or national privileges), but above all it is essential to prevent such practices from being carried out by private actors themselves. Eucken (1952, 267) asked: "What is the point of a freedom of trade officially decreed by the State if the policy of power groups abolishes it in practice?" As a result, the state must also pay attention to all cases of anti-competitive preventive policy, such as loyalty discounts, exclusive contracts, or advertising.

The particular case of the ordoliberal discussion on the role of "patent law" (*Patentrecht*) in the market economy offers an archetypal example of the harm that can be caused by unfair legislation (Eucken 1949, 233; Röpke 1942c, 157). Skeptical about the alleged advantages of patents (promotion of technological progress and protection of invention), Eucken (1952, 268) argued that patents had made it possible to "step up the formation of monopolies and concentration" since they "restrict the quantity of goods offered," as in the field of telecommunications and in the chemical industry. The question remains as to the extent to which patents are, indeed, if not the sole cause, at least one of the forces encouraging concentration and cartelization in these cases. From the ordoliberal viewpoint, patents represented a vehicle for the formation of illegitimate economic power. Thus Röpke (1942c, 303), like Eucken,[16] wished to replace patents with compulsory licences (i.e., monetary compensation due to the inventor). As Robert Van Horn and Matthias Klaes (2010) suggested, the position against patents was characteristic of some liberal economists, particularly American economists like Henry C. Simon or Frank Knight—a position that was to be reversed within the Chicago tradition (notably by Stigler) in favor of patent protection.

The defense of the right to private property (K. c), one of the central principles of the liberal tradition, must also be interpreted from a specific ordoliberal viewpoint. According to the ordoliberal philosophy of history, private property had allowed monopolies "to exercise their power against workers, customers and competitors" (Eucken 1952, 273). A priori, Eucken did not attribute a particularly positive value to private property, holding that it is in the light of the overall functioning of the economic process that it is possible to assess whether private property acquires a desirable economic and social significance and does not represent an abuse or misappropriation:

> The key question is whether market forms and the monetary system can be achieved in such a way that "exploitation" (*Ausbeutung*) is impossible, power

16. On Eucken's view on patents, see Manuel Wörsdörfer (2012b).

> concentration (*Vermachtung*) is impossible and the balance of the overall process is preserved. In other words: *can private property become a useful economic and social instrument of the structure of the order of society?* (Eucken 1952, 273, emphasis in original)

From the ordoliberal viewpoint, the relationship between private property and the competitive order is a circular one. Essential for the exercise of property rights to acquire capital property and to meet consumer demand, private property in a noncompetitive system has nonetheless an effect that Eucken (1952, 274) considered "antisocial" (*unsozial*).[17]

Like the right to private property, the principle of freedom of contract (K. d) should also be analyzed as a neutral principle insofar as it is a condition of the competitive order whose use may be perverted when exercised by groups. The contract then becomes an instrument of economic warfare, an "exquisite instrument of individual domination," to use Böhm's words (1961, 40).

Finally, the civil and commercial liability (*Haftung*) of companies (K. e) is the last constitutive principle. Faced with the spread of joint stock companies (*Aktiengesellschaft*) and limited liability companies (*Gesellschaft mit beschränkter Haftung*), Eucken (1952, 279) noted that liability (i.e., "the possibility of seizing a debtor's assets") was largely in default. However, Eucken did not directly recommend the abolition of these legal forms of companies. Most importantly, the possibility of bankruptcy and liability for losses must remain a credible threat because the proper functioning of the global economic order depended on it. Indeed, according to Eucken (1952, 280), commercial liability has the merit of "exerting a prophylactic effect (*prophylaktisch*) by preventing the liquidation and waste of capital because it motivates a better analysis of the market" based on a rigorous cost analysis which thus prevents economic concentration based on erroneous economic grounds (see also Röpke 1942c, 121).[18]

These constitutive principles embodied the "rules of the game," or "all the constraints" (Grossekettler 1989, 43), for both state and individual

17. Article 14 [Property, inheritance rights and expropriation] of the German Constitution of 1949, which stipulates that "property obliges: its use must contribute at the same time to the good of the community"; can be interpreted along these lines. Despite the proximity between some ordoliberal ideas and the content of the Basic Law (Constantinesco 1960), it nevertheless seems that the concrete influence of the ordoliberals in the legislative field came later (Rabault 2016a).

18. The liability criterion must also be placed in the context of the issue of motivation and private initiative in business. For instance, the five-year study by Adolf A. Berle and Gardiner C. Means (1932) on more than two hundred of the major industrial companies in the United States came to the same conclusions about changes in the form of corporate ownership.

actions. Rigorous application of the constitutive principles was indeed a *necessary* condition for minimizing the potential existence of monopolistic power structures and making the competitive order possible (resolving the social question). Yet it was by no means a *sufficient* condition. Hence an economic policy based on regulative principles was compulsory.

#### 4.3.1.2 Regulative Principles

Eucken formulated "regulative principles" (*regulieren Prinzipien*) in response to the imperfections inherent in an exchange economy. They covered four areas of action, also amended by Eucken in his *Principles* (Eucken 1952, 291–304):

R. 1. Control of monopolistic market structures
R. 2. Redistributing income policy
R. 3. Control of adverse effects (negative externalities)
R. 4. Control of abnormal supply reactions

Eucken made it perfectly clear that "the competitive order *has* its defects" (1952, 300, emphasis in original). Accordingly, regulative principles were required to overcome two types of shortcomings. First, merely securing the legal framework—the constitutive principles—of markets does not completely prevent the emergence of firms with monopolistic tendencies (R.1). Moreover, even when complete competition prevails within an economic order, some market failures requiring correction may occur (R. 2–4).

When Eucken mentioned the control of abnormal supply reactions (R. 4), he had in mind the formation of insufficient wages on the labor market. In such cases, Eucken (1952, 304) argued that setting "minimum wages" would be an adequate policy measure. The unions, in turn, would have an "important function" within the competitive order, namely "compensating for the unequal market position between workers and entrepreneurs" (Eucken 1946c, 21). According to the ordoliberals, an unorganized workforce would be in an excessively unfavorable bargaining position vis-à-vis the employer; indeed, the workers had "always been the weakest party in the market relationship" (Miksch 1948, 320).

Eucken's principle of control of adverse effects (R. 3) can be reduced to the consideration of negative externalities, although he did not explicitly use this concept (Grossekettler 1994, 16; Möschel 2001, 11).[19] In his own

19. The modern understanding of externalities was forged in the late 1950s. Previously, externalities had widely been seen as "exceptional" and thus trivial quibbling about the

lexical field associated with the issue of "economic calculation," Eucken (1952, 301, emphasis in original) referred to the principle of externalities as "repercussions that will not be felt by individuals in *their own* planning area" (*Planungsbereich*). Typical of such cases were the social cost in terms of workers' health and hygiene conditions, as well as the environmental impact of some companies' production. Similarly, Röpke (1940, 291) proved highly skeptical about private exploitation of environmental resources, claiming that it would be necessary to prevent any "rapacious exploitation of natural treasures." While respecting to the full the competitive effort of firms, Eucken (1952, 303) observed that a "commercial police" department should, for instance, ensure that the damage that a soda ash plant could cause to households and surrounding businesses be taken into account, for example, in the regulations of certain branches of industry.

Eucken's principle of redistributive income policy (R. 2) contained important clarifications for positioning ordoliberalism within the liberal tradition. Eucken (1952, 300) called for a "progressive tax rate" aiming at fairer distribution. Röpke (1944b, 147) endorsed this view of tax progressiveness, insisting in particular on a "progressive inheritance tax." Their ambition was to equalize individuals' starting conditions and prevent the concentration of wealth over several generations—a potential factor for economic concentration and therefore for the exercise of power.

Admittedly, Röpke (1942c, 293) recognized that a social policy increasing wages and reducing working time would have paradoxical effects since it could tend to destroy small and medium-sized enterprises by leaving only the large ones able to cope with this increase in costs. However, social emergency requires that the state does not remain totally insensitive to the plight of the poorest: "as long as we have a proletariat, this social policy will indeed retain a certain limited scope of activity, and much intelligent work can still be done in the field of wage policy, trade unionism, workers' protection and social insurance" (Röpke 1942c, 295). Röpke presented this pursuit of greater justice as coherent with changes, first, in the distribution of income by category; second, in the personal distribution of income; and third, in a posteriori correction of the distribution of income. A redistribution policy would be possible without necessarily disrupting the price system (demand inflation) and as long as it was careful not to discourage investment (Eucken 1952, 301; Röpke 1942c, 248). If ordoliberal social policy deserves special mention among the various forms of (neo-)

effectiveness of the properties of the theoretical equilibrium and, as such, were not really perceived as a relevant issue for economic policy (Medema 2020).

liberalism, for instance by contrast with the Austrians' (Chaloupek 2006; Wörsdörfer 2013b), its scope should not be exaggerated. Actually, the ordoliberal social policy in any case remains *secondary*, in the sense that realization of the competitive order represents the first and foremost social policy.

It can reasonably be argued that ordoliberal thought remained somewhat vague about the system of taxation and redistribution to be effectively implemented. Nevertheless, the position adopted does not seem so far removed from the general observation Keynes made about the same period. Indeed, in his "Final Notes on the Social Philosophy to Which General Theory Can Lead," Keynes (1936, 374) stressed that from the nineteenth century on, "significant inequalities of incomes and wealth" can be justified on social and psychological grounds, "but not for such large disparities as exist today." While, on the one hand, we may consider it a weakness not to sharpen the focus on a more precise, even quantified formulation, we might equally well interpret it as a reasoned omission on the part of these economists: from the Keynesian viewpoint, a matter of allowing for political deliberation to set social objectives, while in the ordoliberal perspective, the principle was to leave the necessary degree of freedom for the historical, political, and institutional analysis that must be carried out in situ and judged in each case according to the particular conditions.

### 4.3.2 Taming Market Power

The aim of the ordoliberal policy could not have been clearer: "*Prevention, combating and reversal of the process of concentration of power*" was to be their motto (Böhm 1947, 130, emphasis in original; see also Eucken 1952, 290). Constitutive and regulative principles combined to contribute to achievement of the competitive order. However, one principle in particular—control of monopolistic market structures (R. 1)—was the cornerstone of Eucken's regulatory policy. Indeed, the Monopoly Office had the essential role of preventing the formation, within the exchange economy, of market structures alien to complete competition and whose emergence cannot be prevented by constitutive principles alone.

#### *4.3.2.1 The Monopoly Office as Referee*

If competition policy is to be taken seriously as a means of deconcentrating the economy in general and combating monopolies in particular, then the existence of supervision and sanctions is critical. The ordoliberals envisaged three responses to address price wars or any other type of abuse of dominant position strategies: first, "dissolution" (*Auflösung*) of the firm; second, nationalization of the firm if the monopoly (individual or collective) was unavoidable or of public interest; and, third, maintaining the firm under the control of an independent Office.

The first solution was ideal for the ordoliberals, according precisely with the competitive order (Eucken 1952, 290; Lutz 1956, 163). Yet, in practice, dissolution can raise new problems. In fact, dissolving a cartel previously acting as a collective monopoly would, for instance, lead to an oligopoly market structure, not a competitive one (Eucken 1942a, 90). Similarly, technical conditions such as the existence of a natural monopoly can prevent its dissolution. Dissolving a monopoly could also overly ration supply in certain markets and therefore have socially unjustifiable consequences in terms of both shortages and labor opportunity.

There is no unanimity among the ordoliberal authors regarding nationalization. This ambiguity can be explained by the fact that the nature of the firm's ownership (private or public) was not a decisive criterion with regard to the ordoliberal focus on power; decisive, on the other hand, was the type of management of the economic process. While Röpke (1942c, 248) argued that nationalization was not directly "contrary to the logic of a market economy," and as such could be implemented in some cases,[20] Eucken (1949, 240) claimed that neither nationalization—being tantamount to "merging economic and political power"—nor collective control by the workforce would provide a satisfactory answer to the monopoly problem in the competitive order.

Rejecting both dissolution and nationalization, the ordoliberals opted for the third solution: that of economic supervision by an independent "Monopoly Office" (*Monopolamt*). This Office, comprised of economists and lawyers, would have to control the effective conditions of competition. Eucken (1949, 241) described the Office as a public (state-related) institution, yet independent of the political institutions (government, ministries, parliaments). Indeed, the Office had to be as far as possible "from the persistently dangerous influence exerted by interested parties (although these are weakened in the competitive order)."[21] Thanks to its

20. Initially, Röpke (1942a) argued for the nationalization of all private monopolies in order to keep only public monopolies. In a subsequent text, however, he toned down this position, calling for nationalization only if official surveillance proved insufficient (Röpke 1944b).

21. As Eucken (1951, 35) noted, "once monopolistic bodies have begun to flourish in a state, they gain considerable political influence, so considerable that the state itself becomes incapable of exercising effective monopoly control." If the ordoliberals showed a certain distrust of the state, it was not because of logic intrinsic to its functioning, as

independent status, the ordoliberals believed that the Office would acquire sufficient authority while minimizing the risk of making it the vehicle for a deleterious exercise of private power. In this case, the Office would become the epitome of what Böhm (1947, 131) termed "pitiless de-concentration of the private economy; de-privatisation of any remaining market power." According to the ordoliberals, the Office would be a vital institution in the modern market economy, an institution of economic justice functioning as a real safeguard against the dynamics of concentration. It was, therefore, Eucken (1949, 241) claimed, "just as indispensable as the Supreme Court" (the *Oberste Gericht*).

The Office should fight against concentration mainly through legislative decisions. However, the ordoliberals were aware that it was one thing to create new institutions parallel to the courts—indeed, in keeping with the ordoliberal observation of the law on cartels of November 1923 (*Kartellverordnung*), as mentioned in Chapter 1 of this book—but defining the notion of "abuse" of economic power precisely in legal language was far from easy. Yet, in the case of the Monopoly Office, Eucken underlined that it was "less *against the abuses* of existing power groups that economic policy should therefore focus, than *against the formation* of these entities holding power" (Eucken 1951, 35, emphasis added). To carry out an effective policy of combating monopolistic positions, it was, then, not so much a matter of a posteriori sanctions as, rather, of a priori prevention through assiduous control and supervision.

This market referee was to be a central institution of economic control. However, it would only be able to fulfil its mission if cartels and monopoly were already reduced to a minimum—otherwise it would be overwhelmed. Indeed, the modern state would be truly "unable to establish an effective supervision of monopolies in an economic order in which large parts of the industry are monopolized" (Eucken 1949, 239). The opposite situation is made possible by prior and systematic application of the constitutive principles. According to Böhm's terminology (1961, 44), this would be the *second* "prophylactic" effect exerted by economic policy.[22] Indeed, the Office's task would be greatly facilitated within the competitive order where the formation of monopolistic powers is de facto prevented.

was the case with Hayek or, for example, in the Public Choice. The state can be threatening because it can be the object of predatory strategies on the part of firms. Hence the ordoliberal suspicion ultimately concerned the private sphere.

22. For the record, the *first* prophylactic effect was performed by the principle of commercial liability of firms (K. e) discussed earlier.

> Not only by prohibitions of cartels, but also—and far more importantly—by an economic and legal policy which breaks through the strong forces of competition, as exist in a modern economy, by applying the constitutive principles. In this way the state largely escapes the influence of private pressure groups. (Eucken 1949, 239)

Hence, in addition to the actual action of the Monopoly Office, the ordoliberals relied on the credibility of its threat. This authority would have a preventive effect, further limiting tangible cases by its mere existence, taming the individual lust for the power gained by acquiring monopoly positions, "which is normally so strong," but would be "considerably weakened" or even "eliminated" if the supervision of monopolies became effective (Eucken 1949, 243). This could be labelled the *third* prophylactic effect of the ordoliberal economic policy.

#### *4.3.2.2 The "As If" Competition*

Even when the economic order is already tending toward the competitive order—which minimizes the logic of concentration without totally preventing it—the fight against monopolies is a permanent mission. So what, then, is this Monopoly Office actually to do? One of its central aims is to ensure that competitive practices are effectively oriented toward performance. The "performance-based competition" (*Leistungswettbewerb*) the ordoliberals envisaged would ensure that every entrepreneur, in a dynamic process, was subject to pressure from his competitors (Eucken 1948c, 88; 1949, 231; Rüstow 1942, 274). Eventually, competition would benefit the consumer by offering the widest range of choices that would guide the production process (Eucken 1949, 226; Lenel 1971, 262; Müller-Armack 1956, 83). As a result, the ordoliberals never saw competition as a good thing in itself, and some competitive practices could even harm the competitive order. Cut-throat competition, or "impediment competition" (*Behinderungswettbewerb*) as Eucken (1949, 235) called it, includes embargo strategies, loyalty discounts, predatory pricing, and dumping, which favor the disappearance of competitors and close the door to new entrants—typical cartel strategies. Eucken (1949, 228) defined impediment competition, which is in fact a "struggle for monopoly," as distinct from competitive behavior, as the absence of cost-based price regulation.

The essential task of the Office when identifying these injurious practices must be to compel monopolies and cartels to charge prices comparable to those of competition: indeed "as if" (*als ob*) they were really in a competitive situation. In short, the Office must place firms in a situation "analogous to competition" (*wettbewerbsanalog*), as Eucken (1949, 241) termed it. Here Eucken was drawing on Miksch's work, and in particular on his article "*Die Wirtschaftspolitik des Als-Ob*" published in 1948, where he stressed that theoretical analysis could serve as a guide for imposing a certain scale of pricing on the actual markets.[23]

While "as if" competition was to become the benchmark for determining whether firms were adopting acceptable competitive practices, as Böhm emphasized (Walther 2016, 119), it would also take on a proactive and normative sense in correcting actual market pricing, as Miksch argued (Goldschmidt and Berndt 2005, 973).[24] Hence the Office's management of prices should coordinate the economic process to facilitate return to the theoretical functioning and outcome of the competitive order:

> It is no simple matter to translate the conceptual model of internal coordination [i.e., the competitive order] into reality. However, the comparison of the model with actual historical reality offers the possibility to identify systematically and precisely where a gap exists between the conceptual model and reality, and to determine in each case whether this incongruity can be resolved through transformation of the legal data of the actual economic process. The conceptual model, despite its ideal-typical nature, is by no means a mere utopia. (Miksch 1948, 333)

To arrive at the theoretical outcome of competition, the market price should correspond to the firm's marginal cost. In theory, the Office would have to set the firm's price at the exact level "that ensures that it sells, produces and generally behaves *as if* it found itself in a situation of complete competition" (Eucken 1942a, 90–91, emphasis in original). In practice, Eucken (1949, 243) was fully aware of the difficulty of calculating this cost. Moreover, the technical difficulty of knowing whether or not a marginal cost equalization of the price allowed a firm to cover its fixed costs would always be there (Ahlborn and Grave 2006, 216). In particular, marginal cost pricing for a natural monopoly (increasing scales) would lead to losses, which meant that the "as if" policy was more easily applicable

23. As Claire Mongouachon (2016, 174) underlined, Miksch (1937b) formulated this idea as early as his habilitation thesis.

24. Thus, Miksch and Böhm did not exactly understand the "as if" policy in the same way. On the one hand, Böhm (1947, 130) favored the discretionary power of the Office, for example, by radically prohibiting certain agreements but limited to monopoly, while, on the other hand, Miksch wanted an authority devoted to "information and economic expertise" but which also addressed cases of oligopoly. Nevertheless, the real doctrinal oppositions would only fully emerge within the new wave of the Freiburg School, which took shape after the fifties (Mongouachon 2016, 181–183).

in some contexts than in others. While in principle it was applicable to "wage formation" (*Lohnbildung*), Miksch pointed out that this was a more complex issue than that of markets of goods and services. Indeed, within certain limits, the national labor authority may be involved in wage formation. Thus, fixing wage rates that approximately correspond to the "equilibrium wage which does not cause any long-term unemployment" seemed to Miksch (1948, 335) an accessible goal.

In light of these many shortcomings, Miksch (1948, 333) outlined three criteria to assess the effective competitiveness of a firm, and therefore guide the Office's activity if they were not satisfied. First, economic agents should not be able to fix the market price. Second, the market price should be linked to the real cost of production. Third, the price should follow the general movement of prices on free markets. As long as a firm or a group of firms charge prices "that do not come close to competitive prices, they will have to expect the daily interventions of the office" (Eucken 1949, 245). Miksch (1948) justified this form of external interference in the internal coordination of the market with the fact that the Office does no more than reproduce, or imitate, the "severity" of the constraint exerted by competitive market in normal times. Hence the Office's management of prices would be authoritative but not arbitrary.

The ordoliberals wanted to avoid any intervention in the economic process. Yet, paradoxically, the Office had the power to impose prices to mimic the competitive mechanism if it failed to function properly, taking on the task of guiding the economic process in the direction of the normative criteria. In short, the ordoliberals fundamentally saw the economy as consisting of two types of markets. First of all, there are markets where implementation of the constitutive principles sufficed to ensure completion. This first type, representing the majority of the markets, functions through internal coordination. Second, there are markets requiring specific interventions through the regulatory policy in general and through the control of monopolistic market structures in particular. Although very limited in number, these markets called for external coordination through economic policy because they undermined the legal and moral foundations of the competitive order as a whole, and thus—given the interdependencies—undermined its overall functioning.

### 4.3.3 Crisis Policies: From *Krise* to *Gesellschaftskrise*

The constitutive and regulative principles were central to the ordoliberal program of economic policies and yet they did not cover the whole field. While the ordoliberals did in fact envisage a short-run expansionary kind of policy to restore the economy in periods of severe economic crises, they contemplated a long-run sociological program designed to counteract the alleged spiritual crises of the twentieth century.

#### *4.3.3.1 A Keynesian Moment?*

Looking back on them, the ordoliberal economic policies are now often seen as systematic recipes to be absolutely followed, but this means forgetting that they resulted from critical and historical reflection on the particular case of Germany. Evidence of this attitude is to be seen in the ordoliberals' ways of addressing the Great Depression that hit Germany harder than any other European country.

By the beginning of 1932, the Brüning government was seriously considering fighting recession, deflation, and unemployment by means of public works and job creation. Hence, well before the publication of Keynes's *General Theory* (1936), Germany already had its own "anticipators" of Keynes or "proto-Keynesians," which accounts for the similarities between the German economic policies of the thirties and the general spirit of the Keynesian program in the sense of public stimulus for job creation (Klausinger 1999). Wilhelm Lautenbach, "a scholar and a policy-maker simultaneously" (Backhaus 1985, 177), was the main architect of this German version of Keynesianism as early as 1931. He supported "a radical plan for credit-financed government spending" (Tooze 2001, 170) that found its way through the Brauns Commission, which was created to come up with an answer to the unemployment crisis coming with the Great Depression.

Despite the public works policy envisaged by Brüning and partly carried out by the following Chancellor (von Papen), it was not a systematic policy of public works, and it eventually proved to be extremely modest and without real effects on mass unemployment (Petzina 1969, 69). Indeed, this program of job creation did not get under way until Hitler finally applied and reoriented it toward "massive rearmament" when he came to power (Garvy 1975, 403). While the influence of the Brauns Commission remained very limited and the expansionist policy was not implemented immediately, the investment and public expenditure plans could then count on the strong support of Hjalmar Schacht, president of the Reichsbank (1933–1939).[25]

25. Within a broader perspective, the volume edited by Peter E. Hall (1989) on *The Political Power of Economic Ideas: Keynesianism Across Nations* showed how Western countries' counter-cyclical fiscal policies against unemployment came about primarily

Both Eucken and Röpke participated in the pre-Hitler expert circles and were among the scholars who called for an immediate short-run expansionist program in Weimar Germany (Commun 2018; Feld et al. 2018). In September 1931, Eucken took part in a two-day meeting with the then *Reichsbank* President Hans Luther. There the question was to decide between continuation of the deflationary policy or transition to state job creation, low interest rates, and credit expansion, an issue more debated than ever. Shortly afterward, Röpke was fighting this battle within the Brauns Commission. Drawing a distinction between the initial, or "primary," phase of the Depression and its "secondary" phase, Röpke (1932; 1936a) attempted to combine—and thus reconcile—Hayek's and Keynes's approaches to the business cycle (see Fèvre 2018b). As Germany was entering the latter (secondary) kind of depression, Röpke argued that the state had to lower taxes drastically while raising expenditure and financing public works to produce a strong "initial spark" (*Initialzündung*) that would eventually boost the economy. Indeed, Röpke (1933, 430) emphasized that "the national economy was captive to a form of torpor, from which it could emerge through a state-led impulse."

For Röpke as for Eucken, the urgency and magnitude of the Great Depression made it impossible for the government to remain unresponsive to the situation and wait for the crisis to work itself out, as for instance advocated in the Austrian theory of cycles. And, indeed, Hayek tried to convinced Röpke that it was too soon to be backing an expansionist policy (see Magliulo 2018).

In retrospect, Eucken (1951, 65) insisted that when "there are millions of unemployed, any government will have to pursue a policy of full employment . . . social conscience forbids us to tolerate mass unemployment, and so does reason of state." Eucken (1951, 59) went so far as to suggest that if at that time the government had accepted the plan designed by Lautenbach—"deservedly known as the German Keynes"—then "there might perhaps never have been a National Socialist revolution." Over and above the counterfactual element in Eucken's analysis, due weight should be given to the reason he provided for the authorities' passive conduct:

> The most likely reason why the government did not do so [adopt Lautenbach's plan], was because it was afraid of inflation, which had caused such devastation in Germany ten years previously. (Eucken 1951, 59)

without any reference to Keynes. Franklin Delano Roosevelt's New Deal is an obvious example, but other examples can also be seen in Sweden, France, or Italy (see also Bateman 2006, 283–286).

Remarkably, Eucken challenged the panic fear of inflation—in this case the hyperinflation of the twenties—as a bad political advisor. In any case, Eucken's reflection attested to the fact that the ordoliberals were not, in all circumstances, contrary to a policy of economic recovery that might involve public spending and control of investment. From the early 1930s to the late 1940s, Eucken maintained a similar perspective on the need for a Keynesian-like policy to overcome severe crises. But how, then, are we to take the ordoliberal rejection of the full-employment objective?

Neither Röpke nor Eucken envisaged controlling the overall level of investment as ambitiously or continuously as Keynes did. From an ordoliberal point of view, expansionary policy had to respond to the special case of the Great Depression and be abandoned at the first signs of recovery; otherwise, it would lead to marked inflation. Therefore, according to the ordoliberals, there was room for no more—though no less—than a Keynesian *moment*.

Thus, what drove the ordoliberals to flat dismissal of the full employment philosophy of Keynesian interventionism was adoption of it as a perennial guide in state management of day-to-day economic life. More generally, Röpke and Eucken criticized Keynes for making the full employment policy not only the means to overcome the crisis in the national or international economy—since they themselves were in favor of it at the beginning of the 1930s—but for making it a mode of state management of current economic affairs.

According to them, it is precisely this day-to-day management that poses the risk of a spread of economic planning and political authoritarianism, given the example of the full employment policies implemented by Hitler in 1933, followed by Göring's four-year plan as early as 1936. Indeed, both Eucken (1948c, 179) and Röpke (1944b, 196) associated Keynesianism with a form of policy on the economic process (*Prozesspolitik*) that would be, mutatis mutandis, back on the same tracks as the managed economy implemented by the national socialist state (from 1933 to 1936), eventually leading toward protectionism, nationalism, and central planning. The ordoliberals completed this bizarre cocktail by adding the Beveridge Plan of 1944 to the mix. Although Keynes was decidedly alien to the project of the British welfare state (Marcuzzo 2010; Backhouse and Bateman 2012), from the ordoliberal point of view—here in line with the neoliberal thought collective—they were all eventually paving the way to serfdom, to paraphrase the title of Hayek's famous book.

Eucken believed that unemployment was not the evident consequence of the development of liberal capitalism, but rather the result of the instability of market forms and the monetary system. Eucken aimed to shift the focus of public intervention within the economic process—a state investment plan, for example—to the framework, or "rules of the game," of the economic system itself. Thus, he refused to place full employment at the center of social justice and preferred to pursue other objectives that he deemed sufficient to ensure a high level of employment in return. This issue could only be resolved indirectly through the establishment of a sustainable economic order and not through a "perfect welfare state" (Rüstow 1956, 1). Thus, full employment must be a result, the consequence of an economic policy of stabilizing market forms and never the direct object of specific intervention. Otherwise, this preliminary objective would be contravened:

> Satisfactory control of the overall process and through this "full employment"—yes. Full employment alone, ignoring or concealing the problem of control of the economic order—no. (Eucken 1948a, 45)

Eucken and the ordoliberals envisaged economic policy as "state planning of forms" of economic framework.[26] Yet even in calling for ruled-based policy, they did not imply that state action would be uniform in time and space. On the contrary, Eucken (1949, 228) was very clear about the plasticity of the competitive order, stressing that "it will be realized in a particular way, depending on the current or historical situation" of each country. And even when the right economic policy had been carried out to implement the competitive order in one country in particular, the task was "never finished," for the economy itself is in "constant evolution" and requires a reinvention of the tools and fields of action of economic policy (Miksch 1948, 337). However, the ordoliberals set two limits to this adaptive attitude. Not only was every single measure to be consistent with all the others, but economic policy itself was to be conducted on a reasonably consistent basis over time.

First, the ordoliberals were adamant on the fact that each policy decision would be evaluated in terms of its compliance with other decisions. The historical process of increasing the complexity (i.e., interdependence) of economic activities runs counter to adoption of public policies that are not in line with the dynamics of the overall economic order. The need for coherence in economic policy was truly decisive on the nation-state level. And eventually the principle of coherence should also apply to international governance.

26. This alternative formulation can be found in the German notes for the lectures at the LSE in Eucken, published posthumously (see Eucken 2001, 77).

As a matter of fact, the ordoliberals opposed Keynes's "Plan for an International Clearing Union" (the second version of April 1943) on the ground that it would entail inconsistent global measures. Eucken (1943, 273) recognized that the Keynes Plan did in fact envisage international monetary measures "seriously attempting to promote equilibrium tendencies" among national competitive orders, but it also entailed global control of investment and trade, thus favoring forms of international planning that would lead to "general imbalance in world commodity markets."[27] Ultimately, as Eucken (1943, 273) saw it, Keynes would then be organizing "concentration of power" on an international scale. Eucken's former student Friedrich Lutz (1943, 21) came to similar conclusions to Eucken's regarding the deleterious role of pressure groups on international decisions.[28] Lutz (1943) also emphasized the lack of "logical consistency" regarding economic policy as the chief weakness of modern governments in general and of pre-Bretton Woods discussions in particular. Thus, neither of these plans (White's or Keynes's) would adequately regulate the international monetary system in the long run. Lutz complained that the interdependence of economic orders was not sufficiently considered and always overshadowed by technical sophistication in narrow domains and, indeed, by short-sighted resolutions.

Second, a certain consistency in economic policies over time was a necessary condition for effective anticipation of specific long-run economic plans. Eucken (1952, 285) referred to this principle as "constancy of economic policy." He argued that "the nervous restlessness of economic policy" which counteracts the formation of "an atmosphere of confidence" was a major factor accounting for underinvestment (1952, 288).

Drawing on Lutz's (1945) work on US firms and his own experience of 1940s Germany, Eucken (1952, 288) stressed that firms often disregarded a wide range of profitable investments to implement solely the most profitable ones. He attributed this state of affairs to the inconsistency of

27. Eventually, Eucken (1944, 277) adopted a more nuanced position in his second commentary on the Keynes Plan. He then recognized that in some particular cases, controlling already existing international cartels may be a lesser evil, rather than constant state intervention in these markets. In particular, certain technological shocks could in fact render the market process for raw materials such as rubber or cotton inoperative.

28. Eucken and Lutz arrived at rather similar analyses and conclusions despite their completely different environments. While Eucken presented discussion of Keynes's Plan to a private audience within the Freiburg resistance circles (cf. Chapter 3), Lutz had been in the United States since 1939, eventually becoming full professor at Princeton University. He issued a comparative analysis of Keynes's and White's Plan in the booklet series of the *International Finance Section*.

economic policy inducing firms to undertake investments that could be amortized in the short run (in a three- to five-year time span). Thus, in addition to the constitutive and regulative principles, the proper functioning of the competitive order requires "a certain constancy" (1952, 288) in economic policy. Entrepreneurs can then behave rationally (i.e., conceive long-run economic plans) with regard to opportunities to invest in capital or employ more staff. By contrast, uncertainty accompanying inconsistent economic policy would give "an impulse" (*Anstoß*) to the formation of industrial—horizontal—concentration: large industrial groups being allegedly more resilient to hazard (Eucken 1952, 289).

#### *4.3.3.2 Spiritual Reform and the Competitive Order*

Clearly, the ordoliberals saw competition as the key organizational principle of economic life, thus building their entire political vision around the shaping of the competitive order. As Rüstow (1951, 170) put it, competition was the "most productive and healthiest economic principle." However, he also emphasized that competition carried "obvious drawbacks" and in particular opposed the "principle of solidarity . . . one of the most fundamental and valuable human needs." Lack of solidarity would not be overcome by means of usual social policy but by taking care of the "vital situation" of mankind. Under this heading, the ordoliberals—Röpke and Rüstow foremost—outlined a broad sociological and civilizational agenda aiming to restore the spiritual and existential conditions of persons (as opposed to the masses).[29] The ordoliberal program aimed to go beyond local or symptomatic therapeutics to establish itself as "medicine for the mass society" (Röpke 1942c, 297). It ambitioned nothing less than combining policy for the competitive order with "degregarization, deproletarianization, decollectivization, and enhancement of the peasantry, craftsmanship and decentralization—in short, with a social policy aiming at a more solid sociological-anthropological framework" (Röpke 1944b, 73–74).

To do so, Röpke (1942c, 176) deemed that individuals should be provided with types of property of vital importance, covering a quasi-anthropological range of human needs: ownership of one's dwelling and, to a certain extent, of one's means of production. Röpke (1944b, 69) conceived a structural policy based on sustained action in the direction of the social preconditions that are prerequisites for and outcomes of the market economy, including

29. Werner Bonefeld (2013b) contributed to the reading of Rüstow's *Vitalpolitik* from a Foucauldian viewpoint (see also Dörr et al. 2016).

the "distribution of income and property, [the] size of farms, [the] distribution of the population between town and country, between industry and agriculture and between the different classes." According to Röpke, it would in some respects be necessary to return to an earlier stage of industrial-social development, although this would inevitably entail "highly unrealistic expectations" informed by "preindustrial social structures" (Ptak 2009, 123).[30]

Röpke (1942c, 263) claimed that the agrarian world was the true source of morality; he called it the true "backbone of a healthy nation." The farmer's way of life embodied Röpke's sociological ideal. Obviously, Röpke condemned large-scale, concentrated farms with the same logic as he did with the industrial sector. Here, Röpke outlines clearly restrictive rules. And although these rules do not directly contravene the logic of a competitive market economy, they find their reason outside the commercial sphere, in both the communitarian and natural spheres:

> It is an essential characteristic of peasant agriculture that the size of each farm does not exceed the working capacity of one family . . . ; it is *embedded in the social organization* of the family and the kinship group, of the village, of the cooperative peasant associations and the occupational and neighborly community *to which every thought of competition is alien*; and lastly, following the cycle of nature and its laws. (Röpke 1942c, 202, emphasis added)

According to Röpke, the agrarian world would somehow function as a sociological force counteracting the destructuring tendency of competitive capitalism. The agrarian sector embodies a form of alter- or contra-capitalist way of life. In short, peasant farming would be "the normal complement" to the "industrial and urban side of our civilisation" (Röpke 1942b, 263).

Obviously, the peasant's way of life cannot be generalized to the whole social body. If the artisanal sector is to be brought closer to it, particularly in terms of ownership conditions, everything possible must be done to ensure that the working class and wage workers tend toward this ideal. In order to emerge from the current era of the masses, Röpke (1942c, 219) argued that it would be necessary to make the "working and living conditions of the industrial worker as similar to the positive aspects of the

30. At the beginning of the 1930s, Röpke (1934a, 13–14) had mocked the attempts of "conservative economists" like Adolph Wagner "to turn back the wheels of history." And yet, during the war, Röpke adopted a somewhat similar approach. In the second half of the twentieth century, Röpke grew increasingly conservative on societal issues: close to American neoconservatism, he notably supported South Africa's policy of apartheid (see Goldschmidt and Dörr 2018; Slobodian 2018, chap. 7).

life of the peasant and artisan as possible." What, however, remains questionable here is the compatibility between this sociological program and the competitive order the ordoliberals called for. Indeed, competition in the field of employment, for example, implies a high degree of mobility, of being ready to change one's occupation or function according to the economic situation: Does this not directly contradict the ordoliberal desire for the individual to take root in his family and in his community?

In any case, behind this structural policy lay the ambition to endow work with a new spirit—not only with a view to resisting the socially, sociologically, and spiritually destructuring tendencies of the competitive exchange economy, but also in order to have what might be termed a *fourth* prophylactic effect: that is, to provide individuals from the outset with mental structures that are antagonistic to industrial concentration (praise for the local and the small) and the exercise of power. Eucken (1952, 275) claimed that small-scale private property would be a vector of independence, freedom, and individuality, or, in other words, a source of "social and moral freedom" (Bilger 1964, 108) because it gives everyone the means to exercise their potential as well as a degree of independence essential to cope with the negative effects of the market economy.

Thus, paradoxically, response to the social and spiritual crisis afflicting workers mainly involves reforms outside the economic sphere. Röpke aimed at bypassing the Marxist program of dictatorship of the proletariat through the multiplication and diffusion of small holdings of capital property. He was convinced that "the misery of 'capitalism'" does not lie in the fact that some have capital, but in the fact that others do not and are therefore "proletarians" (Röpke 1942c, 178).[31] Nevertheless, widespread distribution of capital could not suffice to answer to what the ordoliberals perceived as the spiritual emptiness of the masses, for it would also be necessary to educate individuals in the implications, use, and social significance of such property.

The subjective and educational dimension of the Röpkean program also concerned the consumer, who, while often presented in ordoliberal discourse as a victim at the mercy of monopolistic structures, was also guilty of a form of complicity. It was not only the conditions of industrial supply of certain products that crushed artisanal production, but also the subjective conditions of demand and consumption habits. This is why Röpke (1942b, 384, 307) saw "intelligent and effective consumer education" as

31. From this point of view, Röpke's perspective sits well with the "property-owning democracy" later indicated by John Rawls (2001): an institutional system in its own right imagined as an alternative to laissez-faire or different versions of state socialism.

the appropriate means "to weaken the power of the monopolies considerably." For Röpke, nothing was more crucial than the fullest possible clarification of all economic phenomena, the most diffuse and transparent "publicity," and as perfect precision as was possible in examination of the market and the data that determine it. Note that here "publicity" is to be understood in the sense of economic information since the ordoliberals fiercely opposed advertising in its modern form, which they saw as contributing to establishing the economic power of monopolies. No doubt, an "exceptional effort" would be required of the population as a whole in order to achieve a competitive economy, with everyone pursuing this goal as a "kind of national sport" (Böhm 1954, 159). The educational dimension of the ordoliberal program was conveyed in particular by Ludwig Erhard in the postwar period. He represented some of the societal items on the ordoliberal agenda in his speeches and through numerous works intended for the general public.

## 4.4 CONCLUSION: TOWARD A POWER-FREE ECONOMIC ORDER

Rather than growth, security, or justice, the ordoliberals aimed at the disappearance of illegitimate economic power as a flagship objective of economic policy. This goal was not only fundamental in the economic perspective, but also in a more comprehensive societal dimension. The ordoliberal reformulation of the social question required a threefold effort of distinction: from historical liberalism, from socialist planning, and indeed from Keynesian interventionism (associated with the infant British welfare state). In this way the ordoliberal reformulation of the social question stood as culmination of the ordoliberal historical diagnosis highlighted in Chapter 1 of this book.

From the ordoliberal standpoint, standard social policy could at best conceal the social question, at worst aggravate it. Thus, the ordoliberals relegated social policy per se to the background of core state intervention, to the benefit of economic policy and moral reform. In the quest for a composite synthesis emerging from the liberal, socialist, and conservative tradition of thought, the ordoliberals aimed to take up the socialist and Marxist criticism but, at the same time, to empty it of its corollary. For instance, the ordoliberal criticism of the living conditions of workers was hampered by the desire to organize the whole economy according to a competitive process: competition which, as Marx among others had shown, brings pressure to bear on the workers. In the final analysis, it may prove difficult to understand how the two levels of the ordoliberal policy—economic competition and spiritual reform—can effectively be combined in a satisfactory and noncontradictory way. Nevertheless, the ordoliberals drew up an ambitious sociological program to address the spiritual problem of the masses which the industrial countries would inevitably be faced with.

The ordoliberals' fundamental argument asserting the superiority of the competitive order over other types of societal organization ran thus: individuals—in the absence of private economic power—would be both promoters of and subject to the expression of the general will (embodied by the competitive price) which drives the production process according to consumer choices.[32] Three implicit economic arguments follow on from this central societal aim. First, a trend toward enhanced performance in production techniques (in terms of quality/price ratio). Second, better allocation of scarce resources, depending on the effective utility within the overall process (the calculation tool that drives the process). Finally, a trend toward a long-run economic equilibrium (in the sense of coordination of individual actions through plans). However, these three arguments were not based so much on rigorous logical demonstration as on the return to certain conclusions of an economic theory external to ordoliberal thinking, as discussed in Chapter 3.

By holding to the stability of market forms and monetary order, the ordoliberals made the disappearance of economic power within the economic process the key to solving the social problem in both the short and long run. To this end, Eucken outlined a set of constitutive and regulative principles. The state and public authorities were the only legitimate institutions in the exercise of power (for the purposes of maintaining or modifying the economic order) while being themselves the source of their own limitations. Indeed, the objective of an adequate functioning of the price system in the competition order serves as a yardstick for freedom of action, both of the individual and of the public authorities. While the emergence of monopolistic situations can be minimized with assiduous application of economic policy principles, it can under no circumstances be entirely prevented. This is why the Monopoly Office has to force companies to behave as if they were effectively in a competitive situation. The ordoliberals saw competition as the vital instrument for the disempowerment of private economic power—as a tool for regulating the social body in order to eliminate its positions of illegitimate economic power.

32. Formalized interpretations of the ordoliberal perspective can be found in the language of game theory (Vatiero 2010, 2015) and using Edgeworth boxes (Dold and Krieger 2017).

In this chapter, we also assessed to what extent the ordoliberal principles, although having general—universal—relevance, were irrevocably anchored to the German context of the first half of the twentieth century. Certainly, the ordoliberals paid exceptional attention to the stability of the currency and condemned state intervention in the economic process. However, they also argued that interventionism by means of short-run expansionary policy was mandatory in overcoming periods of severe economic crisis. What mattered to the ordoliberals most was nonetheless observing a certain consistency in economic policy, both over time and in terms of coherence binding economic measures together. Thus, the crux of the ordoliberal disagreement with Keynesianism lay precisely in the time span perspective of economic policy. On the one hand, Keynesianism reasoned in terms of the urgency of the moment—famously embodied by Keynes's catchphrase that "in the long run we are all dead" (see Mann 2017). On the other hand, Eucken (1942a, 95, emphasis in original) underlined that the right economic policy for the present "*transitional* economy" (in view to the postwar period) should remain orientated toward the future "*permanent* order" if there was to be any hope of reaching it one day.

# CHAPTER 5
# Epilogue
## *Time for Responsibility*

So far, this book has kept the issue of power well to the fore as the central challenge around which the ordoliberal political economy was structured—in its doctrinal, methodological, and theoretical as well as political aspects. In this fifth and last chapter, we take a sidestep: rather than examining the nature of the ordoliberal project as it took shape over some twenty years, from 1932 to 1950, we offer an overview of the critical scope of ordoliberal discourse over the short but significant period of the early postwar years. The following pages will flesh out the scenario of the ordoliberal campaign against economic planning and in favor of transition toward a market economy in West Germany.

Significant for this purpose is Michel Foucault's conjecture that "Nazism was, in a way, the epistemological and political 'road to Damascus' for the Freiburg School. That is to say, Nazism enabled them to define what I would call the field of adversity that they had to define and cross in order to reach their objective" (Foucault 2008, 106). Foucault's conjecture finds confirmation if we analyze the ordoliberal literature of the early postwar years in West Germany. This literature shows that, in the eyes of the ordoliberals, the planning promoted by the Bizonal administration of the Western Allies represented the continuation of a policy that perpetuated the ills of the Nazi administration. Relying on fixed prices and output/input objectives, the Allies thus ensured that the new West Germany would suffer from the same economic and social problems that plagued the old Nazi regime.

*A Political Economy of Power.* Raphaël Fèvre, Oxford University Press. © Oxford University Press 2021.
DOI: 10.1093/oso/9780197607800.003.0006

The ordoliberals wanted to dispel what they perceived as the huge illusion still held by the West: the ordoliberals wanted to disabuse the West of the notion that the Nazi machinery had been marked by tremendous economic and social efficiency. In truth, as the ordoliberals well knew, Hitler's Germany had been an unsustainable economic order. They argued that West Germany's economic problem did not reside in the fact that Germany lay in ruins after the war, but in the Allies' perpetuation of unsustainable economic policies (i.e., the Nazi planning model). They saw market liberalism as the only way to overcome the economic slump West Germany was locked in. My contention is that the ordoliberals drew the political lessons that could be learned from the economy of the Third Reich: they confronted the Western Allies and the German authorities with the fact that proper denazification could succeed only if Nazi planning methods were rejected.[1] The narrative outline here rests on the hypothesis that ordoliberal ideas gained traction because their authors sought to establish a *continuity* between the economic order of the Nazi and the administration of the Western Allies in the postwar period. Wilhelm Röpke offered perhaps the best summing up of the continuity thesis by highlighting—with a characteristic tone of caustic irony—what he viewed as a truly absurd situation:

> We have seen the strange spectacle of the Western Allies trying to rush the German experts into accepting an economic programme which, in the final analysis, reveals itself as that of the Third Reich. (Röpke 1950a, 339)

As a matter of fact, the continuity ordoliberals were setting forth was not so much based on the fact that part of the Nazi administration remained in place several years after the end of the war. Their argument was rather that, although Nazi Germany and the Allies represented different political ideologies, the Allies were continuing, in West Germany, the economic planning and price controls of Hitler's regime. As such, the continuity thesis was addressed both to the West German political authorities and to the Western Allies who held the fate of Germany in their hands. On what looks rather like an economic policy battlefield, the ordoliberals promoted and circulated their arguments through various media: hence we used various

1. Hayek (1944) was among the loudest liberal voices expressing concern about the West's planning tendencies. If in principle the "slippery slope" argument, which one can also find in Mises and Friedman, is consistent with ordoliberal ideas, the continuity argument I discuss here follows a separate route.

kinds of documentation, including advisory reports, newspaper/magazine articles, and academic publications focusing on a short period of time (1945–1950).

In June 1948, the monetary reform and a law liberalizing prices seemed to mark the unexpected veer of West Germany away from planning toward a market economy.[2] These reforms may be seen as constituting a cunning maneuver of the Anglo-American Bizone in keeping with Western liberal principles and in opposition to the rise of the communist bloc. However, to attribute both policies—the monetary reform and price liberalization—to the Allies would be a mistake. In truth, the Allies pushed forward only the monetary reform. It took the ordoliberals to add price liberalization to the policy mix. As far as the ordoliberals were concerned, the Bizone's sole direct concern was monetary reform and certainly not moving in the direction of liberalism.[3] Indeed, they saw the US government (Balisciano 1998), and even more so Clement Atlee's Labour government in Britain (see Chick 2002), sticking to the principles inherited from the Second World War: the national "love affair[s] with planning"—to borrow Marcia Balisciano's metaphor (1999, 13)—continued to flourish in the early postwar years. Planning found support in Germany not only because of the Allied (military) administrations, but even more so on account of the socialist orientation of the Social Democratic Party (SPD), which dominated the political scene from 1945 to the summer of 1947. Even part of the Christian Democratic Union (CDU/CSU) was inclined to nationalize major industries and pursue a degree of economic planning (Giersch et al. 1992, 32–33). Rationalization of the economy—ranging from complete planning to a Keynesian mixed economy—was then the dominant perspective.

Nevertheless, it was the German authorities who enacted the law liberalizing prices, but not without the lobbying of the ordoliberals. Indeed, Walter Eucken, Leonhard Miksch, Friedrich Lutz, and Franz Böhm worked with the government of the French zone (in which Freiburg im Breisgau was situated), but also with a number of Anglo-American Bizone government commissions in which they exerted a growing influence together with Ludwig Erhard (Glossner 2010, 43).[4] Erhard, the director of

2. The Law on Principles and Pricing Policy After the Monetary Reform (*Gesetz über Leitsätze und Preispolitik nach der Geldreform*).

3. The monetary reform was a unilateral Anglo-American decision (Braun 1990, 154–155; Capie and Wood 2001, 452; Sauermann 1979, 302; Wandel 1979, 321).

4. As an academic in Geneva, Röpke had no direct role to play in administrative circles during these early postwar years. He nevertheless commanded considerable attention as a liberal thinker.

the economic administration newly appointed by the Bizonal Economic Council, is credited with this unexpected "leap into cold water." It is well established that Erhard's admiration for economic liberalism was rooted in ordoliberal ideas. It was indeed the ordoliberals who, advancing their continuity thesis, urged Erhard to combine monetary reform with the liberalization of prices. Otherwise, monetary reform alone would fail to change the economic order in depth and bring prosperity to West German citizens. Despite the decidedly unfavorable postwar situation in which, "politically, liberalism was weak and discredited" (Nicholls 1994, 137), as in a large part of the West, ordoliberal ideas gained substantial ground in the early postwar years, a pivotal period in shaping the economic model first of the Federal Republic of Germany (FRG) and later of unified Germany.

Previous literature offers a detailed picture of the political debates in West Germany in the early post-Second World War years. The rise of ordoliberalism as a leading intellectual force has been explained through a series of political and institutional circumstances (Giersch et al. 1992; Glossner 2010; Hook 2004; Nicholls 1994). Scholars have also emphasized the ordoliberal offer of a simple and "culturally coherent concept of economic theory" in turbulent times as the main reason for its success (Ptak 2009, 120; see also Rieter and Schmolz 1993). However, these explanations are only one side of the story. Indeed, the substance of the ordoliberal diagnosis—in particular the issue of continuity—has been largely neglected in the existing literature.

## 5.1 WEST GERMANY UNDER THE ORDOLIBERAL DIAGNOSIS

In the crucial postwar years, the ordoliberals were faced with a West German economy stuck at an extremely low level of production. To account for this state of affairs, the ordoliberals did not refer to the devastation of war, German laziness and lack of cooperation, or events such as the Allies' breaking down heavily cartelized sectors or promoting agriculture, as has been commonly argued (Allen 1989, 269). For Eucken, Röpke, and other ordoliberals, the fundamental cause of the economic malaise was economic planning: a continuation of what the Nazis had been doing. Bringing the Western Allies as well as German opinion around to this point of view was far from easy, as the Nazi economic machinery still enjoyed a solid reputation in the postwar years.

### 5.1.1 An International Campaign

Magazines and newspapers were the best medium through which ordoliberal expertise could influence "world public opinion" (Röpke 1946b, 511). The Swiss liberal newspaper *Neue Zürcher Zeitung* was the first and foremost platform (and then the German *Frankfurter Allgemeine Zeitung* from its creation in November 1949), but an ordoliberal international campaign started in parallel with publications in British, American, and French outlets.

Worth mentioning is the British weekly political and literary review *Time & Tide*, which was a favored place of publication for Röpke (a dozen publications between 1947 and 1951) and Eucken (1947, 1948d). Important academic articles were also published in various international journals: a notable example is "Repressed Inflation" by Röpke (1947e), which appeared in the newly created academic journal *Kyklos* (see Meijer 1994, 29). Another good example is the two-part article "On the Theory of the Centrally Administrated Economy," by Eucken (1948c) in *Economica*. Eucken and Röpke's English-language articles contributed to the socialist planning debate and the debate on the viability of a mixed economy.[5] While ordoliberal activism originated in the second half of the thirties with the book series known as *Ordnung der Wirtschaft* (see Böhm et al. 1936), it came into its own with the creation, by Franz Böhm and Walter Eucken, of the academic journal *Ordo* in 1948.[6] A central forum for liberal ideas, *Ordo* provided real political visibility. In pursuit of "a well-functioning economic and social order" (Lenel and Meyer 1948, viii), the first contribution to the journal by Eucken (1948a) set forth in broad lines what this new economic order should look like.

Although they attributed a major role to the disastrous effects of the Second World War, the ordoliberals pointed to the problem of the economic order as the primary cause of the weakness of the German economy.[7] And

5. This debate waxed particularly lively in England, chiefly at the London School of Economics (Backhouse 2005, 355).

6. In the same spirit, Röpke had endeavored to found the journal *Occident*, conceived of as a place of publication for liberal European intellectuals, but this project aborted. Indeed, Röpke failed to raise enough funds from Swiss contributors to ensure the sustainability of the project. The funds he did manage to secure were eventually redirected to organization of the first conference (April 1947) of the Mont Pèlerin Society (Steiner 2007).

7. The ordoliberal diagnosis was partially corroborated by subsequent historical studies on that point. Although the German cities, transport infrastructure, and population had been so severely hit, historians concur that Germany's productive potential remained at a level almost as high as its prewar level (Braun 1990, 153; Nicholls 1994, 124–125; Sohmen 1959, 989; Hook 2004, 9). For example, the capital stock

behind the state of the European postwar economy (of Germany in particular) lay two—almost independent—basic reasons for Röpke: "the war has *destroyed* so much, and the economic process is in *disorder*" (Röpke 1947d, 123, emphasis added). What was missing in the German economic order in those early postwar years was "a perfectly functioning 'scarcity gauge,' then although economic activity is still possible the lack of coordination will not be conducive to overcoming scarcity" (Eucken 1948a, 30). The "scarcity gauge" Eucken referred to was the price system, which suffered under the strain of rationing and price-fixing but was also disturbed by serious monetary disequilibria. The main consequence of economic disorder, however, was to be seen in the price structure. Prices, because they were fixed, no longer had any real economic basis; they were "fictitious values" (Röpke 1947e, 247) that had nothing to do with scarcity or need and thus represented factors of inefficiency in the form of an "inadequate utilization of the productive capacity" (Eucken and Meyer 1948, 53).

The official markets suffered from serious disproportions and, in particular, severe shortages. When "the direction of the economy by central administration broke down in 1946–47" (Eucken 1948c, 81), what we would now call an "unofficial" or "secondary" economy emerged: a black market obviously, but also barter and a domestic self-sufficient economy (i.e., households producing their own food and other necessities).[8] These were not just marginal cases. From November 1945 to January 1946, transactions made under the table rose from 20% to 50% in the total amount of exchanges (Bignon 2007, 230).[9] Given this state of affairs, money could no longer fulfil its canonical functions (medium of exchange, unit of account, and store of value), and a barter economy emerged—and with it the problem of the "twofold coincidence of needs" necessary for exchange. Friedrich Lutz (1949b, 122) explained that in such circumstances,

(in billion RM of 1950 prices) rose from 51.8 in 1938 to 71.2—its highest level—by the end of 1943, and terminated at 58.6 in 1946 (Krengel 1963, 123, table I). This is nuanced by Postan (1967, 24): "[t]rue enough, some of this productive capital was in the form of highly specialized munitions plants unsuited to peacetime employment." Nevertheless, what was termed "zero hour" (*Stunde Null*) reflects a somewhat distorted view. Indeed, Germany found itself in a comparatively more favorable situation than that of the other European countries, especially thanks to a better "balance between wartime investment and destruction" (Carlin 1996, 463).

8. Study of this type of coordination was developed to a great degree in the postwar period, with the rise of what were called the *Soviet-type economies*: "all economic activities that are either undertaken directly for private gain or are knowingly illegal in some substantial way" (Alexeev 2008, 384).

9. For a detailed inquiry into German black markets at that time, see Frank Grube and Gerhard Richter (1979).

for both "individuals and business firms . . . a whole series of exchanges were sometimes necessary to obtain the desired commodity."

### 5.1.2 "No Economic Order at All"

The ordoliberals asserted that the economy generated such a complex system of coordination, spawning so much inefficiency, that it was impossible to identify it with either of the two major types of coordination known thus far. Röpke indeed observed "the distortion of *all value relations*, the increasing importance of illegal dealings besides the shrinking 'official sector' and the ever-greater conflict between the impulses of the market and the administration struggling desperately to maintain its authority—all this leads finally to *a chaos* where there is *no economic order at all,* be it collectivist or competitive" (Röpke 1947e, 247, emphasis added). From this point of view, Germany experienced "a border-line case . . . of particular interest" (Eucken 1951, 81).

With the aim of raising worker productivity, but also of eluding the fixed ceiling set on wages, some firms introduced forms of "payment in kind" alongside monetary pay. Without affecting the level of production, according to Eucken and Meyer (1948, 53), these industries increased their wage bill to the detriment of the industries that did not practice such forms of remuneration. And even worse, this payment in kind had the perverse effect of encouraging black markets. Röpke (1947e, 250), as well as Eucken and Meyer, called attention to the negative repercussions that these practices had on the secondary economy: "partial wage payments in kind, furthermore, have increased the turnover in the black market and in the barter deals" (Eucken and Meyer 1948, 53).

The consequent decline in productivity and in the total volume of production led to a vicious circle. The advantages offered by specialization and the division of labor were inadequate, so people turned to unofficial channels. In the ordoliberal analysis, then, as the division of labor was reduced to a more limited scale, the development of "primitive" or "precapitalist" forms of organization were to be seen, including barter and home food production (Eucken 1951, 69). Faced with economic disorder, the people of West Germany eventually turned to expedients that were rational at the individual level—taking on extra work, looking for black markets, and barter—but led to increasing irrationality at the global level of the economy:

> From the *economic* point of view, such extra work is *senseless waste*. From the point of view of the *individual German*, however, it is exceedingly important

> because *it saves him* from misery and frequently even from death by starvation. For that reason this extra work is also *more important to him* than the work at his job. (Eucken and Meyer 1948, 53, emphasis added)

Inefficient as it was at the collective level, this individual behavior gave spontaneous expression to the individual will to engage in free exchange. In Eucken and Meyer's view, a resort to bargaining, rational at the individual level, was the only means for survival. Eucken makes the same point in another article (Eucken 1948a, 43). In the ordoliberal reading, barter was indeed an inefficient system (see Levy and Peart 2008, 689), but Eucken and Meyer raised the issue not so much to condemn it, but rather as a signal indicating spontaneous pressures for free exchange. In short, barter was approached as an additional argument in favor of reform toward a market economy. So much is clearly attested in an incidental sentence—with its significant parenthesis—in Röpke: "the law of supply and demand (sometimes referred to as the 'black markets')" (1948a, 5). Those primitive markets were indeed the only markets where "prices are free" (Lutz 1948, 9).

Instead of pointing their fingers at individual behavior (laziness, for instance) or decrying the ill will of the individuals involved, as some foreign commentators did, Eucken and Meyer, Röpke, and Lutz brought the discussion back to the field of economic systems analysis. The ordoliberals found fault with the current economic system itself, which contravened the "invisible hand" mechanism: Friedrich Lutz (1949b, 122) emphasized that the "economy was 'organized' along lines such that the self-interest of individuals and firms was strictly opposed to the common interest." From 1933 to the time he was writing, the German economy embodied what Miksch (1947, 5) qualified as a "drastic contrast between private and public interests." Lutz (1949b, 122) concluded that "working at a regular job was the least profitable occupation, and mere survival necessitated breaches of the law." In the face of a chaotic economy, it had become indispensable for a great many workers to break the law: the planning system undermined its own foundations.

Thus, we have seen that the ordoliberals dismissed the causes that were commonly said to account for West Germany's low level of productivity. The ordoliberals leveled their critical fire at the economic order in place as the root of West Germany's economic depression; the role of prices in channeling rare resources toward their best use was entirely out of action. The circumstances that lay behind the lack of trade coordination were perceived as a return to primitive forms of organization such as black markets, barter, or personal production of the means of subsistence. But these primitive forms of trade were taken as proof of the potential of market forces waiting to be released.

## 5.2 DENAZIFYING THE ECONOMIC ORDER

The ordoliberals based their rejection of economic planning on the grounds that it constituted continuation of the economic order of the Third Reich. Thus, they accused the Allies of perpetuating a system "inherited from the Nazis" (Röpke 1948b, 1270). The ordoliberal *continuity* thesis rested on two arguments. First, there would be an administrative perpetuation of previous planning methods (i.e., a political *continuity*). Second, there would be propagation of a vicious circle linking price-fixing and repressed inflation (i.e., an economic *continuity*). On the basis of these analyses, the ordoliberals argued that authoritarian methods of economic control must be replaced by market mechanisms by virtue of which democratic aims could be set in the form of consumer democracy.

### 5.2.1 Political *Continuity*: Yet Another Army, an "Army of Officials"

The first major ordoliberal publication asserting the need for a new political order in postwar Germany was Röpke's *Die Deutsche Frage* (1945a), translated the following year for an English readership as *The German Question*. Simultaneously, Röpke (1946a) summarized his main argument in favor of turning West Germany into a democratic federation in *The New York Times*. Röpke's leading recommendation was to decentralize the German state in order to avoid a return to totalitarianism. Political centralization went hand in hand with economic centralization in Röpke's eyes, and this historical trend must be broken.

According to Ludwig Erhard, political and economic centralization pursued with the merging of the British and American zones as of January 1, 1947, was also a major cause of constraints on production. As the then chairman of the Special Department for Money and Credit (*Sonderstelle Geld und Kredit*) constituted in the Bizone, he made it clear that "without a centralized administration and its concomitant powers, for example, the deterioration of Germany's economy would never have assumed such pathological proportions" (Erhard 1947, 25). Erhard's statement was not only directed toward the Allied military administrations, but also against the SPD. Indeed from 1945 to 1947, the SPD dominated the Ministries of Economy in most *Länder* and were especially influential in the British zone (Domes and Wolffsohn 1979, 334).[10] Viktor Agartz commanded great influence at that time: first as the head of the central office for economics (*Zentralamt der Wirtschaft*) in the British zone and, from January 1947, Director of the Bizonal economic administrations. Agartz is a particularly good representative of a trend toward a more sophisticated—“scientifically designed” (Agartz 1946, 8)—planning method than that of war, notably promoting the growth and centralization of the administration.

Since the end of the war, Eucken (1946c, 9) had been decrying the same fact, which he considered an absurdity: German consumers were reckoning on “prices of 1936 which are still basically valid today,” and this absurd economic situation would remain the same, he said, “as long as the direction of economic life continues to be entrusted to a central bureau” (Eucken 1947, 408). Röpke highlighted this continuity in his article entitled “Economic Disease in Germany”: “very few people seem to realize that in all this the Allies are continuing the Nazi tradition,” they “are still drawing on the Nazi model” (1947b, 129). He concluded by summarizing what became the ordoliberal imperative in the early postwar years: “up to the present it does not seem to have occurred to anybody that, in the sphere of economic policy in Germany, ‘denazification’ is just as urgent as in any other sphere” (1947b). Röpke illustrated this similarity in strongly critical terms, attributing the official language of yesterday’s enemies to today’s liberators:

> Allies, when taking Germany into their custody, did not hesitate to adopt the whole formidable machinery of Nazi collectivism with all its principles and conceptions. Although the implications are so serious it is almost amusing to hear leading men among the occupation authorities talking in the jargon of the Nazi economy and using as a matter of course the German equivalents of “apportioning”, “directing”, “controlling” and “priorities.” (Röpke 1947b, 129)

In Röpke’s eyes, the irony is less to be found in the last part of the quotation than in the Allies having thought that the Nazi bureaucratic apparatus was indeed a “formidable mechanism” (1947b, 129). In a special number of the *Annals of the American Academy of Political and Social Science* on “Postwar Reconstruction in Western Germany,” Eucken and Meyer (1948) leveled their criticism at the “Evils of Planned Economy.” They expressed their concern in a language full of military terms, referring to the—German under

10. On the reasons and circumstances that led to the progressive weakening of the SPD—though hegemonic at the end of the war—in favor of the CDU, see James C. van Hook (2004, chap. 3).

the Allies'—administrative body in charge of planning as a "veritable *army* of officials," or "a whole *army* of officials" (Eucken and Meyer 1948, 53, emphasis added). As with Röpke, the stylistic formulas of Eucken and Meyer serve to highlight their continuity thesis.

Rhetorical in character, the ordoliberal narrative was not just an abstract fantasy. The failure of the Allies' economic planning, undertaken on the basis of prices and quotas fixed before the war by the Nazi command economy (*Zwangswirtschaft*), is now recognized by historians as the obstacle to recovery (Giersch et al. 1992, 19–23). From 1936 on, the Nazi economy had been based on Göring's four-year plan. This plan, which showed some affinity with the Soviet-type economy (Temin 1991), relied on major investments (25% of the overall amount) and drastic control of international trade (especially in raw materials), while both prices (including wages) and output were set in key sectors. However, private ownership of enterprises was admitted on a very large scale, so planning was based on—extremely imbalanced—contracting through agencies; that is, a chain of command that went back to the highest authorities of the Reich (Tooze 2006).

The Allies' pursuit of what van Hook (2004, 51) calls a "moderately socialist agenda" and Ptak (2009, 119) "comprehensive economic planning" soon impeded the coordination of productive forces. The Allies' planning authority mixed foreign officials with German administrative and political forces under the guidance of a bureaucratic military organization. If it differed from one zone to another, they jointly encouraged socialization and corporatism as ways to "democratize" the economy (Prowe 1985, 458). By promoting *Länder* control, planning nevertheless took on a *local* dimension. In 1946–1947, the Allied authorities of the military occupation set out to decentralize Germany's industries with the aim of crippling German industrial potential, in accordance with the Potsdam agreements (Schwartz 1957, 642–648; Shapiro 1962, 4). On the evidence of the disastrous experience of First World War reparations, the British and Americans came to favor dismantling as a punishment (Fisch 2004, 272). In the two reports he wrote for the Scientific Advisory Committee of the French zone, Eucken (1946a, 1946c) pointed out the presence of numerous cartels in the German economy, taking as an example the case of I. G. Farben.[11] Eucken's addressed this monopoly problem following a classic pattern of ordoliberal argumentation: beginning with administrative scientific

11. The world's biggest chemical cartel, deeply involved in the Nazi war effort and the Holocaust (see Hayes 1987), is paradigmatic of the American industrial policy in West Germany.

reports (1946a), through articles intended for the wider public (1947), to academic reformulations (1948a).

Thus, Eucken warned against monopoly power and the negative influence of cartels on the economy: a central issue for ordoliberals. On this basis, Eucken should have supported dismantling, and to some extent he did, but not in the way the Allies did.[12] The Allies' decision to put clamps on the German economy by dismantling a cartelized industry was seen by the ordoliberals not just as poorly implemented, but as blurring the most fundamental issue. Like Eucken (1947, 409), Röpke (1947b, 129) noted that the dismantling of the German industry was not the primary or essential reason for West Germany's productive weakness; he was "convinced that the trouble lies much deeper"; "what was needed was a thorough change of the *principles of economic life*" (1947a, 584, emphasis in original).

In his LSE series of lectures in London, Eucken (1951, 81) returned to the tenuous connection between productive capacity, inflation, and global coordination of the economy: "even existing possibilities of production were insufficiently exploited" at that time, because repressed "inflation had rendered the price system incapable of controlling the economy." Over and above the problem of monetary evaluation of goods and wages in a planned economy, there was the question of inflation. In the next section, I will address the indissoluble link that the ordoliberals (in particular Röpke and Eucken) aimed to establish between repressed inflation and planning.

### 5.2.2 Economic *Continuity*: The Planning–Inflation Vicious Circle

Inflation was nothing new in the postwar period for it had been a cause of concern since the end of the First World War (hyperinflation peaked in 1923). Indeed, surveying the post-conflict situation, Ludwig Erhard (1944, 5) was already warning that "the real problem lies in the elimination of superfluous purchasing power from the economy."[13] Inflation within the planned war economies constituted a well-known problem, proving,

12. The (mainly American) adverse prescriptions against the German economy—namely the Morgenthau plan and the JCS 1067 directive—gradually weakened from 1946: even if the US military authorities (OMGUS) went furthest in blaming the German people (see Solchany 1997, 29–32), Tobias Vogelgsang (2016, 162–163) demonstrated how, between the two competing views within the American position, the anti- vs. pro-industry factions, the latter soon prevailed over the former.

13. On the pre-1945 German debates and the road "from Nazi war finance to monetary overhang," see Keith Tribe (2001, 25–39).

according to Gunnar Myrdal's own admission, "one main defect of . . . national planning" (Myrdal 1951, 35).

Röpke offered an innovative study of this phenomenon, typical of a war economy, which he called "repressed" inflation (as opposed to "open" inflation).[14] For Röpke, this was nothing less than "the great economic malady of our times" (1947e, 242). Repressed inflation arises from a tension between two contradictory forces (which are not of the same nature), that of the supply and demand mechanism in search of a price adjustment, and that of fixing these prices by public authorities. Repressed inflation persists as long as the second force prevails over the first one:

> As a consequence of the war and of bad economic management after the war we observe almost everywhere a serious inflation in the sense of a great increase of the volume of money relative to a very slow recovery of production. . . . [Government] forbids the excess of demand to result in increased prices . . . there are now two sorts of pressure working against each other: the pressure of inflation driving prices, costs, and exchanges upward and the pressure of "control" which tries to neutralize that upward pressure. The question is how long the government can sit on the gusher of inflation, and what will happen as long as it is able to do so. (Röpke 1947e, 242)

If repressed inflation does not mean prices increase (as they remain fixed), in what sense is it inflation *at all*? In a situation of repressed inflation, demand exceeds supply in all markets. In short, the fundamental mechanism can be summarized as follows. In the attempt to achieve full employment, state planning results in an investment shock. The overabundant money supply, far in excess of the amount of available goods, sends prices rising. By definition, markets then cannot clear through prices (open inflation). An excess of purchasing power follows, and the authorities are forced to ration consumption, as with quotas or coupon allocations, in order to avoid

14. Röpke was the first to use the English expression "repressed inflation." Hitherto a variety of terms had been used for the phenomenon, including "suppressed," "retarded," or "frustrated" inflation (by Henry C. Simons or Frank Hahn). Before, Röpke used the German term "*zurückgestaute Inflation*" in commenting on the French economist Jacques Rueff's *L'Ordre Social* (Röpke 1947h). Albert O. Hirschman (1948, 599) observed that Röpke's concept "has since been widely used in the analysis of postwar monetary conditions," applying it himself to the situation in postwar Italy. Alongside Walter Eucken (1948c, 79), Gottfried Haberler (1948, 11) and Abba Lerner (1949, 195–196) were among the first to discuss the term, illustrating Röpke's contemporary impact on the field. Without any reference to Röpke's work, F. W. Paish's article (1953) and above all Harold K. Charlesworth's book (1956) provided the first systematic studies on the subject.

massive shortages. People cannot obtain goods; therefore, the extra money becomes worthless and prices fail to function as relevant signals: money is no longer desired. The extra money results in forced savings. The only way out of this sequence is to maintain the available amount of purchasing power by increasing the volume of goods to bridge the gap: the ordoliberals decried the lack of incentives—to invest, to work harder, etc.—to achieve a rise in output (Eucken 1948d, 900; Lutz 1948, 10; Röpke 1947e, 248).

Eucken (1948c, 79) adopted Röpke's analysis to describe (in retrospect) the situation in Germany since 1936. But in doing so, Eucken implicitly abandoned the war–inflation connection to concentrate on the link that he considered more fundamental, that between a planned economy and inflation: "because in one sphere, where a sufficient order is most needed, namely that of currency, the problem of order was inadequately solved, planning was called into being in every other sphere of economic life" (Eucken 1947, 409). War had this effect only insofar as a wartime economy was planned: the perpetuation of "measures of repression" (Röpke 1947e, 242). Röpke also stressed this inevitable interconnection:

> First, repressed inflation is the monetary counterpart of collectivism because *all experiences bear out the well-founded assumption that collectivism invariably leads to inflation*. Secondly, as we saw, collectivism is connected with *repressed* inflation because *the measures of repression constitute what we call collectivism*, i.e., an economic system which replaces the spontaneous order of the free market by an order which some name "conscious" while, in fact, it is based on command and the sanctions assuring obedience. (Röpke 1947e, 243, emphasis added)

Röpke was arguing in terms of the empirical evidence and logical tautology in this passage, delineating the interrelatedness between the two terms "repressed inflation" and "collectivism." Similarly, Eucken made of this connection the great lesson to be drawn from the economic experience of the Third Reich: planning feeds on monetary surplus. This reading was by no means prevalent at the time. Shortly after, two prominent American economists were still claiming that German inflation was caused "wholly and exclusively by two destructive wars which left the economy in monetary chaos" (Hansen and Musgrave 1951, 39).

What worried Eucken was not so much that inflation was a consequence of planning but rather the reverse, that inflation led to planning: "Not only did the inflation destroy the price system and hence all free types of economic order, not only did *they engender or decisively foster the tendency to central planning*, but they were also *a precondition* of the existence of central planning" (Eucken 1951, 69, emphasis added). This was in line with Röpke's earlier statement that "collectivism and inflation became intertwined: it was inflation which made possible the waste and disorder of collectivism which made it possible to have inflation without turn-away prices, wages, and exchange rates" (1947b, 130). Röpke made the correlation clear, stressing the compensatory effect that came into play between the two phenomena, one coming to the aid of the other and vice-versa. It seemed to him that "collectivism serves just as well for an attempt to mitigate the open harms of inflation as inflation serves for an attempt to mitigate the open harms of collectivism" (Röpke 1947e, 244).[15] Collectivism developed to curb inflation and may justify its existence with this end; this led Röpke (1947f, 115) to the conclusion that "defence of controls rests on the assumption of inflation." The greater circulation of money, to some extent, counterbalances disturbances in the supply of certain goods. To some extent, the overabundant money supply fed an ignis fatuus of prosperity and success.

If the effects on production were disastrous, ordoliberal criticism of this type of inflation eventually extended to issues of social justice and economic democracy:

> Under collectivism, it is no longer true that money embodies the liberty of choice and the freedom to buy under conditions equal to all. Collectivist money means that money is next to worthless unless it is accompanied with rights and privileges accorded by the political authority. If the rationing is *equal* for all it is money *plus* ration coupons which decide its real value. If the rationing is *differentiated* according to a system of needs and merits defined by the government it is money *plus* ration coupons *plus* the social and political position of the owner which determines its ultimate value. (Röpke 1947e, 245, emphasis in original)

In a word, according to Röpke (1947e, 246), "under collectivism, money begins to smell." The value of money is no longer intrinsically guaranteed, but quite other factors, like the status or position of the person holding it, become decisive in the purchase of goods and services. From an ordoliberal viewpoint, such a situation favored personalism and authoritarian control over democratic consumer values. As a consequence, the ordoliberals put aside their original interwar mistrust of parliamentary democracy in favor of an approach that would prove of great significance in the subsequent West German context: democracy should be achieved first and foremost in

15. Or, in Eucken's (1951, 74) words, "planned economy . . . correlates with inflation."

the economic sphere; hence, achievement of a democratic regime depended above all on the advent of sovereign consumers.

### 5.2.3 Toward a Consumer Democracy?

Through their analysis of repressed inflation, Röpke and the ordoliberals insisted on the monetary order as one central channel for expression of individual decisions in the market economy. This channel was then obstructed by administrative control of the economy. Back in the interwar period, Röpke (1942d, 253) had already used the metaphor of money as a "ballot-paper" embodying a "*plébiscite de tous les jours*" (in original French) through buying and selling decisions.[16] In his opinion, therefore, the true model of democracy is not to be found in the political sphere but in the economic domain. Indeed, as each "ballot-paper" ensured proportional representation of every person, including minorities, Röpke (1942b, 138) claimed that "market democracy . . . surpasses the most perfect political democracy." In the same vein, Böhm emphasized that the creation of market prices would be tantamount to a "*voting* process, taking place, by the day, hour and even minute"; hence he called the free market economy "the *most perfect expression of mass democracy*; its degree of precision is impossible to reproduce within *political* life"(Böhm 1947, 127–128, emphasis in original).[17]

In short, from an ordoliberal perspective, the market economy was not only the best expression of political democracy, nor just its most natural complement, but more essentially its main vector and safeguard. The market economy was the first step in a political model in accordance with what the ordoliberals saw to be the core of Western values, as opposed to the communist model that East Germany saw setting in. On this basis, should it be concluded that the ordoliberals pursued a model of "economic democracy?" In Chapter 1 we saw that the ordoliberals had leveled their critical fire at the parliamentary democracy of the interwar period, a political system that fueled economic concentration and eventually saw Hitler appointed Chancellor. Was there a new turn in the ordoliberals' appreciation of (economic) democracy after 1945?

16. Röpke was not the first to use the metaphor associating money with ballot-papers: Mises (1922) is probably responsible for giving wider circulation to this expression coined by the American economist Frank A. Fetter at the beginning of the twentieth century (Persky 1993, 185).

17. Much later, Böhm (1961, 30) continued to insist on the daily plebiscite embodied by consumer choices through the competitive price mechanism.

On the one hand, the ordoliberals were convinced that a lot of improvement could—and needed to—be made within capitalist firms in terms of greater "self-governance of the workforce," better working conditions, and indeed larger shares in the firms' profits (Rüstow 1951, 171). On the other hand, they were staunchly opposed to economic democracy understood as "equal participation of workers in all the decisions taken by firms, cartels, chambers of commerce or industry" (Böhm 1954, 153; see also Rüstow 1951, 171). According to the ordoliberals, this desire for "absolute equality between capital and labour" (Böhm 1954, 156) within managerial representation was the Trojan horse of neo-mercantilism—a form of governance that could only work to the detriment of consumers. In this respect, the ordoliberals were opposed to a cornerstone of what today we call *Rhine capitalism*: consensual co-management within the firm. In contrast to "economic democracy" as understood from the postwar period to the present day, it seems more appropriate to use Röpke's term and to speak of "consumer democracy" to describe the political-economic model the ordoliberals envisaged. Essentially, the ordoliberals located the true site for individual sovereignty not in individuals' identity as producers (whether managers or workers), but in their consumer identity.

From the ordoliberal standpoint, the competitive order alone—neither the interventionist welfare state nor authoritarian planning—was the adequate framework for the advent of the consumer democracy they envisaged. Eucken (1946b) and Miksch (1948) insisted on the incompatibility between socialism (broadly understood) and the values of liberal democracy. In other words, an incompatibility of socialism with what Miksch (1948, 332) called "the foundations of Western Christian culture" and, in particular, with the aspiration to individual freedom (see also Böhm 1954, 159). Indeed, Miksch claimed that Western values were in harmony with the results of a competitive market economy:

> The high value of internal coordination [the competitive order] is based on the fact that it combines maximum economic efficiency with maximum freedom and personal autonomy. The *economic sovereignty of consumers makes internal coordination the economic counterpart of political democracy.* (Miksch 1948, 332, emphasis in original)

In this text, Miksch emphasized the similarity and complementarity between what he called the "internal coordination" (the free market) of the economy and political democracy (see also Miksch 1950a). One of their main common points was rejection of every kind of illegitimate position of power. Again, Röpke had already stressed this crucial bond between the political and economic orders. However, to conclude that because of this connection the ordoliberals assimilated both orders by indicating that market was, ultimately, "only a political order" (Joerges 2006, 249) seems overstated. Actually, the ordoliberals did emphasize the specificity of each of these two spheres, ruling out reduction of the former (the economic order) to the latter (the political order). In any case, Röpke made a point of underlining the incongruity of reasoning in terms of completely different logics in two interdependent spheres:

> There always exists a definite, more or less fixed relationship between a political and an economic system which makes it impossible to combine just any political system with just any economic system, and vice versa. . . . In the long run economic dictatorship can as little exclude political and intellectual control as, conversely, political and intellectual dictatorship can exclude economic control. It is hardly forgivable naïveté to believe that a state can be all powerful in the economic sphere without also being autocratic in the political and intellectual domain and vice versa. (Röpke 1942c, 87–90)

The ordoliberals understood democracy not so much as the sovereignty of voting citizens who express themselves through representative bodies. Rather, they understood it in terms of certain values of the open society where, within a set of common constraints, everyone is free to pursue the objectives they have individually set themselves, in particular through their purchasing decisions on the market. Röpke did not speak directly of sovereign consumers, but of a "consumer democracy" in which the general interest would be achieved when the interest of all consumers—for each individual is a consumer—would prevail over the private interests of producers. Consumer sovereignty proved pivotal in the justification of Erhard's social market economy and its ability to shape a desirable future society in the postwar years (see Olsen 2018, chap. 3).[18]

In final analysis, everything turned out as if the ordoliberals had shifted the exercise of popular sovereignty from the political to the economic sphere. Accordingly, Miksch (1947, 5) claimed that providing West Germany with a market economy was a vital democratic "public task" (*öffentliche Aufgabe*). Thus, sovereignty no longer existed so much

18. The English-born economist William H. Hutt is attributed with the first occurrence of the concept of "consumer sovereignty." In the same years, the Austrian Hayek and the ordoliberal Röpke came up with comparable formulations. On Hutt's concept and its central place in the Anglo-Saxon context of the LSE, see Maxime Desmarais-Tremblay (2020).

through representativeness, or the impact of the popular will on political decisions—because the ordoliberals saw the genesis of norms lying with an elite of experts (Wörsdörfer 2012a)—but went directly through the capacity for choice in the market: hence the requirement that it should function flawlessly. From an ordoliberal point of view, establishment of this economic democracy was the condition not only necessary, but to some extent sufficient, for the development of a (future) political democracy in West Germany.

## 5.3 THE 1948 REFORMS IN THE EARLY COLD WAR CONTEXT

Having reconstructed the ordoliberal diagnosis of and discussion on the functioning of the postwar economic order in West Germany, this last section investigates the content and context of the 1948 reforms. In determining price liberalization in particular, ordoliberal expertise was key. Just as critical was the ordoliberals' fierce defense of the 1948 reforms in the early Cold War context, which they ensured by championing the German "economic miracle."

### 5.3.1 Ordoliberal Expertise

Printed in the United States with top-secret security, the Deutsche Mark (DM) was brought in to replace the Reichsmark (RM) in the early hours of June 21, 1948. Initially conceived as a new currency for all of Germany, it came up against the misgivings of the Soviet authorities, so the new currency was restricted to West Germany. The priority was to reduce the quantity of money drastically by nullifying public and private debts, together with (forced) savings. Monetary reform had been in the cards for a long time, and the Americans worked on the details at considerable length on the basis of the Colm-Dodge-Goldsmith Plan of 1946.[19]

The surprise came some days later, on June 24, when Erhard proclaimed the end of the controlled economy in the journal of the Frankfurt

19. For a detailed explanation of the monetary reform package, see Herbert Giersch et al. (1992, 36–38). In view of the coming reform, the *Bank Deutscher Länder*—the forerunner of the *Deutsche Bundesbank*—had been established on March 1, 1948, to take on monopoly of issue. For a history of the independence of West Germany's Central Bank, see Bibow (2009).

administration, without waiting for Allied approval and, indeed, against the advice of the Anglo-American counselors.[20] Erhard's reform won the day, eliminating controls for four hundred products and slackening the measures on wages. In the autumn of 1948, price controls were lifted on other basic products (fruits, vegetables, coffee, tea, etc.), but also on manufactured goods and services such as insurance (see table IV in Mendershausen 1949, 664). In an address delivered before the Economic Council (*Wirtschaftsrat des Vereinigten Wirtschaftsgebietes*) in Frankfurt on April 21, 1948, Erhard made the case for his policies: monetary reform alone would not cure the ills of West Germany's economy. Price-fixing, "as the pioneer of a controlled economy," was not to survive the reform: "our task is not to dilute the price freeze, but to get rid of it altogether" (Erhard 1948, 29).

When they wrote their article, Eucken and Meyer (1948) were aware that a monetary and fiscal reform was imminent, but they did not know all the details. Their worries were about the other measures that were to accompany the monetary reform:

> The first and most important requisite for a reconstruction of the German economy is the introduction of a yardstick for economic calculations. . . . If an important part of the prices remains at a fixed level, the interaction of misorientation of the productive forces, formation of a new surplus of money, appearance of a black market, and the necessity of barter will begin again. (Eucken and Meyer 1948, 61; see also Böhm 1947, 134)

Given the hardships experienced by the population, in particular after the terrible winter of 1946–1947 (Solchany 2003, 362), the Allies and German authorities were faced with a choice: either enhance centralization and planning techniques or venture upon a market economy. "The opinion that a centrally planned economy is superior to a free market economy is now open to very serious doubts" according to Alfred Müller-Armack (1947, 20), an economist and politician who rallied to the ordoliberals precepts in the postwar period and coined the expression "Social Market Economy" (*Soziale Marktwirtschaft*). Like the ordoliberals, Müller-Armack now came firmly down in favor of a market economy, stressing that West Germany "shall inevitably have to take steps towards market freedom" (1947, 20).[21]

20. This episode is closely analyzed in the literature (Broyer 2003b, 210; Carlin 1996, 464; Nicholls 1994, 215–218; Uterwedde 2009, 25).

21. Here the ordoliberals were unanimous, urging a shock therapy, which the authorities found premature at the time. What they called for was the simultaneous liberalization of prices and wages (Röpke 1947e, 251). We nevertheless find here an

In a similar vein Röpke wrote that "the paralysis cannot be overcome within the framework of the present collectivist system" (Röpke 1948a, 5).

A general end to price controls nevertheless "met with incomprehension" (Glossner 2010, 128) and was seen as potentially dangerous by both political leaders (Stolper and Roskamp 1979, 384) and the public (Hoppe 1991, 79). But Erhard found support in the analyses by Eucken and Miksch. From October 1947, the Special Commission (*Sonderstelle Geld und Kredit*) worked specifically on future reforms. The commission member responsible for price and wage policy, Leonhard Miksch, held a position of primary importance for the support of the ordoliberal recommendations (Mierzejewski 2004, 65–67). Together with Erhard, Miksch drafted the liberalization measures. Ludwig Erhard's rallying to the ordoliberal precepts and to the social market economy owed much to personal contact with Eucken and Miksch as well as, to a lesser extent, to Röpke.[22] In fact, both Eucken and Miksch—alongside Böhm, Lampe, and Müller-Armack—belonged to the Scientific Advisory Committee (*Wissenschaftlicher Beirat*) of the Bizone economic administration, of which Erhard had been director from March 2, 1948. Membership in the committee was designed to maintain a balanced representation of the various ideological positions,[23] but the liberal majority argued in favor of price liberalization and an end to administrative control over raw materials. It wished to promote market competition and was wary of the risk of concentrations while watching out for the possibility of abuse.

The committee's first report therefore showed a clear orientation in the direction of liberalization:

> The currency reform only makes sense if it is accompanied by a fundamental change from previous *dirigisme*. It would be worthless and even dangerous if it

example of contrasting positions among German liberals, with Röpke, Eucken, and Miksch pressing for it in the face of Müller-Armack's prudence (see Nicholls 1994, 184, 203, 206, 259).

22. Erhard and especially Konrad Adenauer, elected federal chancellor in 1949, regularly called on his expertise. On the—limited—influence of Röpke on Erhard, see Mierzejewski (2006). In addition to these contacts, the political context also played a crucial role: as Patricia Commun (2003, 193) explains, the two reforms of June 1948 were "made possible by the Soviet walkout, abandoning the quadripartite government on 6 March 1948."

23. Erhard took charge of this committee, which he had not set up himself. For a list of the original twenty-three members of the Scientific Committee—professors mainly of economics (seventeen), but also of law (three), political science (two), and philosophy (one)—as well as their stance in favor of liberalism (accounting for three-quarters) or planning, see Sylvain Broyer (2003b, 208).

> were introduced merely as an isolated, technical operation. Effective demand will be restricted as a result of the currency reform so that the complete control of consumption and economic activity will be superfluous. ("Measures for Controlling Consumption" 1979, 449)

The tendency to favor market solutions was not shared among all the members of the Committee, however. A minority of the Committee opposed such recommendations: "to try to move in this direction [economic equilibrium] through a system of free market prices is impractical" ("Measures for Controlling Consumption" 1979, 452). This minority, consisting of G. Keiser, G. Weisser, K. Schiller, and W. Kromphardt, especially feared that liberalization would cause a major inflation. In stark contrast with ordoliberals claims, they argued in favor of a mixed economy, which was to pursue a full-employment policy. Consistent with the Marshall Plan which had just been implemented, Weisser and Schiller wanted to improve the techniques of planning. To do so, Kromphardt, following his market division theory (*Marktspaltung*), offered to legalize black markets, with the aim of extending the official allocation management system (coupons, etc.) to these—formerly—unofficial markets. Kromphardt thought his solution would "reduce the transaction costs and widen bottlenecks in the administrated core of the economy" (Giersch et al. 1992, 35).[24]

The arguments developed by the minority were rooted in the program of the SPD, which was looking for a kind of synthesis between Marxist historical grammar and Keynesian-type of manning the economy, but without conceiving a clear theoretical picture of these claims (Abelshauser 1986, 90). In any case, the social-democrat views expressed by the minority of the Committee were practically disregarded in the reform.

### 5.3.2 Championing the "Economic Miracle"

The reforms of 1948 proved, as the ordoliberals were eager to stress, "a tremendous success" (Lutz 1949b, 122; see also Eucken 1948d, 900; Röpke 1950a, 339). The monetary reform led to a drastic reduction in the quantity of money in circulation. In short, "money became scarce" (Eucken 1951, 69), and, indeed, the money supply had been reduced by about 90%. Overall, the monetary reform reintroduced the essential conditions for a competitive economic order as the ordoliberals conceived it:

24. On the overall debates inside the *Wissenschaftlicher Beirat*, see Anthony J. Nicholls (1994, chap. 9).

> The reform restored an adequate unit of account, allowed the economy to be controlled by prices and gave rise to an economic order that provided a framework for the organization of a large-scale division of labour. (Eucken 1951, 69)

In this context, consumer choices had regained their weight and influence on the production process through the free price mechanism. This situation offered only advantages according to Eucken. When the money in circulation was scarce, firms and households alike would be paying more attention to product quality. He also noted that, after the reforms, absenteeism at work decreased, productivity increased, and real production costs fell. As a result, "under the new conditions created by monetary reform and the partial return to a free market, production has increased rapidly" (Eucken 1951, 69).

The enthusiasm shown by Eucken and Lutz was shared by Erhard and Röpke. The former stressed the shift of plan-making capacity from the central authorities to economic agents: "it seems to me that these last eight to ten weeks since the Currency Reform has witnessed the *drawing up of more plans* i.e., more premeditation and provision for the future than all the years of a regimented economy" (Erhard 1948, 35–36, emphasis added). Röpke, on the other hand, once again emphasized the complementarity of the two reforms and the indispensability of price liberalization. Monetary reform alone would not solve Germany's economic problems, as he made clear in his influential 1950 report *Ist die deutsche Wirtschaftspolitik richtig?* (*Is the German Economic Policy the Right One?*) commissioned by Chancellor Adenauer: "it is an incomprehensible distortion of the true facts and a failure to recognize intrinsic economic implications if one depicts the currency reform as being more important or as the solely effective part of the overall reform" (Röpke 1950b, 41).

All this seems to show that, if the ordoliberals were so keen to defend the reforms, it is because a return to administrated prices appeared a very real threat. In the seven months following the reforms, the prices of agricultural products increased by 25%, and of manufactured goods by 35% (Klopstock 1949, 287).[25] And, between late 1948 and early 1949, macroeconomic stability was threatened by steadily increasing prices. The reforms soon came under attack by American and British experts and researchers, also from the point of view of social justice and of the ills of increasing inequality (Hutchison 1979, 436). Faced with these hardships, the trade

25. Jacques Rueff (1949, 105–106) had also noted the inevitable inflationary pressure following price liberalization which he had himself been advocating for France since 1947.

unions, supported by part of the politicians, were pressing for the reintroduction of price controls (Bignon 2007, 248). In March 1949, Horst Mendershausen (1949, 658)—an economist who served with the US Military Government of Germany in the capacity of Assistant Chief of Price Control from 1947 to 1948—considered a return to price control as very likely, but nothing was to come of it.

Thus, the reform was not an all-around success, and Germany's "economic miracle" (*Wirtschaftswunder*) would only come effectively in the mid-1950s, driven by external factors.[26] As historian Jean Solchany (2003, 364) pointed out, not all the effects of this liberalization were beneficial: the cost of living remained high, as did unemployment (about 10% of the active population), leading to strikes in 1950. The inflow of more than 12 million refugees beginning in 1945 should also be taken into account (Commun 2004, 23). Finally, the substantial aid granted by the Marshall Plan (initiated in 1947) made a significant contribution (Buchheim 1993; Wolf 1993, 30) and was, according to some observers (Borchardt 1991, 92; Braun 1990, 154), the fundamental factor in West Germany's economic recovery.

The Berlin blockade began on June 22, 1948, right between the dates of the West German reforms, making explicit, if there were indeed any need, the conflicting foreign interests at work on German soil. While the fate of Germany was indeed crucial to political and economic stability in Europe (Dijk 2004, 78; Wala 2004, 73), the German Federal Republic was to become a model of growth that could stand up to the rise of European communism (Allen 1989, 270). But to conclude that Germany found itself being used as an experiment for rival economic policies—as Grenier and Orléan (2007) did—goes too far. The West Germans were not merely passive subjects but also key actors in the Cold War. In this respect, we saw how isolated the ordoliberals were at that time in their favoring market liberalism against any kind of planning, a position which Allied authorities (Anglo-American and French), but also many political parties (foremost the SPD), were still very distant from.

26. This chapter gives little room to diverse appraisals of the effective causes of the "economic miracle." Werner Abelshauser (1975) was among the first to cast doubt on this excessively well-disposed retrospective view toward liberal action, attributing no real importance to the economic policies of the time. The literature wavers between these two positions. With great good sense, Jean Solchany (2003, 366–370) calls for a more nuanced explanation (see also Plumpe 2004, 299–300). He considers the combined effect of government policy and the German industrial structure little affected (Hook 2004, 4–5) as well as a favorable international context, attested by the recovery of the European countries as a whole. If the word "miracle" was used, it was also because the renewed growth came later but more strikingly than in the other countries.

As a matter of fact, the ordoliberals' publications, like those by Röpke (1947d, 1947g) and Eucken (1948d, 901), as well as a twenty-page essay for the *International Finance Section* of Princeton University by Lutz (1948, 3, 7, 11), were linking the success of the Marshall Plan with the rise of liberal economies. Röpke insisted on the importance of the issue as a matter of life or death: "if the West fails in Western Germany it will fail everywhere" (1948a, 31). Worried about communist subversion of West Germany, the ordoliberals tried to clarify the *continuity* between the Nazis and the Allies in order to stop any drift toward communism.

## 5.4 CONCLUSION: ENTERING THE ECONOMIC POLICY BATTLEFIELD

Although Germany's productive capacity remained considerable after the Second World War, the population was utterly indigent. In their diagnosis, the ordoliberals took this paradox as evidence that the economy was "highly pathological," eventually leading to "the complete dissolution of the national economy" (Röpke 1947e, 246–247): the Allies were perpetuating a planning system much like that of the Third Reich. To win on the economic policy battlefield, the ordoliberals' best defense was a direct attack: they rejected economic planning on the ground that it was a continuation of the Third Reich's economic order. Thus, they accused the Allies of perpetuating a system inherited from the Nazis. The ordoliberals presented this *continuity* thesis along two different lines. First, there was a *political* continuity: an administrative perpetuation of previous methods of planning. Second, there was an *economic* continuity, which became visible in the conjunction between price fixing and (repressed) inflation. The ordoliberals constructed that continuity to argue that planning should end and be replaced by a certain form of market liberalism. True denazification could only be achieved once its method of coordinating the economy was rejected.

Two main conclusions can be drawn from our presentation of the continuity thesis. First, drawing lessons from the economic experience of the Third Reich, the ordoliberals acquired the epistemological and theoretical resources that enabled them to address institutional change in Germany politically. In other words, the ordoliberals appeared particularly well prepared and theoretically equipped to play their part on the economic policy battlefields of the seminal postwar years in West Germany precisely because they were able to take advantage, within a radically different historical context, of capital they acquired under Nazism (as Michel Foucault conjectured).[27] If, however, ordoliberals discussed the problem of inflation even before 1933, it was the experience of Nazi Germany that provided them with a full picture of the mechanism linking the phenomenon of open and repressed inflation to the structure of the economic order and the functioning of the economic process.

Second, the continuity thesis brings out the mainly political nature of the struggle against inflation. As the ordoliberals saw it, inflation fostered by the reproduction of the planned economy imposed by the Allies came on top of the inflation inherited from the Third Reich and war years. Over and above the distortions in economic calculation and distribution that the ordoliberals stressed (Helmut 2001, 337), they considered inflation fundamentally dangerous—politically speaking—because it paved the way to planning, with a potential assault on the competitive economic order. In the light of this observation, it was expedient to introduce a new currency (monetary reform) but at the same time free prices (*Leitsätzegesetz*), so that the latter could reflect needs and scarcity. Retrospectively, monetary reform and price liberalization appear as an obvious set of economic policies: however, the choice to bring in *both of them together* in 1948 was by no means self-evident. Thus, Erhard's initiative to concomitantly adopt the reforms based on the ordoliberals' prescriptions helped them to take the credit—at least symbolically—for an economic miracle linked to the political birth of the Federal Republic of Germany. According to Böhm (1954, 167), the Germans were then entering a new era, leaving behind their old pattern of "a people which has never really liked competition, and which has been used to regard . . . every concentration as a growth of the social ethos." Well aware of this historical turning point, Jürgen Habermas (1971, 32–33) later stressed, in a disillusioned tone of amusement, that by becoming "one of the six or seven most liberal countries" in the postwar world, Federal Germany "for the first time in centuries, became a contemporary of Western Europe."

The continuity thesis enables us to specify the interactions of ordoliberal ideas on the ideological battlefield of the early Cold War. The ordoliberal crusade for market liberalism was also intended as a crusade against communism. The real impact of ordoliberal ideas should be sought in their capacity to shape the agenda of the West German state and, more in general, to exert considerable influence on the postwar ideological context: West Germany's "leap into cold water," which the ordoliberals urged and celebrated, also contributed, on a much wider scale, to the West–East leap into the Cold War.

27. In an ironic turn of events, ordoliberal ideas themselves were the object of a (failed) campaign to show that the Nazis were "sympathetic to the ordoliberal concept of competition" during what Ekkehard A. Köhler and Daniel Nientiedt (2017, 625) called the "Muthesius controversy" of the fifties.

# Conclusion

## *Ordoliberalism, from Crystallization to Ossification*

In July 1949, all the ordoliberals took part in the second meeting of the Mont Pèlerin Society in Seelisberg, Switzerland. Miksch reported in his diary a conversation he had with the economist L. Albert Hahn, a German émigré who had been teaching at the New School for Social Research in New York. On the sidelines of the conference, Hahn had tried to convince the ordoliberals of the gigantic gap that would separate their analysis from Anglo-Saxon economics—a gap widened by the isolation caused by the Nazi regime and the war. Thus, Hahn urged the ordoliberals to concentrate exclusively on reading the international literature for a while and stop writing altogether.

A few days after this discussion, and as the Seelisberg conference was coming to an end, Miksch recognized that there was indeed a huge gap, but in the opposite sense to what Hahn had meant:

> Just as myself, Eucken had the impression that we could not learn as much from abroad as Hahn thought. The reasoning in morphological order elements developed by the Freiburg School is missing elsewhere. This morphological system is greatly superior. It was a good thing we did not speak better English, otherwise we would have reasoned them into the ground. (from Miksch's 1949 diary, translated and reproduced in Kolev et al. 2020, 459)

*A Political Economy of Power.* Raphaël Fèvre, Oxford University Press. © Oxford University Press 2021.
DOI: 10.1093/oso/9780197607800.003.0007

In retrospect, the ordoliberals' sheer overconfidence may seem almost ludicrous. But from their viewpoint, did not they have good reasons to be satisfied? Had they not offered the arguments that convinced Erhard to embark on the price liberalization reform less than a year earlier, thus initiating among Western countries the fastest transition from war planning to (free) market economy? In any case, the Seelisberg episode illustrates the confidence and sense of superiority the ordoliberals derived from their own views and concepts, as well as their relative lack of interest in the then flourishing US economic literature.

What piques our historical curiosity about the ordoliberal agenda that would continue to prevail in the Northern countries of Europe until our own days can perhaps best be captured in the following paradox: it was at the very moment when the ordoliberals were moving toward an irrevocable divorce from the scientific canons of postwar economics that they were imposing their domination over the praxis of economic policy in West Germany. The historical analysis presented in this book may suggest some elements accounting for this apparent contradiction.

When the term "*ordoliberalismus*" was coined in 1950, the project drawn up by Eucken, Röpke, and others stood at a tipping point. Ordoliberal political economy emerged as a questioning of the capitalist system in the years of interwar crisis, eventually shaping the economic policy decisions of the newly born German Federal state in the aftermath of the Second World War. Being to some extent absorbed within Ludwig Erhard's political discourse and partly applied in the name of the "Social Market Economy" (*Soziale Marktwirtschaft*), the seminal ideas of the ordoliberal *political economy of power* lost their specificity.

This book has retraced the constitution of German ordoliberalism from the perspective of this tipping point. To this end, it has shed light on the intellectual foundations of the ordoliberal political economy in all its dimensions—historical, epistemological, theoretical, and, indeed, political.

The book's emphasis on the unity of ordoliberalism may have left some readers dissatisfied. One might argue, for instance, that Walter Eucken and Wilhelm Röpke differed on several issues, or that Franz Böhm's legal approach belonged to a rather different field of inquiry than that of economics; it is also possible to object that some of the younger ordoliberals, like Fredrich Lutz, were inspired by Anglo-Saxon methods and approaches to economics. These are, indeed, all points worthy of consideration. Yet over and above the particular characteristics that distinguish each and every single author, ordoliberalism was perceived by its exponents as a coherent doctrine and was generally received as such. Therefore, rather than trying to establish distinctions, in this book we have tried to reconstruct the set of ideas, problems, and solution emerging from what remained basically a shared project.

What endowed the ordoliberal agenda with a singularity all of its own was the central importance it attributed to the issue of power. Obviously, there had been some precedents: a number of authors—such as Marx, Weber, or Keynes—had brilliantly recognized that power relations were an essential dimension of the functioning of modern capitalist society. However, the ordoliberals made of the manifestations of power in the social sphere the central issue that bridged the entire scope of their reflections, underpinning the common elements and relative coherence in the four dimensions of their political economy. In short, the ordoliberals' preoccupation with power issues worked as a strong binding element for their common project.

Showing that ordoliberalism can be interpreted as a political economy of power, however, does not mean that it did actually deal with the issue of power in a comprehensive and exhaustive way. Indeed, the ordoliberals paid little attention to some issues that seem indispensable to anyone wishing to analyze the social impact of economic and political power, such as (among other) the wealth–power nexus or the role of the financial market in the power relations of the real economy. Despite these puzzling omissions, the political economy of power forged by the ordoliberals proved a central resource for the model of society adopted by West Germany—a project that contemporary Germany continues to claim as the distinctive basis of its economic discourse. However, the persisting relevance of ordoliberalism on the political scene has not been accompanied by a capacity to take deep roots in the postwar academic milieu. In short, it proved a political hit but an academic flop—a curious imbalance that might to some extent be explained by the definition of ordoliberalism that this book has provided.

At the center of the ordoliberal discourse stood this—simply formulated but immense—challenge: How was the modern industrialized economy to be endowed with an efficient and yet humane order? This crucial issue dominated ordoliberal deliberations throughout the nearly twenty years of major disorders examined in this book. On the basis of historical and epistemological, as well as theoretical considerations, the ordoliberals constructed their model of a competitive order secured by strong public authorities in order to control unrest and abuses of power within civil society. In doing so, the ordoliberals addressed an issue which is at the heart of political theory; namely, the complex relation between power and social order.

Eventually, ordoliberalism contributed to the development of a form of economic rationale for the (West German) state, presenting itself as architect of an overall vision of society from the perspective of its economic performance. Yet in many respects, the way the ordoliberals framed their main questions and answers was no longer within the recognized arena of mid-twentieth century economics. Indeed, the scope of the ordoliberal political economy broke away from later developments of economics as a technique, as a discipline oriented toward the construction of formalized micro- and macroeconomic models that use statistical estimates to (in)validate their hypotheses. In other words, in developing a political economy of power, the ordoliberals adopted an approach that clashed with the scientific canons then taking shape in the postwar period.

As economics entered the second half of the twentieth century, the gap between ordoliberalism and mainstream economics grew increasingly wider. The international shift in the way of conceiving economics—and no longer political economy—was probably the main reason for the decline of the ordoliberal scientific agenda. Indeed, while power considerations were constitutive of the early discourse of modern political economy (Kurz 2018; Schabas 2009), power had been increasingly relegated to the margins of the legitimate arena of economic analysis throughout the twentieth century. And indeed mainstream economics would be characterized by "a strange lack of power considerations" (Rothschild 1971, 7), applying a very narrow conception of economic power and reflecting its lack of interest in the multidimensionality of this plural concept (Klein 1980; Monvoisin and Rochon 2007; Ozanne 2016).

Nevertheless, this process was neither uniform nor absolute, as has been argued throughout this book. Indeed, looking back to the interwar period one can see how central the issue of economic power was to ordoliberal economic thought—ironically enough Keynes, on the opposite front, to some extent shared the same agenda (Fèvre 2018a). The combined effect of the interwar crisis of liberalism and the rise of authoritarian regimes caused the ordoliberals to enlarge their conception of economic power by taking in the overall political and juridical structure of the economy. Power is by definition an issue which goes beyond the scope of disciplinary fields; consequently, the ordoliberals were bound to extend political economy to history, law, philosophy of science, political philosophy, and sociology. What was later termed "economics imperialism" (Radnitzky and Bernholz 1987; Mäki et al. 2018) from the 1960s onward took shape against the disciplinary openness to other disciplines that was part of the ordoliberals' original identity.

Fundamentally, the ordoliberal contributions were deeply alien from the disciplinary tools and canons of the "formalist" turn economics went through in the mid-twentieth century (Ward 1972; Rutherford and Morgan 1998; Blaug 2003). And, indeed, the ordoliberal attempt to forge a realistic approach to economic theory could not be easily reconciled with the implicit methodology—positivist and falsificationist—of the profession epitomized by Milton Friedman's influential *Essay in Positive Economics* (1953), to mention just one crucial example. This new form of economic theory embraced the unrealism of hypotheses, building its central structure around the behavior of self-interested but clairvoyant individuals engaged in instantaneous trade on perfectly competitive markets tending toward equilibrium. Once again, economic theory relegated power issues to the background of accessory situations, just as the first marginalists had at the turn of the last century (Dockès 1999, 2). Soon enough, most West German economists embraced econometrics and the tools of the neoclassical synthesis. If the University of Freiburg remained an ordoliberal citadel, as did a few other places, by the 1960s, mainstream economics had become largely dominant in federal Germany, both in empirically oriented economics departments and in research institutes (Hesse 2012, 87–88; Grimmer-Solem 2014, 91–92; Düppe 2020, 320–326).

As the years went by, the economic discipline went through a series of major changes which extend far beyond the scope of this book. One transformation that is highly relevant to the story narrated here is the so-called counter-revolution that took place between the late seventies and the early eighties. Monetarism and the New Classical Macroeconomics—championed respectively by Milton Friedman and Robert L. Lucas—undertook a crusade against any remaining form of Keynesianism (Johnson 1971; Tobin 1981; Leeson 2001; Laidler 2015; Wren-Lewis 2016). Thus, these years marked a "remarkable and dramatic change in attitudes toward the role of the state in economic activity" (Backhouse 2005, 355). Through new concepts and theories (e.g., the natural rate of unemployment, rational choice theory, adaptive and rational expectations, real cycles), mainstream economics renewed the prescriptions of laissez-faire liberalism by other means. Politically speaking, it drove the authorities to reduce income taxes and cut public spending, to privatize industries and public services, and to deregulate the legal framework of the commercial and financial sectors.

Voices were periodically raised against the narrow technical development of mainstream economics combined with its overt anti-state agenda. The controversy waxed strong again during the recent period of crisis (2007–2012), though without apparently leading to the refoundation of economics that some wished to see.[1] Yet one unexpected outcome of the crisis was the revival of the Keynesian–ordoliberal divide at the forefront

1. See, among many others, Geoffrey Hodgson (2009) and Colander et al. (2009).

of European public debate (Esch 2014; Young 2014b; Ojala and Harjuniemi 2016). By definition, times of economic crisis help to promote positive, active visions of the role of the state. However, it is somewhat surprising to see post-2007 political discourses echoing programs born in the interwar period and developed for the postwar era some fifty years ago. There is perhaps some irony in the vision of ordoliberalism resurfacing as an ossified model resting on austerity measures, in a form that is a far cry from the first ordoliberals' "third way," the purpose of which was to free market economy from the deleterious exercise of illegitimate powers.

# BIBLIOGRAPHY


Abelshauser, Werner. 1975. *Wirtschaft in Westdeutschland 1945–1948*. Stuttgart: Deutsche Verlags-Anstalt.

Abelshauser, Werner. 1986. "Les nationalisations n'auront pas lieu. La controverse sur l'instauration d'un nouvel ordre économique et social dans les zones occidentales de l'Allemagne de 1945 à 1949." *Le Mouvement Social* 134: 81–96.

Abelshauser, Werner. 2004. "L'école historique et les problèmes d'aujourd'hui." In *Histoire et économie politique en Allemagne de Gustav Schmoller à Max Weber: Nouvelles perspectives sur l'école historique de l'économie*. Edited by Hinnerk Bruhns, translated by Françoise Laroche, 19–38. Paris: Éditions de la Maison des sciences de l'homme.

Abrams, Lynn. 2007. *Bismarck and the German Empire: 1871–1918*, 2nd edn. New York: Routledge.

Agartz, Viktor. 1946. *Sozialistische Wirtschaftspolitik. Rede auf dem Parteitag der Sozialdemokratischen Partei Deutschlands am 9. Mai 1946 in Hannover*. Hamburg: Hönix-Verlag Christen.

Ahlborn, Christian, and Carsten Grave. 2006. "Walter Eucken and Ordoliberalism: An Introduction from a consumer welfare perspective." *Competition Policy International* 2 (2): 197–217.

Alexeev, Michael. 2008. "Second economy (unofficial economy)." In *The New Palgrave Dictionary of Economics*, 2nd edn. Edited by Steven N. Durlauf and Lawrence E. Blume, 384–390. Basingstoke: Nature Publishing Group.

Allen, Christopher S. 1989. "The underdevelopment of Keynesianism in the Federal Republic of Germany." In *The Political Power of Economic Ideas: Keynesianism Across Nations*. Edited by P. A. Hall, 263–290. Princeton: Princeton University Press.

Almodovar, António, and Pedro Teixeira. 2008. "The ascent and decline of Catholic economic thought, 1830–1950s." *History of Political Economy* 40 (5): 62–87.

Ananyin, Oleg. 2003. "Comment intégrer l'économie comparative dans l'économie?" *Revue D'études Comparatives Est-Ouest* 34 (2): 5–29.

Arena, Richard, Sheila C. Dow, and Matthias Klaes, eds. 2009. *Open Economics: Economics in Relation to Other Disciplines*. London: Routledge.

Arnsperger, Christian. 2008. *Critical Political Economy: Complexity, Rationality, and the Logic of Post-Orthodox Pluralism*. London: Routledge.

Arrous, Jean. 1990. "Socialisme et planification: O. Lange et F. A. von Hayek." *Revue Française d'Économie* 5 (2): 61–84.

Audier, Serge. 2008. *Aux origines du néo-libéralisme : Le colloque Lippmann*. Paris: Le Bord de l'eau.

Audier, Serge. 2012. *Néolibéralisme(s)*. Paris: Grasset.

Audier, Serge. 2013. "Les paradigmes du 'Néolibéralisme.'" *Cahiers Philosophiques* 133 (2): 21–40.

Augustine. 1998. *The City of God against the Pagans*. Edited by Robert D. Dyson. Cambridge: Cambridge University Press.

Bachelard, Gaston. 1938/1970. *La formation de l'esprit scientifique. Contribution à une psychanalyse de la connaissance objective*, 7th edn. Paris: Vrin.

Backhaus, Jürgen G. 1985. "Keynesianism in Germany." In *Keynes' Economics, Methodological Issues*. Edited by Tony Lawson and Hashem Pesaran, 209–253. London and Sydney: Routledge.

Backhaus, Jürgen G. 1989. "Sombart's modern capitalism." *Kyklos* 42 (4): 599–611.

Backhaus, Jürgen G., Günther Chaloupek, and Hans Frambach, eds. 2019. *The First Socialization Debate (1918) and Early Efforts Towards Socialization*. Cham: Springer.

Backhouse, Roger E. 2005. "The rise of free market economics: Economists and the role of the state since 1970." In *The Role of Government in the History of Economic Thought*. Edited by Steven G. Medema and Peter J. Boettke, 37: 355–392. History of Political Economy (Annual Supplement). Durham: Duke University Press.

Backhouse, Roger E., and Bradley W. Bateman. 2012. "Keynes and the welfare state." *History of Economic Thought and Policy* 1 (1): 7–20.

Backhouse, Roger E., and Jeff Biddle. 2000. "The concept of applied economics: A history of ambiguity and multiple meanings." In *Toward a History of Applied Economics*. Edited by Roger E. Backhouse and Jeff Biddle, 32: 1–24. History of Political Economy (Annual Supplement). Durham: Duke University Press.

Backhouse, Roger E., and Steve G. Medema. 2009. "Defining economics: The long road to acceptance of the Robbins definition." *Economica* 76 (1): 805–820.

Balisciano, Marcia L. 1998. "Hope for America: American notions of economic planning between pluralism and neoclassicism, 1930–1950." In *From Interwar Pluralism to Postwar Neoclassicism*. Edited by Malcolm Rutherford and Mary Morgan, 30: 153–178. History of Political Economy (Annual Supplement). Durham: Duke University Press.

Balisciano, Marcia L. 1999. *American Economic Planning, 1930–1950: The Rise and Fall of Ideology*. PhD dissertation. London: London School of Economics and Political Science.

Ban, Cornel. 2012. "Heinrich von Stackelberg and the diffusion of ordoliberal economics in Franco's Spain." *History of Economic Ideas* 20 (3): 137–157.

Baranzini, Roberto. 2011. "La concurrence et le tâtonnement à la lumière du réalisme walrassien: Une note sir les six premières sections des Éléments." In *Léon Walras et l'équilibre économique général: Recherches récentes*. Edited by Roberto Baranzini, André Legris, and Ludovic Ragni, 153–168. Paris: Economica.

Baranzini, Roberto, and Raphaël Fèvre. 2019. "Walras as an ordoliberal?" *European Journal of the History of Economic Thought* 26 (2): 380–413.

Barjot, Dominique. 2013. "Les cartels, une voie vers l'intégration européenne ?" *Revue Économique* 64 (6): 1043–1066.

Barone, Enrico. 1908/1975. "The ministry of production in the collectivist state." In *Collectivist Economic Planning: Critical Studies on the Possibilities of Socialism*. Edited by Friedrich A. Hayek, 245–290. Abingdon: Routledge.

Barroche, Julien. 2013. "L'État contre lui-même." *Raisons Politiques* 49 (1): 153–171.

Bateman, Bradley W. 2006. "Keynes and Keynesianism." In *The Cambridge Companion to Keynes*. Edited by Roger E. Backhouse and Bradley W. Bateman, 271–290. Cambridge: Cambridge University Press.

Bauer, Otto. 1919/2016. *Der Weg zum Sozialismus*. Bremen: Wiener Verlag.

Baume, Sandrine. 2006. "Le Parlement face à ses adversaires." *Revue Française de Science Politique* 56 (6): 985–998.

Becker, Pia, and Julian Dörr. 2016. "Rückkehr der Macht in die Ökonomik? Zur Stellung des Machtbegriffs in der Wirtschaftstheorie." In *Macht. Aktuelle Perspektiven aus Philosophie und Sozialwissenschaften*. Edited by Phillip H. Roth, 263–286. Frankfurt: Campus.

Behrens, Peter. 2015. "The ordoliberal concept of 'abuse' of a dominant position and its impact on Article 102 TFEU." Abuse Regulation in Competition Law, Proceedings of the 10th ASCOLA Conference Tokyo, 2015.

Benda, Julien. 1927/1946. *La Trahison des clercs*, 8th edn. Paris: Grasset.

Berlan, Aurélien. 2012. *La fabrique des derniers hommes : Retour sur le présent avec Tönnies, Simmel et Weber*. Paris: La Découverte.

Berle, Adolf A., and Gardiner C. Means. 1932/1991. *The Modern Corporation and Private Property*. New Brunswick: Transaction.

Bettendorf, L. J. H., and Ben J. Heijdra. 2003. *The Monopolistic Competition Revolution in Retrospect*. Cambridge: Cambridge University Press.

Bibow, Jörg. 2009. "On the origin and rise of central bank independence in West Germany." *European Journal of the History of Economic Thought* 16 (1): 155–190.

Bibow, Jörg. 2013. "At the crossroads: The euro and its central bank guardian (and saviour?)." *Cambridge Journal of Economics* 37 (3): 609–626.

Bibow, Jörg. 2018. "How Germany's anti-Keynsianism has brought Europe to its knees." *International Review of Applied Economics* 32 (5): 569–588.

Biebricher, Thomas. 2014a. "The return of ordoliberalism in Europe: Notes on a research agenda." *Rivista i-lex* 9 (21): 1–24.

Biebricher, Thomas. 2014b. "Power in neoliberal thought." *Journal of Political Power* 7 (2): 193–210.

Biebricher, Thomas. 2019. *The Political Theory of Neoliberalism*. Stanford: Stanford University Press.

Biebricher, Thomas, and Frieder Vogelmann, eds. 2017. *The Birth of Austerity: German Ordoliberalism and Contemporary Neoliberalism*. New York: Rowman & Littlefield International.

Bignon, Vincent. 2007. "La crise monétaire allemande de 1945–1948." In *La monnaie dévoilée par ses crises*. Edited by Bruno Théret, 2: 221–248. Paris: Éditions de l'EHESS.

Bilger, François. 1964. *La pensée économique libérale dans l'Allemagne contemporaine*. Paris: Librairie générale de droit et de jurisprudence.

Blaug, Mark. 2003. "The formalist revolution of the 1950s." *Journal of the History of Economic Thought* 25 (2): 145–156.

Blumenberg-Lampe, Christine, ed. 1986. *Der Weg in die soziale Marktwirtschaft: Referate, Protokolle, Gutachten der Arbeitsgemeinschaft Erwin von Beckerath, 1943–1947*. Stuttgart: Klett-Cotta.

Blümle, Gerold, and Nils Goldschmidt. 2006. "From economic stability to social order: The debate about business cycle theory in the 1920s and its relevance for the development of theories of social order by Lowe, Hayek and Eucken." *European Journal of the History of Economic Thought* 13 (4): 543–570.

Blyth, Mark. 2013. *Austerity: The History of a Dangerous Idea*. Oxford: Oxford University Press.

Böhm, Franz. 1928. "Das Problem der privaten Macht." *Die Justiz* 3: 324–345.

Böhm, Franz. 1933/2010. *Wettbewerb und Monopolkampf*. Edited by Ernst-Joachim Mestmäcker. Baden-Baden: Nomos.

Böhm, Franz. 1937. *Die Ordnung der Wirtschaft als geschichtliche Aufgabe und rechtsschöpferische Leistung*. Ordnung der Wirtschaft. Stuttgart: Kohlhammer.

Böhm, Franz. 1942. "Der Wettbewerb als Instrument staatlieber Wirtschaftslenkung." In *Der Wettbewerb als Mittel volkswirtschaftlicher Leistungssteigerung und Leistungsauslese*. Edited by Günter Schmölders, 51–98. Schriften der Akademie für Deutsches Recht. Gruppe Wirtschaftswissenschaft. Berlin: Duncker & Humblot.

Böhm, Franz. 1947/2017. "Kartellauflösung und Konzernentflechtung. Spezialistenaufgabe oder Schicksalsfrage / Decartelisation and de-concentration: A problem for specialists or a fateful question?" In *The Birth of Austerity: German Ordoliberalism and Contemporary Neoliberalism*. Edited by Thomas Biebricher and Frieder Vogelmann, translated by Michelle Everson, 121–135. New York: Rowman & Littlefield International.

Böhm, Franz. 1948. "Das Reichsgericht und die Kartelle." *ORDO: Jahrbuch für die Ordnung von Wirtschaft und Gesellschaft* 1: 197–213.

Böhm, Franz. 1950. "Die Idee des Ordo im Denken Walter Euckens: Dem Freunde und Mitherausgeber zum Gedächtnis." *ORDO: Jahrbuch für die Ordnung von Wirtschaft und Gesellschaft* 3: 15–64.

Böhm, Franz. 1954. "Monopoly and competition in Western Germany." In *Monopoly and Competition and Their Regulation: Papers and Proceedings of a Conference Held by the International Economic Association in 1951*. Edited by Edward H. Chamberlin, translated by J. Kahane, 141–167. London: Macmillan.

Böhm, Franz. 1957. "Die Forschungs-und Lehrgemeinschaft zwischen Juristen und Volkswirten an der Universität Freiburg in den dreißiger und vierziger Jahren des 20. Jahrhunderts." In *Aus der Geschichte der Rechts-und Staatswissenschaften zu Freiburg i. Br*. Edited by Hans J. Wolff, 95–113. Freiburg: Eberhard Albert.

Böhm, Franz. 1961. "Demokratie und ökonomische Macht." In *Kartelle und Monopole im modernen Recht*. Edited by Johann Wolfgang , 1–46. Karlsruhe: C. F. Müller.

Böhm, Franz. 1966/1989. "Rule of law in a market economy." In *Germany's Social Market Economy: Origins and Evolution*. Edited by Alan Peacock and Hans Willgerodt, 46–67. London: Macmillan for the Trade Policy Research Centre.

Böhm, Franz, Walter Eucken, and Hans Großmann-Doerth. 1936/1989. "Unsere Aufgabe (Our Task) / The Ordo Manifesto of 1936." In *Germany's Social Market Economy: Origins and Evolution*. Edited by Alan Peacock and Hans Willgerodt, 15–26. London: Macmillan for the Trade Policy Research Centre.

Böhm, Franz, Friedrich A. Lutz, and Fritz W. Meyer. 1961. "Vorwort." *ORDO: Jahrbuch für die Ordnung von Wirtschaft und Gesellschaft* 12: 31–48.

Bonatti, Luigi, and Andrea Fracasso. 2013. "The German model and the European crisis." *Journal of Common Market Studies* 51 (6): 1023–1039.

Bonefeld, Werner. 2012. "Freedom and the strong state: On German ordoliberalism." *New Political Economy* 17 (5): 1–24.

Bonefeld, Werner. 2013a. "Adam Smith and ordoliberalism: On the political form of market liberty." *Review of International Studies* 39 (02): 233–250.

Bonefeld, Werner. 2013b. "Human economy and social policy: On ordo-liberalism and political authority." *History of the Human Sciences* 26 (2): 106–125.

Bonefeld, Werner. 2017. *The Strong State and the Free Economy*. London: Rowman & Littlefield International.

Bönker, Frank, and Hans-Jürgen Wagener. 2001. "Hayek and Eucken on state and market economy." In *Institutional Economics in France and Germany: German*

*Ordoliberalism Versus the French Regulation School*. Edited by Agnès Labrousse and Jean-Daniel Weisz, 183–199. Heidelberg: Springer.

Borchardt, Knut. 1991. *Perspectives on Modern German Economic History and Policy*. Cambridge: Cambridge University Press.

Bostaph, Samuel. 2003. "Wieser on economic calculation under socialism." *Quarterly Journal of Austrian Economics* 6 (2): 3–34.

Bouton-Touboulic, Anne-Isabelle. 1999. "Les valeurs d''ordo' et leur réception chez Saint Augustin." *Revue des études augustiniennes* 45 (2): 295–334.

Braun, Hans-Joachim. 1990. *The German Economy in the Twentieth Century*. London: Routledge.

Bridel, Pascal. 1993. "Introduction to the special issue 'The socialist calculation debate after the upheavals in Eastern Europe.'" *Revue Européenne des Sciences Sociales* 31 (96): 5–12.

Broyer, Sylvain. 2003a. "Ordnungstheorie et ordolibéralisme: Les leçons de la tradition. Du caméralisme à l'ordolibéralisme: Ruptures et continuités?" In *L'ordolibéralisme allemand: Aux sources de l'économie sociale de marché*. Edited by Patricia Commun, 79–99. Cergy-Pontoise: CIRAC/CICC.

Broyer, Sylvain. 2003b. "Retour à l'économie de marché: Les débats du conseil scientifique attaché à l'administration économique de la Bizone." In *L'ordolibéralisme allemand: Aux sources de l'économie sociale de marché*. Edited by Patricia Commun, 201–213. Cergy-Pontoise: CIRAC/CICC.

Broyer, Sylvain. 2007. "Die Hinterlassenschaft der historischen Schule in Walter Euckens Ordnungstheorie und dem deutschen Ordoliberalismus / La pensée théorique et politique de Walter Eucken à la lumière des écoles historiques allemandes." Thèse de doctorat, Lyon 2 Lumière.

Bruch, Rüdiger vom. 2004. "Gustav Schmoller entre science sociale et réforme sociale." In *Histoire et économie politique en Allemagne de Gustav Schmoller à Max Weber: Nouvelles perspectives sur l'école historique de l'économie*. Edited by Hinnerk Bruhns, translated by Françoise Laroche, 39–52. Paris: Éditions de la Maison des sciences de l'homme.

Bruhns, Hinnerk. 1996. "Max Weber, l'économie et l'histoire." *Annales. Histoire, Sciences Sociales* 51 (6): 1259–1287.

Bruhns, Hinnerk, ed. 2004. *Histoire et économie politique en Allemagne de Gustav Schmoller à Max Weber: Nouvelles perspectives sur l'école historique de l'économie*. Paris: Éditions de la Maison des sciences de l'homme.

Buchheim, Christoph. 1993. "Marshall Plan and currency reform." In *American Policy and the Reconstruction of West Germany, 1945–1955*. Edited by Jeffry M. Diefendorf, Axel Frohn, and Hermann-Josef Rupieper, 69–83. Washington: German Historical Institute.

Burgin, Angus. 2012. *The Great Persuasion: Reinventing Free Markets Since the Depression*. Cambridge: Harvard University Press.

Caldwell, Bruce. 1982/2003. *Beyond Positivism*. London and New York: Routledge.

Caldwell, Bruce. 1997. "Hayek and socialism." *Journal of Economic Literature* 35 (4): 1856–1890.

Calvez, Jean-Yves. 2000. *L'Eglise et l'économie. La doctrine sociale de l'Eglise*. Paris: L'Harmattan.

Campagnolo, Gilles. 2003. "Les trois sources philosophiques de la réflexion ordolibérale." In *L'ordolibéralisme allemand: Aux sources de l'économie sociale de marché*. Edited by Patricia Commun, 133–148. Cergy-Pontoise: CIRAC/CICC.

Campagnolo, Gilles. 2004. *Critique de l'économie politique classique: Marx, Menger et l'Ecole historique allemande*. Paris: Presses Universitaires de France.

Campagnolo, Gilles. 2005. "Note sur le raisonnement marginal version Carl Menger." *Revue Française de Sociologie* 46 (4): 799–806.

Campagnolo, Gilles. 2011. "Enquête sur la "querelle des méthodes.'" In *Recherches sur la méthode dans les sciences sociales et en économie politique en particulier*. By Carl Menger, 421–530. Paris: Éditions de l'EHESS.

Capie, Forrest, and Geoffrey Wood. 2001. "The birth, life and demise of a currency: 50 years of the Deutsche Mark." *Economic Journal* 111 (472): 449–461.

Caré, Sébastien. 2016. "La dérive des continents néolibéraux: Essai de typologie dynamique." *Revue de Philosophie Économique* 17 (1): 21–55.

Carlin, Wendy. 1996. "West german growth and institutions, 1945–90." In *Economic Growth in Europe Since 1945*. Edited by Nicholas Crafts and Gianni Toniolo, 455–497. Cambridge: Cambridge University Press.

Cerny, Philip G. 2016. "In the shadow of ordoliberalism: The paradox of neoliberalism in the 21st century." *European Review of International Studies* 3 (1): 78–91.

Chaloupek, Günther. 1990. "The Austrian debate on economic calculation in a socialist economy." *History of Political Economy* 22 (4): 659–675.

Chaloupek, Günther. 2006. "Approaches of the Austrian School to the soziale frage before World War I—Wieser and Böhm-Bawerk." *Journal of Economic Studies* 33 (3): 177–188.

Chamberlin, Edward H. 1933/1948. *Theory of Monopolistic Competition*, 6th edn. Cambridge: Harvard University Press.

Charlesworth, Harold Karr. 1956. *The Economics of Repressed Inflation*. London: Allen & Unwin.

Cherrier, Beatrice. 2009. "Gunnar Myrdal and the scientific way to social democracy, 1914–1968." *Journal of the History of Economic Thought* 31 (01): 33–55.

Chick, Martin. 2002. *Industrial Policy in Britain 1945–1951: Economic Planning, Nationalisation and the Labour Governments*. Cambridge: Cambridge University Press.

Christ, Kevin. 2018. "A measure of judgments: Wilhelm Röpke's methodological heresy." *ORDO: Jahrbuch für die Ordnung von Wirtschaft und Gesellschaft* 69: 35–50.

Ciaffa, Jay A. 1998. *Max Weber and the Problems of Value-Free Social Science: A Critical Examination of the Werturteilsstreit*. London: Bucknell University Press.

Clapham, John H. 1922. "Of empty economic boxes." *Economic Journal* 32 (127): 305–314.

Clavert, Frédéric. 2009. "Un néo-mercantilisme allemand? Hjalmar Schacht et la politique économique, monétaire et financière du IIIe Reich." In *La pensée économique allemande*. Edited by Alain Alcouffe and Claude Diebolt, 357–374. Paris: Economica.

Clark, John M. 1940. "Toward a concept of workable competition." *American Economic Review* 30 (2): 241–256.

Colander, David, Michael Goldberg, Armin Haas, Katarina Juselius, Alan Kirman, Thomas Lux, and Brigitte Sloth. 2009. "The financial crisis and the systemic failure of the economics profession." *Critical Review* 21 (2–3): 249–267.

Commun, Patricia. 2003. "La conversion de Ludwig Erhard à l'ordolibéralisme (1930–1950)." In *L'ordolibéralisme allemand: Aux sources de l'économie sociale de marché*. Edited by Patricia Commun, 175–199. Cergy-Pontoise: CIRAC/CICC.

Commun, Patricia. 2004. “Le miracle économique : mythe ou réalité ? Les conditions du retour à la croissance, 1945–1950.” *Documents, Revues des Questions Allemandes* 4: 19–30.

Commun, Patricia. 2014. “German ordoliberalism: order vs. disorder in Röpke's early works.” *Rivista i-lex* 9 (21): 27–39.

Commun, Patricia. 2016. *Les ordolibéraux: Histoire d'un libéralisme à l'allemande*. Paris: Les Belles Lettres.

Commun, Patricia. 2018. “Wilhelm Röpke's report on the Brauns Commission: Advocating a pragmatic buisness cycle policy.” In *Wilhelm Röpke (1899–1966): A Liberal Political Economist and Conservative Social Philosopher*. Edited by Patricia Commun and Stefan Kolev, 121–132. Cham: Springer.

Commun, Patricia, and Stefan Kolev, eds. 2018. *Wilhelm Röpke (1899–1966): A Liberal Political Economist and Conservative Social Philosopher*. Cham: Springer.

Constantinesco, Leontin-Jean. 1960. “La constitution économique de la République fédérale allemande.” *Revue Économique* 11 (2): 266–290.

Cubeddu, Raimondo, and Alberto Vannucci. 1993. “Economic planning and the Austrian School.” *Revue Européenne des Sciences Sociales* 31 (96): 85–131.

Dardot, Pierre, and Christian Laval. 2009. *La nouvelle raison du monde : Essai sur la société néolibérale*. Paris: Découverte.

Dathe, Uwe. 2009. “Walter Euckens Weg zum Liberalismus (1918–1934).” *ORDO: Jahrbuch für die Ordnung von Wirtschaft und Gesellschaft* 60: 53–86.

Dathe, Uwe, and Nils Goldschmidt. 2003. “Wie der Vater, so der Sohn? Neuere Erkenntnisse zu Walter Euckens Leben und Werk anhand des Nachlasses von Rudolf Eucken in Jena.” *ORDO: Jahrbuch für die Ordnung von Wirtschaft und Gesellschaft* 54: 49–74.

Dehay, Eric. 1995. “La justification ordo-libérale de l'indépendance des banques centrales.” *Revue Française d'Économie* 10 (1): 27–53.

Dehay, Eric. 2003. “L'indépendance de la banque centrale en Allemagne: Des principes ordolibéraux à la pratique de la Bundesbank.” In *L'ordolibéralisme allemand: Aux sources de l'économie sociale de marché*. Edited by Patricia Commun, 243–254. Cergy-Pontoise: CIRAC/CICC.

Dekker, Erwin. 2016. *The Viennese Students of Civilization*. New York: Cambridge University Press.

Delsol, Chantal. 1992. *L'État subsidiaire: Ingérence et non-ingérence de l'État, le principe de subsidiarité aux fondements de l'histoire européenne*. Paris: Presses Universitaires de France.

Demme, Géraldine. 2013. “ 8e réforme de la Loi contre les entraves à la concurrence (GWB).” *Regards sur l'Économie Allemande* 109: 25–34.

Denord, François. 2007. *Néo-libéralisme version française : Histoire d'une idéologie politique*. Paris: Demopolis.

Denord, François, Rachel Knaebel, and Pierre Rimbert. 2015. “L'ordolibéralisme allemand, cage de fer pour le Vieux Continent.” *Le Monde diplomatique* 8: 21.

Denord, François, and Antoine Schwartz. 2010. “L'économie (très) politique du traité de Rome.” *Politix* 23 (89): 35–56.

Desmarais-Tremblay, Maxime. 2020. “W. H. Hutt and the conceptualization of consumers' sovereignty.” *Oxford Economic Papers* 72 (4): 1050–1071.

Dickinson, Henry D. 1930. “The economic basis of socialism.” *Political Quarterly* 1 (4): 561–572.

Dickinson, Henry D. 1933. “Price formation in a socialist community.” *Economic Journal* 47 (170): 237–250.

Dietze, Constantin von, Walter Eucken, and Adolf Lampe. 1943/2008. "Wirtschafts- und Sozialordnung." In *Grundtexte zur Freiburger Tradition der Ordnungsökonomik*. Edited by Nils Goldschmidt and Michael Wohlgemuth, 99–115. Tübingen: Mohr Siebeck.

Dijk, Ruud v. 2004. "Winning the peace: The United States, Western Germany, and the ambiguities of 'dual containment,' 1945–1950." In *The United States and Germany in the era of the Cold War, 1945–1990*. Edited by Detlef Junker, 78–84. Cambridge: Cambridge University Press.

Dobb, Maurice. 1933. "Economic theory and the problems of a socialist economy." *Economic Journal* 43 (172): 588–598.

Dockès, Pierre. 1999. *Pouvoir et autorité en économie*. Paris: Economica.

Dockès, Pierre. 2008. *Hobbes: économie, terreur et politique*. Paris: Economica.

Dold, Malte, and Tim Krieger. 2017. "Competition or conflict? Beyond traditional ordo-liberalism." Discussion Paper Series, *Wilfried-Guth-Stiftungsprofessur für Ordnungs- und Wettbewerbspolitik* 2017-02.

Dold, Malte, and Tim Krieger, eds. 2019. *Ordoliberalism and European Economic Policy: Between Realpolitik and Economic Utopia*. London: Routledge.

Domes, Jürgen, and Michael Wolffsohn. 1979. "Setting the course for the Federal Republic of Germany: Major policy decisions in the bi-zonal economic council and party images, 1947–1949."*Journal of Institutional and Theoretical Economics* 135 (3): 332–351.

Dörr, Julian, Nils Goldschmidt, Gisela Kubon-Gilke, and Werner Sesselmeier, eds. 2016. *Vitalpolitik, Inklusion und der sozialstaatliche Diskurs: Theoretische Reflexionen und sozialpolitische Implikationen*. Berlin: LIT Verlag Münster.

Draghi, Mario. 2013. "Opening remarks at the session 'Rethinking the Limitations of Monetary Policy.'" https://www.ecb.europa.eu/press/key/date/2013/html/sp130618.en.html.

Drexl, Josef. 2011. "La Constitution économique européenne: L'actualité du modèle ordolibéral." *Revue Internationale de Droit Économique* 25 (4): 419.

Dullien, Sebastian, and Ulrike Guérot. 2012. "The long shadow of ordoliberalism: Germany's approach to the euro crisis." *ECFR, Policy Brief* 49.

Dupeux, Louis. 1992. "'Révolution Conservatrice' et modernité." In *La Révolution Conservatrice allemande sous la République de Weimar*. Edited by Louis Dupeux, 17–44. Paris: Kimé.

Düppe, Till. 2011. *The Making of the Economy: A Phenomenology of Economic Science*. Lanham: Lexington Books.

Düppe, Till. 2015. "Border cases between autonomy and relevance: Economic sciences in Berlin—A natural experiment." *Studies in History and Philosophy of Science Part A* 51: 22–32.

Düppe, Till. 2020. "War after war: Wilhelm Krelle, 1916–2004." *Journal of the History of Economic Thought* 42 (3): 307–334.

Durbin, Evan F. M. 1936. "Economic calculus in a planned economy." *Economic Journal* 46 (184): 676–690.

Dürr, Ernst-Wolfram. 1954. *Wesen und Ziele des Ordoliberalismus*. Winterthur: PG Keller.

Ebner, Alexander. 2006. "The intellectual foundations of the social market economy: Theory, policy, and implications for European integration." *Journal of Economic Studies* 33 (3): 206–223.

Ege, Ragip, and Harald Hagemann. 2012. "The modernisation of the Turkish University after 1933: The contributions of refugees from Nazism." *European Journal of the History of Economic Thought* 19 (6): 944–975.

Erhard, Ludwig. 1944/1982. "Kriegsfinanzierung und Schuldenkonsolidierung (War finance and debt consolidation) / The Economic Needs of Postwar Germany." In *Standard Texts on the Social Market Economy: Two Centuries of Discussion*. Edited by Horst Friedrich Wünsche, translated by Derek Rutter, 5–8. Stuttgart: Gustav Fischer Verlag.

Erhard, Ludwig. 1947/1982. "Politischer Föderalismus und wirtschaftlicher Zentralismus / The Functions and Limits of Central Economic Administration." In *Standard Texts on the Social Market Economy: Two Centuries of Discussion*. Edited by Horst Friedrich Wünsche, translated by Derek Rutter, 23–25. Stuttgart: Gustav Fischer Verlag.

Erhard, Ludwig. 1948/1982. "The new facts (Speech to the 2nd CDU Congress of the British Occupation Zone in Recklinghausen - Auguste 28th)." In *Standard Texts on the Social Market Economy: Two Centuries of Discussion*. Edited by Horst Friedrich Wünsche, translated by Derek Rutter, 35–36. Stuttgart: Gustav Fischer Verlag.

Erhard, Ludwig. 1957/1958. *Prosperity Through Competition*. New York: Frederick A. Praeger.

Esch, Femke A. 2014. "Exploring the Keynesian–Ordoliberal divide. Flexibility and convergence in French and German leaders' economic ideas during the euro-crisis." *Journal of Contemporary European Studies* 22 (3): 288–302.

Eucken, Walter. 1923. *Kritische Betrachtungen zum deutschen Geldproblem*. Jena: G. Fischer.

Eucken, Walter. 1929. *Kredit und Konjunktur*. Berlin: Duncker & Humblot.

Eucken, Walter. 1932a. "Religion–Wirtschaft–Staat." *Die Tatwelt* 8 (7): 82–89.

Eucken, Walter. 1932b/2017. "Staatliche Strukturwandlungen und die Krisis des Kapitalismus / Structural transformations of the state and the crisis of capitalism." In *The Birth of Austerity: German Ordoliberalism and Contemporary Neoliberalism*. Edited by Thomas Biebricher and Frieder Vogelmann, translated by Keith Tribe, 51–72. London: Rowman & Littlefield International.

Eucken, Walter. 1933. "Denken–Warum?" *Die Tatwelt* 9 (10): 148–152.

Eucken, Walter. 1934/1954. *Kapitaltheoretische Untersuchungen*. Tübingen: Mohr Siebeck.

Eucken, Walter. 1938a. "Die Überwindung des Historismus." *Schmollers Jahrbuch* 62 (2): 63–86.

Eucken, Walter 1938b. *Nationalökonomie – wozu?* Leipzig: Felix Meiner Verlag.

Eucken, Walter. 1940a/1950. *Die Grundlagen der Nationalökonomie*, 6th edn. Berlin: Springer.

Eucken, Walter. 1940b/1950. *The Foundations of Economics*. Translated by Terence W. Hutchison. London: W. Hodge.

Eucken, Walter. 1940c. "Wissenschaft im Stile Schmollers." *Weltwirtschaftliches Archiv* 52 (3): 468–506.

Eucken, Walter. 1942a/2017. "Wettbewerb als Grundprinzip der Wirtschaftsverfassung / Competition as the basic principle of the economic constitution." In *The Birth of Austerity: German Ordoliberalism and Contemporary Neoliberalism*. Edited by Thomas Biebricher and Frieder Vogelmann, translated by Keith Tribe, 81–98. London: Rowman & Littlefield International.

Eucken, Walter. 1942b. "Wettbewerb als Grundprinzip der Wirtschaftsverfassung." In *Der Wettbewerb als Mittel volkswirtschaftlicher Leistungssteigerung und Leistungsauslese*. Edited by Günter Schmölders, 29–50. Schriften der Akademie für Deutsches Recht. Gruppe Wirtschaftswissenschaft. Berlin: Duncker & Humblot.

Eucken, Walter. 1943/1986. "Bemerkungen zum Währungplan von Keynes." In *Der Weg in die soziale Marktwirtschaft: Referate, Protokolle, Gutachten der Arbeitsgemeinschaft Erwin von Beckerath, 1943–1947*. Edited by Christine Blumenberg-Lampe, 268–274. Stuttgart: Klett-Cotta.

Eucken, Walter. 1944/1986. "Einige weitere Bemerkungen zur internationalen Währungsfrage." In *Der Weg in die soziale Marktwirtschaft: Referate, Protokolle, Gutachten der Arbeitsgemeinschaft Erwin von Beckerath, 1943–1947*. Edited by Christine Blumenberg-Lampe, 275–278. Stuttgart: Klett-Cotta.

Eucken, Walter. 1946a/1999. "Industrielle Konzentration." In *Ordnungspolitik*. Edited by Walter Oswalt, 25–37. Münster: LIT Verlag.

Eucken, Walter. 1946b/2013. "Letter to Professor F. A. Hayek, March 12, 1946." In *Hayek: A Collaborative Biography: Part 1 Influences from Mises to Bartley*. Edited by Robert Leeson, translated by Sigrid Saou, 138–143. Hampshire: Palgrave Macmillan.

Eucken, Walter. 1946c/1999. "Über die Gesamtrichtung der Wirtschaftspolitik." In *Ordnungspolitik*. Edited by Walter Oswalt, 1–24. Münster: LIT Verlag.

Eucken, Walter. 1946d/1999. "Über die Verstaatlichung der Privaten Banken." In *Ordnungspolitik*. Edited by Walter Oswalt, 38–58. Münster: LIT Verlag.

Eucken, Walter. 1947. "Reflections on the problem of monopoly." *Time & Tide*, April 27: 408–409.

Eucken, Walter. 1948a/1989. "Das ordnungspolitische Problem / What kind of economic and social system?" In *Germany's Social Market Economy: Origins and Evolution*. Edited by Alan Peacock and Hans Willgerodt, 27–45. London: Macmillan for the Trade Policy Research Centre.

Eucken, Walter. 1948b/1982. "Die Soziale Frage / The social question." In *Standard Texts on the Social Market Economy: Two Centuries of Discussion*. Edited by Horst Friedrich Wünsche, translated by Derek Rutter, 267–276. Stuttgart: Gustav Fischer Verlag.

Eucken, Walter. 1948c. "On the theory of the centrally administered economy: An analysis of the German experiment. (Part I & II)." Translated by Terence W. Hutchison. *Economica* 15 (58, 59): 79–100, 173–193.

Eucken, Walter. 1948d. "The german currency reform." *Time & Tide*, September 4: 900–901.

Eucken, Walter. 1948e. "Obituary: Heinrich von Stackelberg (1905–1946)." *Economic Journal* 58 (229): 132–136.

Eucken, Walter. 1949/2006. "The competitive order and its implementation." Translated by Christian Ahlborn and Carsten Grave in *Competition Policy International* 2 (2): 219–245.

Eucken, Walter. 1950a. "Preface [to the English Edition]." In *The Foundations of Economics*. Translated by Terence W. Hutchison, 9–11. London: W. Hodge.

Eucken, Walter. 1950b. "Technik, Konzentration und Ordnung der Wirtschaft." *ORDO: Jahrbuch für die Ordnung von Wirtschaft und Gesellschaft* 3: 3–17.

Eucken, Walter. 1951. *This Unsuccessful Age: Or the Pains of Economic Progress*. London: W. Hodge.

Eucken, Walter. 1952/2004. *Grundsätze der Wirtschaftspolitik*. Edited by Edith Eucken and K. Paul Hensel, 7th edn. Tübingen: Mohr Siebeck.

Eucken, Walter. 2001/2012. *Wirtschaftsmacht und Wirtschaftsordnung*. Edited by Walter Oswalt, 2nd edn. Münster: Lit Verlag.

Eucken, Walter, and Franz Böhm. 1948. "Vorwort - Die Aufgabe des Jahrbuchs." *ORDO: Jahrbuch für die Ordnung von Wirtschaft und Gesellschaft* 1: 7–11.

Eucken, Walter, and Fritz W. Meyer. 1948. "The economic situation in Germany." *Annals of the American Academy of Political and Social Science* 260: 53–62.

Fear, Jeffrey R. 2008. "Cartels." In *The Oxford Handbook of Buisness History*. Edited by Geoffrey Jones and Jonathan Zeitlin, 268–292. Oxford: Oxford University Press.

Feld, Lars P., Ekkehard A. Köhler, and Daniel Nientiedt. 2015. "Ordoliberalism, pragmatism and the eurozone crisis: How the German tradition shaped economic policy in Europe." *European Review of International Studies* 2 (3): 48–61.

Feld, Lars P., Ekkehard A. Köhler, and Daniel Nientiedt. 2017. "The 'Dark Ages' of German macroeconomics and other alleged shortfalls in German economic thought." *Working Paper 17/03. Freiburger Diskussionspapiere zur Ordnungsökonomik.*

Feld, Lars P., Ekkehard A. Köhler, and Daniel Nientiedt. 2018. "The German Anti-Keynes? On Walter Eucken's macroeconomics." *Working Paper 18/11. Freiburger Diskussionspapiere zur Ordnungsökonomik.*

Fèvre, Raphaël. 2015. "Du libéralisme historique à la crise sociale du XXe siècle : La lecture de Wilhelm Röpke." *Revue Économique* 66 (5): 901–932.

Fèvre, Raphaël. 2018a. "Keynes and Eucken on power and capitalism." In *Power in Economic Thought*. Edited by Manuela Mosca, 321–348. London: Palgrave Macmillan.

Fèvre, Raphaël. 2018b. "Was Wilhelm Röpke really a proto-keynesian?" In *Wilhelm Röpke (1899–1966): A Liberal Political Economist and Conservative Social Philosopher*. Edited by Patricia Commun and Stefan Kolev, 109–120. Cham: Springer.

Fèvre, Raphaël. 2018c. "Denazifying the economy: Ordoliberals on the economic policy battlefield (1946–50)." *History of Political Economy* 50 (4): 679–707.

Fèvre, Raphaël. 2020. "Power as an epistemological obstacle: Walter Eucken's quest for an interest-proof economic science." *Journal of Economic Methodology* 27 (4): 330–350.

Fisch, Jörg. 2004. "From weakening an enemy to strengthening an ally: The United States and German reparations." In *The United States and Germany in the Era of the Cold War, 1945–1990*. Edited by Detlef Junker, 271–277. Cambridge: Cambridge University Press.

Fisher, Irving. 1935/1997. *100% Money*. Edited by William J. Barber, Robert W. Dimand, and Kevin Foster. The Works of Irving Fisher, vol. 11. London: Pickering & Chatto.

Foucault, Michel. 2008. *The Birth of Biopolitics: Lectures at the Collège de France, 1978–1979*. Basingstoke: Palgrave Macmillan.

Fourcade, Marion. 2013. "The economy as morality play, and implications for the eurozone crisis." *Socio-Economic Review* 11 (3): 620–627.

Frambach, Hans. 2012. "Johann Heinrich von Thünen: A founder of modern economics." In *Handbook of the History of Economic Thought*. Edited by Jürgen G. Backhaus, 299–322. New-York: Springer.

Friedman, Milton. 1953/1966. *Essays in Positive Economics*. Chicago: University of Chicago Press.

Friedrich, Carl J. 1955. "The political thought of neo-liberalism." *American Political Science Review* 49 (2): 509–525.

Fuertes, Juan Velarde. 1996. "Stackelberg and his role in the change in Spanish economic policy." *Journal of Economic Studies* 23 (5/6): 128–140.

Fusfeld, Daniel R. 2008. "Methodenstreit." In *The New Palgrave Dictionary of Economics*, 2nd edn. Edited by Steven N. Durlauf and Lawrence E. Blume, 585–586. Basingstoke: Nature Publishing Group.

Galbraith, John Kenneth. 1948. "Monopoly and the concentration of economic power." In *A Survey of contemporary economics*. Edited by Howard S. Ellis, 99–128. Philadelphia: Blakiston.

Garvy, George. 1975. "Keynes and the economic activists of pre-Hitler Germany." *Journal of Political Economy* 83 (2): 391–405.

Georgiou, Christakis. 2016. "The eurozone crisis and the European corporate elite: Bringing corporate actors into focus." *Economy and Society* 45 (1): 51–76.

Gerken, Lüder. 2000. *Walter Eucken und sein Werk: Rückblick auf den Vordenker der sozialen Marktwirtschaft*. Tübingen: Mohr Siebeck.

Giersch, Herbert, Karl-Heinz Paqué, and Holger Schmieding. 1992. *The Fading Miracle: Four Decades of Market Economy in Germany*. New York: Cambridge University Press.

Gioia, Vitantonio. 2000. "L'école historique allemande d'économie." In *Nouvelle histoire de la pensée économique*. Edited by Alain Béraud and Gilbert Faccarello, 3: 30–73. Paris: La Découverte.

Glossner, Christian L. 2010. *Making of the German Post-war Economy: Political Communication and Public Reception of the Social Market Economy After World War Two*. London: I. B.Tauris.

Goldschmidt, Nils. 2002. *Entstehung und Vermächtnis ordoliberalen Denkens: Walter Eucken und die Notwendigkeit einer kulturellen Ökonomik*. Münster: Lit.

Goldschmidt, Nils. 2003. "Theorie auf normativer Basis: Anmerkungen zum ordoliberalen Konzept von Walter Eucken." In *L'ordolibéralisme allemand: Aux sources de l'économie sociale de marché*. Edited by Patricia Commun, 119–132. Cergy-Pontoise: CIRAC/CICC.

Goldschmidt, Nils, ed. 2005a. *Wirtschaft, Politik und Freiheit: Freiburger Wirtschaftswissenschaftler und der Widerstand*. Tübingen: Mohr Siebeck.

Goldschmidt, Nils. 2005b. "Zur Einführung: Hans Großmann-Doerth und die Freiburger Schule." In *Das selbstgeschaffene Recht der Wirtschaft. Zum Gedenken an Hans Großmann-Doerth (1894–1944)*. Edited by Uwe Blaurock, Nils Goldschmidt, and Alexander Hollerbach, 9–18. Tübingen: Mohr Siebeck.

Goldschmidt, Nils. 2013. "Walter Eucken's place in the history of ideas." *Review of Austrian Economics* 26 (2): 127–147.

Goldschmidt, Nils. 2016. "Gibt es eine ordoliberale Entwicklungsidee? Walter Euckens Analyse des gesellschaftlichen und wirtschaftlichen Wandels." In *Geschichte der Entwicklungstheorien*. Edited by Heinz D. Kurz, 182–200. Berlin: Duncker & Humblot.

Goldschmidt, Nils, and Arnold Berndt. 2005. "Leonhard Miksch (1901–1950): A forgotten member of the Freiburg School." *American Journal of Economics and Sociology* 64 (4): 973–998.

Goldschmidt, Nils, and Julian Dörr. 2018. "Wilhelm Röpke on liberalism, culture, and economic development." In *Wilhelm Röpke (1899–1966): A Liberal Political Economist and Conservative Social Philosopher*. Edited by Patricia Commun and Stefan Kolev, 203–217. Cham: Springer.

Goldschmidt, Nils, and Jan-Otmar Hesse. 2013. "Eucken, Hayek, and the road to serfdom." In *Hayek: A Collaborative Biography: Part 1 Influences from Mises to Bartley*. Edited by Robert Leeson, 123–146. Hampshire: Palgrave Macmillan.

Gough, Barry. 2014. *Pax Britannica: Ruling the Waves and Keeping the Peace Before Armageddon*. London: Springer.

Gregg, Samuel. 2015. "A Value Judgment on 'A Value Judgment on Value Judgments.'" *Journal of Markets and Morality* 18 (2): 483–495.

Grenier, Jean-Yves, and André Orléan. 2007. "Michel Foucault, l'économie politique et le libéralisme" *Annales. Histoire, Sciences Sociales* 62 (5) : 1155–1182.

Grimmer-Solem, Erik. 2003. *The Rise of Historical Economics and Social Reform in Germany, 1864–1894*. Oxford: Oxford University Press.

Grimmer-Solem, Erik. 2014. "From sciences of state to modern economics." In *Routledge Handbook of the History of Global Economic Thought*. Edited by Vincent Barnett, 86–94. London: Routledge.

Grimmer-Solem, Erik, and Roberto Romani. 1998. "The Historical School, 1870–1900: A cross-national reassessment." *History of European Ideas* 24 (4–5): 267–299.

Grossein, Jean-Pierre. 2005. "Max Weber à Robert Liefmann." *Revue Française de Sociologie* 46 (4): 923–928.

Grossekettler, Heinz G. 1989. "On designing an economic order. The contributions of the Freiburg School." In *Twentieth-Century Economic Thought*. Edited by Donald A. Walker, 2: 38–84. Aldershot Brookfield: Edward Elgar.

Grossekettler, Heinz G. 1994. "On designing an institutional infrastructure for economies: The Freiburg Legacy after 50 years." *Journal of Economic Studies* 21 (4): 9–24.

Grossekettler, Heinz G. 1996. "Franz Böhm as a pioneering champion of an economic theory of legislative science." *European Journal of Law and Economics* 3 (4): 309–329.

Grossekettler, Heinz G. 2005. "Franz Böhm (1895–1977)." In *The Elgar Companion to Law and Economics*, 2nd edn. Edited by Jürgen G. Backhaus, 489–498. Cheltenham: Edward Elgar.

Großmann-Doerth, Hans. 1933/2005. "Selbstgeschaffenes Recht der Wirtschaft und staatliches Recht." In *Das selbstgeschaffene Recht der Wirtschaft: Zum Gedenken an Hans Grossmann-Doerth (1894–1944)*. Edited by Uwe Blaurock, Nils Goldschmidt, and Alexander Hollerbach, 77–96. Tübingen: Mohr Siebeck.

Grube, Frank, and Gerhard Richter. 1979. *Die Schwarzmarktzeit: Deutschland zwischen 1945 und 1948*. Hamburg: Hoffmann u. Campe.

Guesnerie, Roger, Jean-Hervé Lorenzi, Michel Mougeot, and David Encaoua. 2006. *Politiques de la concurrence*. Rapports du conseil d'analyse économique 60. Paris: La Documentation française.

Haarmann, Moritz P. 2015. *Wirtschaft—Macht—Bürgerbewusstsein: Walter Euckens Beitrag zur sozioökonomischen Bildung*. Hannover: Springer.

Haberler, Gottfried. 1948. "Causes and cures of inflation." *Review of Economics and Statistics* 30 (1): 10–14.

Habermas, Jürgen. 1971/1987. *Profils philosophiques et politiques*. Translated by Françoise Dastur, Jean-René Ladmiral, and Marc B. de Launay. Paris: Gallimard.

Hagemann, Harald. 2001. "The Verein für Sozialpolitik from its foundation (1872) until World War I." In *The Spread of Political Economy and the Professionalisation of Economists*. Edited by Massimo M. Augello and Marco Enrico Luigi Guidi, 166–189. London: Routledge.

Hagemann, Harald. 2004. "The German historical approach to economics." *Research in the History of Economic Thought and Methodology* 22: 399–411.

Hagemann, Harald. 2010. "The post-1945 development of economics in Germany." In *The Development of Economics in Western Europe Since 1945*. Edited by A. W. Bob Coats, 110–124. London: Routledge.

Hagemann, Harald. 2016. "Concluding remarks." In *The German Historical School and European Economic Thought*. Edited by José Luís Cardoso and Michalis Psalidopoulos, 223–236. New York: Routledge.

Hagemann, Harald, and Matthias Rösch. 2005. "German economists in parliament (1848–1918)." In *Economists in Parliament in the Liberal Age*. Edited by Massimo M. Augello and Marco Enrico Luigi Guidi, 163–190. Hampshire: Ashgate.

Hall, Peter A., ed. 1989. *The Political Power of Economic Ideas: Keynesianism Across Nations*. Princeton: Princeton University Press.

Hammersley, Martyn. 2017. "On the role of values in social research: Weber vindicated?" *Sociological Research Online* 22 (1): 1–12.

Hansen, Alvin H., and Richard A. Musgrave. 1951. *Fiscal Problems of Germany: A Report Prepared During the Summer of 1951*. Presented to the Minister of the Federal Republic of Germany. Berlin: Druck.

Harding, Christopher, and Julian Joshua. 2010. *Regulating Cartels in Europe*. Oxford: Oxford University Press.

Hartwell, Ronald M. 1995. *A History of the Mont Pelerin society*. Indianapolis: Liberty Fund.

Havertz, Ralf. 2019. "Right-wing populism and neoliberalism in germany: The AfD's embrace of ordoliberalism." *New Political Economy* 24 (3): 385–403.

Hayek, Friedrich A., ed. 1935/1975. *Collectivist Economic Planning: Critical Studies on the Possibilities of Socialism*. Clifton: Routledge.

Hayek, Friedrich A. 1937. "Economics and knowledge." *Economica* 4 (13): 33–54.

Hayek, Friedrich A. 1940. "Socialist calculation: The competitive 'solution.'" *Economica* 7 (26): 125–149.

Hayek, Friedrich A. 1944/2007. *The Road to Serfdom*. Edited by Bruce J. Caldwell. The Collected Works of F. A. Hayek, vol. 2. Chicago: University of Chicago Press.

Hayek, Friedrich A. 1945. "The use of knowledge in society." *American Economic Review* 35 (4): 519–530.

Hayes, Peter. 1987/2001. *Industry and Ideology: I. G. Farben in the Nazi Era*, 2nd edn. Cambridge: Cambridge University Press.

Hédoin, Cyril. 2013. *L'institutionnalisme historique et la relation entre théorie et histoire en économie*. Paris: Classiques Garnier.

Helmut, Leipold. 2001. "The contribution of neoliberal ordnungstheorie to transformation policy." In *Institutional Economics in France and Germany: German Ordoliberalism Versus the French Regulation School*. Edited by Agnès Labrousse and Jean-Daniel Weisz, 334–346. Heidelberg: Springer.

Hennecke, Hans-Jörg. 2005. *Wilhelm Röpke—Ein Leben in der Brandung*. Stuttgart: Schäffer-Poeschel.

Hennis, Wilhelm. 1991. "The pitiless 'sobriety of judgement': Max Weber between Carl Menger and Gustav von Schmoller: The academic politics of value freedom." Translated by Keith Tribe. *History of the Human Sciences* 4 (1): 27–59.

Hensel, K. Paul. 1949. "Ordnungspolitische Betrachtungen zur katholischen Soziallehre (im Sinne der Päpstlichen Enzykliken Rerum Novarum und Quadrogesimo Anno)." *ORDO: Jahrbuch für die Ordnung von Wirtschaft und Gesellschaft* 2: 229–269.

Hensel, K. Paul. 1951. "Das Verhältnis Politischer Wissenschaft zur Politik." *ORDO: Jahrbuch für die Ordnung von Wirtschaft und Gesellschaft* 4: 3–17.

Hensel, K. Paul. 1966/1989. "Problems of worker democracies." In *Germany's Social Market Economy: Origins and Evolution*. Edited by Alan Peacock and Hans Willgerodt, 124–139. London: Macmillan for the Trade Policy Research Centre.

Herrmann-Pillath, Carsten. 1991. "Der Vergleich von Wirtschafts- und Gesellschaftssystemen: Wissenschaftsphilosophische und methodologische Überlegungen zur Zukunft eines ordnungstheoretischen Forschungsprogrammes." *ORDO. Jahrbuch für die Ordnung von Wirtschaft und Gesellschaft* 42: 15–68.

Herrmann-Pillath, Carsten. 1994. "Methodological aspects of Eucken's work." *Journal of Economic Studies* 21 (4): 46–60.

Hesse, Jan-Otmar. 2012. "The 'Americanisation' of West German Economics after the Second World War: Success, failure, or something completely different?" *European Journal of the History of Economic Thought* 19 (1): 67–98.

Hesse, Jan-Otmar, and Eva-Maria Roelevink. 2015. "Cartel law and the cartel register in German twentieth-century history." In *Regulating Competition: Cartel Registers in the Twentieth-Century World*. Edited by Susanna Fellman and Martin Shanahan, 191–207. New York: Routledge.

Hicks, John R. 1935. "Review of marktform und gleichgewicht." *Economic Journal* 45 (178): 334–336.

Hien, Josef, and Christian Joerges, eds. 2017. *Ordoliberalism, Law and the Rule of Economics*. Oxford: Hart Publishing.

Hien, Josef, and Christian Joerges. 2018. "Dead man walking? Current European interest in the ordoliberal tradition." *European Law Journal* 24 (2–3): 142–162.

Hirschman, Albert O. 1948. "Inflation and deflation in Italy." *American Economic Review* 38 (4): 598–606.

Hirschman, Albert O. 1991. *The Rhetoric of Reaction*. Cambridge, MA: Harvard University Press.

Hobbes, Thomas. 1651/1996. *Leviathan*. Edited by Richard Tuck. Cambridge: Cambridge University Press.

Hobsbawm, Eric J. 2014. *L'âge des extrêmes*. Bruxelles: A. Versaille.

Hodgson, Geoffrey M. 2001. *How Economics Forgot History: The Problem of Historical Specificity in Social Science*. London: Psychology Press.

Hodgson, Geoffrey M. 2009. "The Great Crash of 2008 and the reform of economics." *Cambridge Journal of Economics* 33 (6): 1205–1221.

Hook, James C. van. 2004. *Rebuilding Germany: The Creation of the Social Market Economy, 1949–1957*. Cambridge: Cambridge University Press.

Hoppe, Hans-Hermann. 1991. "De-socialization in a united Germany." *Review of Austrian Economics* 5 (2): 77–104.

Horn, Karen. 2019. "The difficult relationship between historical ordoliberalism and Adam Smith." *Working Paper 19/03. Freiburger Diskussionspapiere zur Ordnungsökonomik*.

Husserl, Edmund. 1970. *The Crisis of European Sciences and Transcendental Phenomenology: An Introduction to Phenomenological Philosophy*. Translated by David Carr. Evanston: Northwestern University Press.

Hutchison, Terence W. 1979. "Notes on the effects of economic ideas on policy: The example of the German social market economy." *Journal of Institutional and Theoretical Economics* 135 (3): 426–441.

Jacoby, Wade. 2014. "The politics of the eurozone crisis: Two puzzles behind the German consensus." *German Politics and Society* 32 (2): 70–85.

Janssen, Hauke. 2009. "Zwischen Historismus und Neoklassik: Alexander Rüstow und die Krise in der deutschen Volkswirtschaftslehre." *ORDO. Jahrbuch für die Ordnung von Wirtschaft und Gesellschaft* 60: 101–118.

Jarausch, Konrad Hugo, and Larry E. Jones. 1990. "German liberalism reconsidered: Inevitable decline, bourgeois hegemony, or partial achievement?" In *In Search of a Liberal Germany: Studies in the History of German Liberalism from 1789 to the Present*. Edited by Konrad Hugo Jarausch and Larry E. Jones, 1–24. New York: Berg.

Joerges, Christian. 2006. "La constitution économique européenne en processus et en procès." *Revue Internationale de Droit Économique* 20 (3): 245–284.

Johnson, Harry G. 1971. "The Keynesian revolution and the monetarist counter-revolution." *American Economic Review* 61: 1–14.

Kaldor, Nicholas. 1936. "Review of Marktform und Gleichgewicht." *Economica* 3 (10): 227–230.

Keppler, Jan H. 1994. *Monopolistic Competition Theory: Origins, Results, and Implications*. Baltimore: Johns Hopkins University Press.

Keppler, Jan H. 2002. "Stackelberg Heinrich von." In *Dictionnaire des grandes œuvres économiques*. Edited by Jérôme Lallement, Michel de Vroey, and Xavier Greffe, 553–560. Paris: Editions Dalloz-Sirey.

Keppler, Jan H. 2004. "La quête d'une théorie de la concurrence empiriquement pertinente." *Revue Économique* 55 (3): 557–567.

Keynes, John M. 1936/1973. *The General Theory*. The Collected Writings of John Maynard Keynes, vol. VII. Edited by Elizabeth Johnson and Donald Moggridge. London: Macmillan.

Kitchen, Martin. 2012. *A History of Modern Germany: 1800 to the Present*, 2nd. Malden: Wiley-Blackwell.

Klausinger, Hansjörg. 1999. "German anticipations of the Keynesian revolution? The case of Lautenbach, Neisser and Röpke." *European Journal of the History of Economic Thought* 6 (3): 378–403.

Klein, Philip A. 1980. "Confronting power in economics: A pragmatic evaluation." *Journal of Economic Issues* 14 (4): 871–896.

Kleinwächter, Friedrich. 1883. *Die Kartelle. Ein Beitrag zur Frage der Organisation der Volkswirtschaft*. Innsbruck: Wagner.

Klinckowstroem, Wendula G. v. 2000. "Walter Eucken: Eine biographische Skizze." In *Walter Eucken und sein Werk: Rückblick auf den Vordenker der sozialen Marktwirtschaft*. Edited by Lüder Gerken, 53–111. Tübingen: Mohr Siebeck.

Klopstock, Fred H. 1949. "Monetary reform in Western Germany." *Journal of Political Economy* 57 (4): 277–292.

Klump, Rainer. 2003. "On the phenomenological roots of German ordnungstheorie: What Walter Eucken owes to Edmund Husserl." In *L'ordolibéralisme allemand: Aux sources de l'économie sociale de marché*. Edited by Patricia Commun, 149–162. Cergy-Pontoise: CIRAC/CICC.

Klump, Rainer, and Manuel Wörsdörfer. 2010. "An ordoliberal interpretation of Adam Smith." *ORDO: Jahrbuch für die Ordnung von Wirtschaft und Gesellschaft* 61: 29–51.

Klump, Rainer, and Manuel Wörsdörfer. 2011. "On the affiliation of phenomenology and ordoliberalism: Links between Edmund Husserl, Rudolf and Walter Eucken." *European Journal of the History of Economic Thought* 18 (4): 551–578.

Knight, Frank H. 1921/1971. *Risk, Uncertainty and Profit*. Chicago: The University of Chicago Press.

Knight, Frank H. 1936. "The place of marginal economics in a collectivist system." *American Economic Review* 26 (1): 255–266.

Köhler, Ekkehard A., and Stefan Kolev. 2013. "The conjoint quest for a liberal positive program: 'Old Chicago,' Freiburg, and Hayek." In *F. A. Hayek and the Modern Economy*. Edited by Sandra J. Peart and David M. Levy, 211–228. New York: Palgrave Macmillan.

Köhler, Ekkehard A., and Daniel Nientiedt. 2017. "The Muthesius controversy: a tale of two liberalisms." *History of Political Economy* 49 (4): 607–630.

Kolev, Stefan. 2010. "Hayek as an ordo-liberal." *HWWI Research Paper* 5–11: 1–22.

Kolev, Stefan. 2013. *Neoliberale Staatsverständnisse im Vergleich*. Stuttgart: Lucius & Lucius.

Kolev, Stefan. 2015. "Ordoliberalism and the Austrian School." In *The Oxford Handbook of Austrian Economics*. Edited by Christopher J. Coyne and Peter J. Boettke, 419–444. New York: Oxford University Press.

Kolev, Stefan. 2017. *Neoliberale Staatsverständnisse im Vergleich*. Berlin: De Gruyter.

Kolev, Stefan. 2018a. "Paleo- and neoliberals: Ludwig von Mises and the 'Ordo-interventionists.'" In *Wilhelm Röpke (1899–1966): A Liberal Political Economist and Conservative Social Philosopher*. Edited by Patricia Commun and Stefan Kolev, 65–92. Cham: Springer.

Kolev, Stefan. 2018b. "The abandoned Übervater: Max Weber and the neoliberals." *CHOPE Working Paper no. 2018-21*.

Kolev, Stefan, Nils Goldschmidt, and Jan-Otmar Hesse. 2020. "Debating liberalism: Walter Eucken, F. A. Hayek and the early history of the Mont Pèlerin Society." *Review of Austrian Economics*, 33 (4): 433–463.

Konow, James. 1994. "The political economy of Heinrich von Stackelberg." *Economic Inquiry* 32 (1): 146–165.

Krarup, Troels. 2019. "'Ordo' versus 'Ordnung': Catholic or Lutheran Roots of German ordoliberal economic theory?" *International Review of Economics* 66 (3): 1–19.

Krengel, Rolf. 1963. "Some reasons for the rapid economic growth of the German Federal Republic." *Banca Nazionale del Lavoro Quaterly Review* 64: 121–144.

Kuhnert, Stephan. 2008. "The man who heated up economic discussion with a stove: Walter Eucken's challenge to the social sciences.'" In *The Struggle to Constitute and Sustain Productive Orders: Vincent Ostrom's Quest to Understand Human Affairs*. Edited by Mark Sproule-Jones, Barbara Allen and Filippo Sabetti, 111–124. Lanham: Lexington Books.

Kurz, Heinz D. 2016. *Economic Thought: A Brief History*. New York: Columbia University Press.

Kurz, Heinz D. 2018. "Elements of a science of power: Hobbes, Smith and Ricardo." In *Power in Economic Thought*. Edited by Manuela Mosca, 109–142. London: Palgrave Macmillan.

Labrousse, Agnès. 2009. "La querelle des méthode: Une affaire close?" In *La pensée économique allemande*. Edited by A. Alcouffe and C. Diebolt, 143–170. Paris: Economica.

Labrousse, Agnès, and Jean-Daniel Weisz, eds. 2001. *Institutional Economics in France and Germany: German Ordoliberalism Versus the French Regulation School*. Heidelberg: Springer.

Laidler, David. 2015. "Three revolutions in macroeconomics: Their nature and influence." *European Journal of the History of Economic Thought* 22 (1): 1–25.

Lakomski, Odile. 1999. "L'hypothèse de J.A. Schumpeter: La monnaie comme comptabilité sociale." *Cahiers d'Économic Politique* 35: 91–103.

Lallement, Jérôme. 2004. "Sraffa et la théorie marshallienne de la valeur: La postérité d'une critique." *Economies et Sociétés, PE* 38 (8–9): 1559–1580.

Lange, Oskar. 1936. "On the economic theory of socialism: Part one." *Review of Economic Studies* 4 (1): 53–71.

Lange, Oskar. 1937. "On the economic theory of socialism: Part two." *Review of Economic Studies* 4 (2): 123–142.

Lange, Oskar. 1945. "The scope and method of economics." *Review of Economic Studies* 13 (1): 19–32.

Lantink, Frans Willem. 2018. "Cultural pessimism and liberal regeneration? Wilhelm Röpke as an ideological in-between in German social philosophy." In *Wilhelm Röpke (1899–1966): A Liberal Political Economist and Conservative Social Philosopher*. Edited by Patricia Commun and Stefan Kolev, 187–200. Cham: Springer.

Lavoie, Don. 1985. *Rivalry and Central Planning: The Socialist Calculation Debate Reconsidered*. Cambridge: Cambridge University Press.

Lechevalier, Arnaud. 2015. "Eucken under the pillow: The ordoliberal imprint on social Europe." In *Social Europe: A Dead End*. Edited by Arnaud Lechevalier and Boet Wielgohs, 49–102. Copenhagen: DJøF Publishing.

Leen, A. R. 2003. "Röpke revisited from a modern-austrian perspective: The moral heart of capitalism." In *Economic Policy in an Orderly Framework: Liber Amicorum for Gerrit Meijer*. Edited by Wim Heijmann, 271–283. Münster: Lit.

Leeson, Robert. 2001. *The Eclipse of Keynesianism: The Political Economy of the Chicago Counter-Revolution*. New York: Springer.

Leipold, Helmut. 1990. "Neoliberal ordnungstheorie and constitutional economics." *Constitutional Political Economy* 1 (1): 47–65.

Lemke, Thomas. 2001. "'The birth of bio-politics': Michel Foucault's lecture at the College de France on Neo-Liberal Governmentality." *Economy and Society* 30 (2): 190–207.

Lenel, Hans Otto. 1971/1989. "Does Germany still have a social market economy?" In *Germany's Social Market Economy: Origins and Evolution*. Edited by Alan Peacock and Hans Willgerodt, 261–272. London: Macmillan for the Trade Policy Research Centre.

Lenel, Hans Otto, and Fritz W. Meyer, eds. 1948. "Vorwort: Die Aufgabe des Jahrbuchs." *ORDO: Jahrbuch für die Ordnung von Wirtschaft und Gesellschaft* 1: 7–11.

Leontief, Wassily. 1936. "Stackelberg on Monopolistic Competition." *Journal of Political Economy* 44 (4): 554–559.

Lerner, Abba P. 1934. "Economic theory and socialist economy." *Review of Economic Studies* 2 (1): 51–61.

Lerner, Abba P. 1937. "Statics and dynamics in socialist economics." *Economic Journal* 47 (186): 253–270.

Lerner, Abba P. 1949. "Some theoretical aspects." *Review of Economics and Statistics* 31 (3): 193–200.

Levy, David M., and Sandra J. Peart. 2008. "Socialist calculation debate." In *The New Palgrave Dictionary of Economics*, 2nd edn. Edited by Steven N. Durlauf and Lawrence E. Blume, 685–692. Basingstoke: Nature Publishing Group.

Liefmann, Robert. 1927/1932. *Kartelle, Konzerne und Trusts / Cartels, Concerns and Trusts*. London: Methuen.

Lindenfeld, David F. 2008. *The Practical Imagination: The German Sciences of State in the Nineteenth Century*. Chicago: University of Chicago Press.

Lindseth, Peter L. 2004. "The paradox of parliamentary supremacy: Delegation, democracy, and dictatorship in Germany and France, 1920s–1950s." *Yale Law Journal* 113 (7): 1341–1415.

Louzek, Marek. 2011. "The battle of methods in economics. The classical methodenstreit—Menger vs. Schmoller." *American Journal of Economics and Sociology* 70 (2): 439–463.

Lutz, Friedrich A. 1932. *Das Konjunkturproblem in der Nationalökonomie*. Jena: G. Fischer.

Lutz, Friedrich A. 1933. "Von der Geisteshaltung der jüngeren Generation. I. Die Ideologie des Tatkreise." *Die Tatwelt* 9: 99–112.

Lutz, Friedrich A. 1935/1989. "The functioning of the gold standard." In *Germany's Social Market Economy: Origins and Evolution*. Edited by Alan Peacock and Hans Willgerodt, 219–241. London: Macmillan for the Trade Policy Research Centre.

Lutz, Friedrich A. 1936. *Das Grundproblem der Geldverfassung*. Ordnung der Wirtschaft. Stuttgart: Kohlhammer.

Lutz, Friedrich A. 1938. "The outcome of the saving-investment discussion." *Quarterly Journal of Economics* 52 (4): 588–614.

Lutz, Friedrich A. 1940a. "Review: Die Grundlagen der Nationalökonimie." *American Economic Review* 30 (3): 587–588.

Lutz, Friedrich A. 1940b. "The structure of interest rates." *The Quarterly Journal of Economics* 55 (1): 36–63.

Lutz, Friedrich A. 1943. *International Monetary Mechanisms: The Keynes and White Proposals*. Princeton: International Finance Section, Dept. of Economics and Social Institutions, Princeton University.

Lutz, Friedrich A. 1944. "History and theory in economics." *Economica* 11 (44): 210–214.

Lutz, Friedrich A. 1945. "The interest rate and investment in a dynamic economy." *American Economic Review* 35 (5): 811–830.

Lutz, Friedrich A. 1948. *The Marshall Plan and European Economic Policy*. Princeton: International Finance Section, Dept. of Economics and Social Institutions, Princeton University.

Lutz, Friedrich A. 1949a. "Geldpolitik und Wirtschaftsordnung." *ORDO: Jahrbuch für die Ordnung von Wirtschaft und Gesellschaft* 2: 207–228.

Lutz, Friedrich A. 1949b. "The German currency reform and the revival of the German economy." *Economica* 16 (62): 122–142.

Lutz, Friedrich A. 1950. "Introduction." To *The Foundations of Economics* by Walter Eucken. London: W. Hodge.

Lutz, Friedrich A. 1956/1989. "Observations on the problem of monopolies." In *Germany's Social Market Economy: Origins and Evolution*. Edited by Alan Peacock and Hans Willgerodt, 152–170. London: Macmillan for the Trade Policy Research Centre.

Maas, Harro. 2009. "Disciplining boundaries: Lionel Robbins, Max Weber, and the borderlands of economics, history, and psychology" *Journal of the History of Economic Thought* 31 (04): 500–517.

Magliulo, Antonio. 2018. "Before Hitler: The expansionary programme of the Brauns Commission." In *Hayek: A Collaborative Biography: Part XIII: "Fascism "and Liberalism in the (Austrian) Classical Tradition*. Edited by Robert Leeson, 129–159. Cham: Springer International.

Maier, Hans, ed. 2014. *Die Freiburger Kreise: Akademischer Widerstand und Soziale Marktwirtschaft*. Paderborn: Ferdinand Schöningh.

Mäki, Uskali, Adrian Walsh, and Manuela Fernández Pinto, eds. 2018. *Scientific Imperialism: Exploring the Boundaries of Interdisciplinarity*. Abingdon: Routledge.

Mandeville, Bernard. 1714/1988. *The Fable of the Bees*. Edited by Frederick B. Kaye. Indianapolis: Liberty Fund.

Mann, Geoff. 2017. *In the Long Run We Are All Dead: Keynesianism, Political Economy, and Revolution*. London: Verso.

Marburg, Theodore F. 1964. “Government and business in Germany: Public policy toward cartels.” *Business History Review* 38 (01): 78–101.

Marcuzzo, Maria C. 2008. “The ‘first’ imperfect competition revolution.” In *A Companion to the History of Economic Thought*. Edited by Warren J. Samuels, Jeff E. Biddle, and John B. Davis, 294–306. Oxford: John Wiley & Sons.

Marcuzzo, Maria C. 2010. “Whose welfare state? Beveridge versus Keynes.” In *No Wealth But Life: Welfare Economics and the Welfare State in Britain, 1880–1945*. Edited by Roger E. Backhouse and Tamotsu Nishizawa, 189–206. Cambridge: Cambridge University Press.

Marx, Karl. 1844/1999. *Manuscrits de 1844*. Paris: Flammarion.

Marx, Karl. 1847/1996. *Misère de la philosophie*. Edited by Jean Kessler. Paris: Payot & Rivages.

Masala, Antonio, and Özge Kama. 2018. “Between two continents: Wilhelm Röpke’s years in Istanbul.” In *Wilhelm Röpke (1899–1966): A Liberal Political Economist and Conservative Social Philosopher*. Edited by Patricia Commun and Stefan Kolev, 11–29. Cham: Springer.

Mason, Edward S. 1939. “Price and production policies of large-scale enterprise.” *American Economic Review* 29 (1): 61–74.

Matthijs, Matthias. 2016. “Powerful rules governing the euro: The perverse logic of German ideas.” *Journal of European Public Policy* 23 (3): 375–391.

Matthijs, Matthias, and Kathleen McNamara. 2015. “The euro crisis’ theory effect: Northern saints, southern sinners, and the demise of the eurobond.” *Journal of European Integration* 37 (2): 229–245.

Mayhew, Anne. 1980. “Schumpeterian capitalism versus the ‘Schumpeterian Thesis.’” *Journal of Economic Issues* 14 (2): 583–592.

McGowan, Lee. 2010. *The Antitrust Revolution in Europe: Exploring the European Commission’s Cartel Policy*. Cheltenham: Edward Elgar.

“Measures for controlling consumption, supply and prices after the currency reform (First report of the Advisory Board at the Economic Administration of the United Economic Area; Königstein, April 18, 1948).” 1979. *Journal of Institutional and Theoretical Economics* 135 (3): 449–453.

Medema, Steven G. 2020. “‘Exceptional and unimportant’? Externalities, competitive equilibrium, and the myth of a Pigovian tradition.” *History of Political Economy* 52 (1): 135–170.

Megay, Edward N. 1970. “Anti-pluralist liberalism: The German neoliberals.” *Political Science Quarterly* 85 (3): 422–442.

Meiers, Franz-Josef. 2015. “‘Made in Germany’: Categorical imperatives of ordoliberalism.” In *Germany’s Role in the Euro Crisis*, 11–16. Heidelberg: Springer.

Meijer, Gerrit. 1994. “Walter Eucken’s contribution to economics in an international perspective.” *Journal of Economic Studies* 21 (4): 25–37.

Meijer, Gerrit. 2005. “Some aspects of the relationship between the Freiburg School and the Austrian School.” In *Modern Applications of Austrian Thought*. Edited by Jürgen G. Backhaus, 139–150. New York: Routledge.

Meijer, Gerrit. 2007. “Value and exchange in economic theorizing: The contribution of the Freiburg School.” *Review of Austrian Economics* 20 (2–3): 171–185.

Mendershausen, Horst. 1949. “Prices, money and the distribution of goods in postwar Germany.” *American Economic Review* 39 (3): 646–672.

Menger, Carl. 1883/1986. *Investigations into the method of the social sciences with special reference to economics*. Translated by Francis J. Nock. New York: New York University Press.

Merkel, Angela. 2016. "Rede von Bundeskanzlerin Merkel beim Festakt zum 125. Geburtstag von Walter Eucken am 13. January 2016." https://www.bundeskanzlerin.de/Content/DE/Rede/2016/01/2016-01-14-rede-walter-eucken.html.

Mierzejewski, Alfred C. 2004. *Ludwig Erhard: A Biography*. Chapel Hill: University of North Carolina Press.

Mierzejewski, Alfred C. 2006. "Water in the desert? The influence of Wilhelm Röpke on Ludwig Erhard and the social market economy." *Review of Austrian Economics* 19 (4): 275–287.

Miettinen, Timo. 2016. "Governing with ideas: On the phenomenolgoical roots of the ordoliberal tradition." *Metodo. International Studies in Phenomenology and Philosophy* 4 (1): 111–129.

Miksch, Leonhard. 1937a/1982. "Competition and economic constitution." In *Standard Texts on the Social Market Economy: Two Centuries of Discussion*. Edited by Horst Friedrich Wünsche, translated by Derek Rutter, 147–151. Stuttgart: Gustav Fischer Verlag.

Miksch, Leonhard. 1937b. *Wettbewerb als Aufgabe: Grundsätze einer Wettbewerbsordnung*. Ordnung der Wirtschaft. Stuttgart: Kohlhammer.

Miksch, Leonhard. 1942. "Möglichkeiten und Grenzen der gebundenen Konkurrenz." In *Der Wettbewerb als Mittel volkswirtschaftlicher Leistungssteigerung und Leistungsauslese*. Edited by Günter Schmölders, 99–106. Schriften der Akademie für Deutsches Recht. Gruppe Wirtschaftswissenschaft. Berlin: Duncker & Humblot.

Miksch, Leonhard. 1947. "Wirtschaftspolitik in der Demokratie." *Die Zeit*, July 3: 5.

Miksch, Leonhard. 1948. "Die Wirtschaftspolitik des Als-Ob." *Zeitschrift für die gesamte Staatswissenschaft* 105 (2): 310–338.

Miksch, Leonhard. 1950a. "Die sittliche Bedeutung der inneren Koordination." *ORDO: Jahrbuch für die Ordnung von Wirtschaft und Gesellschaft* 3: 29–73.

Miksch, Leonhard. 1950b. "Walter Eucken." *Kyklos* 4 (4): 279–290.

Mirowski, Philip, and Dieter Plehwe, eds. 2009. *The Road from Mont Pèlerin: The Making of the Neoliberal Thought Collective*. Cambridge: Harvard University Press.

Mises, Ludwig von. 1920/2012. *Economic Calculation in the Socialist Commonwealth*. Translated by S. Adler. Auburn: Mises Institute.

Mises, Ludwig von. 1922/1951. *Socialism*. Translated by J. Kahane. New Haven: Yale University Press.

Mises, Ludwig von. 1949/1998. *Human Action, The Scholar's Edition*. Auburn: Ludwig von Mises Institute.

Moeller, Hero. 1950. "Liberalismus." *Jahrbücher für Nationalökonomie und Statistik* 162 (3): 214–240.

Moinat, Frédéric. 2005. "Sciences humaines, sciences de la nature et procédé d'idéalisation chez Husserl." *Phänomenologische Forschungen* 2005: 41–63.

Möller, Hans. 1948. "Heinrich Freiherr von Stackelberg und sein Beitrag für die Wirtschaftswissenschaft." *Zeitschrift für die gesamte Staatswissenschaft* 105 (3): 395–428.

Mongin, Philippe. 2006. "Value judgments and value neutrality in economics." *Economica* 73 (290): 257–286.

Mongouachon, Claire. 2011. "L'ordolibéralisme: Contexte historique et contenu dogmatique." *Concurrences* 4: 70–78.

Mongouachon, Claire. 2012. "Les débats sur la Constitution économique en Allemagne." *Revue Française de Droit Constitutionnel* 90: 303–337.

Mongouachon, Claire. 2016. "Pour une concurrence régulée : L'apport de Leonhard Miksch." In *L'ordolibéralisme, aux origines de l'École de Fribourg-en-Brisgau*. Edited by Hugues Rabault, 161–188. Paris: L'Harmattan.

Monvoisin, Virginie, and Louis-Philippe Rochon. 2007. "Economic power and the real world: A post-keynesian analysis of power." *International Journal of Political Economy* 35 (4): 5–30.

Möschel, Wernhard. 2001. "The proper scope of government viewed from an ordoliberal perspective: The example of competition policy." *Journal of Institutional and Theoretical Economics* 157: 3–13.

Möschel, Wernhard. 2006. "Les sanctions de droit privé des comportements anticoncurrentiels: Aspects du droit allemand." *Revue Internationale de Droit Comparé* 58 (3): 735–746.

Mosse, George Lachmann, and Edith Magyar. 1999. *De la grande guerre au totalitarisme : La brutalisation des sociétés européennes*. Paris: Hachette.

Müller-Armack, Alfred. 1947/1982. "Die Wirtschaftsordnung, sozial gesehen / The social aspect of the economic system." In *Standard Texts on the Social Market Economy: Two Centuries of Discussion*. Edited by Horst Friedrich Wünsche, translated by Derek Rutter, 9–22. Stuttgart: Gustav Fischer Verlag.

Müller-Armack, Alfred. 1956/1989. "Soziale Marktwirtschaft / The meaning of the social market economy." In *Germany's Social Market Economy: Origins and Evolution*. Edited by Alan Peacock and Hans Willgerodt, 82–86. London: Macmillan for the Trade Policy Research Centre.

Myrdal, Gunnar. 1951. "The trend towards economic planning." *Manchester School* 19 (1): 1–42.

Nau, Heino Heinrich. 2000. "Gustav Schmoller's historico-ethical political economy: Ethics, politics and economics in the younger German Historical School, 1860–1917." *European Journal of the History of Economic Thought* 7 (4): 507–531.

Nedergaard, Peter, and Holly Snaith. 2015. "'As I drifted on a river I could not control': The unintended ordoliberal consequences of the eurozone crisis." *Journal of Common Market Studies* 53 (5): 1094–1109.

Neumann, Manfred. 2001. *Competition Policy: History, Theory and Practice*. Cheltenham: Edward Elgar.

Neurath, Otto. 1919/1973. "Durch die Kriegwirtschaft zur Naturalwirtschat / Through War Economy to Economy in Kind." In *Empiricism and Sociology*. Edited by Marie Neurath and Robert S. Cohen, 123–157. Dordrecht: D. Reidel.

Nicholls, Anthony J. 1994. *Freedom with Responsability: The Social Market Economy in Germany, 1918–1963*. Oxford: Clarendon Press.

Niehans, Jürg. 1992. "Heinrich von Stackelberg: Relinking German economics to the mainstream." *Journal of the History of Economic Thought* 14 (2): 189–208.

Nientiedt, Daniel. 2019a. "German Economists and Value Freedom: The Case of Walter Eucken." Paper presented at the 46th HES Annual Meetings in Columbia (New York), June 20-23.

Nientiedt, Daniel. 2019b. "Metaphysical justification for an economic constitution? Franz Böhm and the concept of natural law." *Constitutional Political Economy* 30 (1): 114–129.

Nientiedt, Daniel, and Ekkehard A. Köhler. 2016. "Liberalism and democracy: A comparative reading of Eucken and Hayek." *Cambridge Journal of Economics* 40 (6): 1743–1760.

Nörr, Knut W. 1995. "Franz Böhm, ein Wegbereiter des Privatrechtsgedankens." *ORDO: Jahrbuch für die Ordnung von Wirtschaft und Gesellschaft* 46: 27–39.

Nörr, Knut W. 1996. "On the concept of the 'economic constitution' and the importance of Franz Böhm from the viewpoint of legal history." *European Journal of Law and Economics* 3 (4): 345–356.

Nörr, Knut W. 2000. "Franz Böhm and the theory of the private law society." In *Theory of Capitalism in the German Economic Tradition: Historism, Ordo-liberalism, Critical Theory, Solidarism*. Edited by Peter Koslowski, 148–191. Heidelberg: Springer.

Ojala, Markus, and Timo Harjuniemi. 2016. "Mediating the German ideology: Ordoliberal framing in European press coverage of the eurozone crisis." *Journal of Contemporary European Studies* 24 (3): 414–430.

Oksala, Johanna. 2016. "Foucault, Husserl and the philosophical roots of German neoliberalism." *Continental Philosophy Review* 49: 1–12.

Olender, Michael. 2012. "Germany's euro crisis: Preferences, management, and contingencies." *Review of European and Russian Affairs* 7 (2): 1–17.

Oliver, Henry M. 1960a. "German neoliberalism." *Quarterly Journal of Economics* 74 (1): 117–149.

Oliver, Henry M. 1960b. "Ordo and coercion: A logical critique." *Southern Economic Journal* 27 (2): 81–91.

Olsen, Niklas. 2018. *The Sovereign Consumer: A New Intellectual History of Neoliberalism*. Cham: Springer.

Oswalt-Eucken, Irene. 1994. "Freedom and economic power: Neglected aspects of Walter Eucken's Work." *Journal of Economic Studies* 21 (4): 38–45.

Ozanne, Adam. 2016. *Power and Neoclassical Economics: A Return to Political Economy in the Teaching of Economics*. Basingstoke: Palgrave Macmillan.

Paish, F. W. 1953. "Open and repressed inflation." *Economic Journal* 63 (251): 527–552.

Pareto, Vilfredo. 1906/1966. *Manuel d'économie politique*. Edited by Giovanni Busino. Œuvres complètes, vol. VII. Genève: Librairie E. Droz.

Peacock, Alan T. 1950. "Recent German contributions to economics." *Economica* 17 (66): 175–187.

Peacock, Alan T. 1952. "Introduction." To *The Theory of the Market Economy*. By Heinrich F. von Stackelberg, xiv–xxiii. New York: Oxford University Press.

Pelle, Anita. 2016. "The Freiburg scholars and interwar Germany." In *Economic Thought and History: An unresolved relationship*. Edited by Monika Poettinger and Gianfranco Tusset, 100–120. New York: Routledge.

Persky, Joseph. 1993. "Retrospectives: Consumer sovereignty." *Journal of Economic Perspectives* 7 (1): 183–191.

Petersen, Jens. 2019. *Rechtsordnung und Wirtschaftsordnung nach Eucken*. Berlin: De Gruyter.

Petzina, Dieter. 1969. "Germany and the Great Depression." *Journal of Contemporary History* 4 (4): 59–74.

Peukert, Helge. 2000. "Walter Eucken (1891–1950) and the Historical School." In *Theory of Capitalism in the German Economic Tradition: Historism, Ordo-liberalism, Critical Theory, Solidarism*. Edited by Peter Koslowski, 93–147. Heidelberg: Springer.

Peukert, Helge. 2001. "The Schmoller renaissance." *History of Political Economy* 33 (1): 71–116.

Phillips, Almarin, and Rodney E. Stevenson. 1974. "The historical development of industrial organization." *History of Political Economy* 6 (3): 324–342.

Piettre, André. 1962. "L'économie allemande est-elle vraiment libérale ?" *Revue Économique* 13 (3): 339–354.

Plumpe, Werner. 2004. "Opting for the structural break: The West German currency reform and its consequences." In *The United States and Germany in the Era of the Cold War, 1945–1990*. Edited by Detlef Junker, 293–300. Cambridge: Cambridge University Press.

Polanyi, Karl. 1944. *The Great Transformation*. New York: Rinehart.

Pongracic, Ivan. 1997. "How different were Röpke and Mises?" *Review of Austrian Economics* 10 (1): 125–132.

Postan, M. M. 1967/2013. *An Economic History of Western Europe 1945–1964*. London: Routledge.

Powers, Charles H. 1997. "Justice, social welfare, and the state in the eyes of Gustav von Schmoller." In *Essays on Social Security and Taxation. Gustav von Schmoller and Adolph Wagner Reconsidered*. Edited by Jürgen G. Backhaus, 173–201. Marburg: Metropolis.

Pribram, Karl. 1935. *Cartel Problems: An Analysis of Collective Monopolies in Europe with American Application*. Washington: Brookings Institution.

Pribram, Karl. 1983. *A History of Economic Reasoning*. Baltimore: Johns Hopkins University Press.

Pribram, Karl. 1986. *Les Fondements de la pensée économique*. Paris: Économica.

Priddat, Birger P. 2004. "Gustav Schmoller : L'économie comme moralité institutionnalisée." In *Histoire et économie politique en Allemagne de Gustav Schmoller à Max Weber: Nouvelles perspectives sur l'école historique de l'économie*. Edited by Hinnerk Bruhns, translated by Françoise Laroche, 53–74. Paris: Éditions de la Maison des sciences de l'homme.

Prowe, Diethelm. 1985. "Economic democracy in post-world war II Germany: Corporatist Crisis Response, 1945–1948." *Journal of Modern History* 57 (3): 451–482.

Ptak, Ralf. 2009. "Neoliberalism in Germany." In *The Road from Mont Pèlerin: The Making of the Neoliberal Thought Collective*. Edited by Philip Mirowski and Dieter Plehwe, 98–138. Cambridge: Harvard University Press.

Rabault, Hugues. 2016a. "L'idée de 'constitution économique' chez Walter Eucken." In *L'ordolibéralisme, aux origines de l'École de Fribourg-en-Brisgau*. Edited by Hugues Rabault, 51–94. Paris: L'Harmattan.

Rabault, Hugues, ed. 2016b. *L'ordolibéralisme, aux origines de l'École de Fribourg-en-Brisgau*. Paris: L'Harmattan.

Rabault, Hugues. 2016c. "Pour introduire à l'ordolibéralisme." In *L'ordolibéralisme, aux origines de l'École de Fribourg-en-Brisgau*. Edited by Hugues Rabault, 13–28. Paris: L'Harmattan.

Radnitzky, Gerard, and Peter Bernholz, eds. 1987. *Economic Imperialism: The Economic Approach Applied Outside the Field of Economics*. New York: Paragon House.

Rainelli, Michel. 2000. "Comportements et formes de la concurrence." In *Nouvelle histoire de la pensée économique*. Edited by Alain Béraud and Gilbert Faccarello, 3: 125–161. Paris: La Découverte.

Rawls, John. 2001. *Justice as Fairness: A Restatement*, 2nd revised edn. Cambridge: Harvard University Press.

Reinhoudt, Jurgen, and Serge Audier. 2017. *The Walter Lippmann Colloquium: The Birth of Neo-Liberalism*. Cham: Palgrave Macmillan.

Reiss, Julian. 2014. "Struggling over the soul of economics: Objectivity versus expertise." In *Experts and Consensus in Social Science*. Edited by Carlo Martini and Marcel Boumans, 131–152. Cham: Springer International.

Richter, Rudolf. 2015. "German 'ordnungstheorie' from the perspective of the new institutional economics." In *Essays on New Institutional Economics*, 161–183. Heidelberg: Springer.

Rieter, Heinz, and Matthias Schmolz. 1993. "The ideas of German ordoliberalism 1938–45: Pointing the way to a new economic order." *European Journal of the History of Economic Thought* 1 (1): 87–114.

Robbins, Lionel. 1932/1984. *An Essay on the Nature and Significance of Economic Science*, 3nd edn. London: Macmillan.

Robbins, Lionel. 1934/2011. *The Great Depression*. New Brunswick: Transaction.

Robbins, Lionel. 1938. *L'économie planifiée et l'ordre international*. Translated by Marie-Thérèse Génin. Paris: Librairie de Médicis.

Robinson, Joan. 1933/1969. *The Economics of Imperfect Competition*, 2nd edn. New York: St. Martin's Press.

Röpke, Wilhelm. 1931. "Praktische Konjunkturpolitik. Die Arbeit der Brauns-Kommission." *Weltwirtschaftliches Archiv* 34: 423–464.

Röpke, Wilhelm. 1932. *Krise und Konjunktur*. Leipzig: Quelle und Meyer.

Röpke, Wilhelm. 1933. "Trends in German business cycle policy." *Economic Journal* 43 (171): 427–441.

Röpke, Wilhelm. 1934a. *German Commercial Policy*. London: Longmans Green.

Röpke, Wilhelm. 1934b/2005. "Kapitalismus und Imperialismus / Capitalisme et Impérialisme." Translated by Michaël Girod in *Carnets de bord en sciences humaines* 8: 48–56.

Röpke, Wilhelm. 1935. "Fascist economics." *Economica* 2 (5): 85–100.

Röpke, Wilhelm. 1936a. *Crises and Cycles*. London: W. Hodge.

Röpke, Wilhelm. 1936b. "Socialism, planning, and the business cycle." *Journal of Political Economy* 44 (3): 318–338.

Röpke, Wilhelm. 1936c. "Tendances actuelles de l'économie politique." Translated by Isabella Hofer. *Revue d'économie politique* 36: 1284–1307.

Röpke, Wilhelm. 1937/1940. *Die Lehre von der Wirtschaft / Explication économique du monde moderne*. Paris: Librairie de Médicis.

Röpke, Wilhelm. 1942a. "A value judgment on value judgments." *Revue de la Faculté des Sciences Economiques d'Istanbul* 3 (1–2): 1–19.

Röpke, Wilhelm. 1942b/1945. *Die Gesellschaftskrisis der Gegenwart / La crise de notre temps*. Translated by Hugues Faesi and Charles Reichard. Neuchâtel: La Baconnière.

Röpke, Wilhelm. 1942c/1950. *Die Gesellschaftskrisis der Gegenwart / The Social Crisis of Our Time*. Chicago: University of Chicago Press.

Röpke, Wilhelm. 1942d. *International Economic Disintegration*. London: W. Hodge.

Röpke, Wilhelm. 1944a/1946. *Civitas humana*, 2nd edn. Paris: Librairie de Médicis.

Röpke, Wilhelm. 1944b/2002. *The Moral Foundations of Civil Society*, 2nd revised edition. New Brunswick: Transaction.

Röpke, Wilhelm. 1945a/1946. *Die Deutche Frage / The German Question*. Translated by Ernest Walter Dickes. London: G. Allen and Unwinn.

Röpke, Wilhelm. 1945b/1959. *Internationale Ordnung—heute / International Order and Economic Integration*. Dordrecht: Springer.

Röpke, Wilhelm. 1946a. "New Germans must shape the new Germany." *New York Times*, October 13, 1946.

Röpke, Wilhelm. 1946b. "The German dust-bowl." *Review of Politics* 8 (04): 511–527.

Röpke, Wilhelm. 1947a. "Anglo-American agreement on Germany." *Time & Tide*, June 7: 584–585.

Röpke, Wilhelm. 1947b. "Economic disease in Germany." *Time & Tide*, February 1 and 8: 129–130, 162–163.

Röpke, Wilhelm. 1947c. *La fonction de la petite et moyenne entreprise dans l'économie publique*. Berne: Publications de l'Union suisse des arts et Métiers.

Röpke, Wilhelm. 1947d/1969. "Marshall Plan and economic policy." Reprinted and translated from the *Neue Zürcher Zeitung*, November 23. In *Against the Tide*, 123–132. Chicago: H. Regnery.

Röpke, Wilhelm. 1947e. "Repressed inflation." *Kyklos* 1 (3): 242–253.

Röpke, Wilhelm. 1947f/1969. "'Repressed inflation': The ailment of the modern economy." Reprinted and translated from the *Neue Zürcher Zeitung*, June 14–15. In *Against the Tide*, 111–122. Chicago: H. Regnery.

Röpke, Wilhelm. 1947g. "The key to the Marshall Plan." *Time & Tide*, September 6: 952–953.

Röpke, Wilhelm. 1947h. "Offene Und Zurückgestaute Inflation." *Kyklos* 1 (1): 57–71.

Röpke, Wilhelm. 1948a. "Germany after the London Conference." *Time & Tide*, January 3 and 10: 5–6, 30–31.

Röpke, Wilhelm. 1948b. "Socialism and European Union." *Time & Tide*, December 11, 1948: 1269–1270.

Röpke, Wilhelm. 1949a. *L'âme de l'économie: Ordre et stimulation*. Genève: Radar.

Röpke, Wilhelm. 1949b. "Zur Theorie Des Kollektivismus: Ein Kritischer Literaturbericht." *Kyklos* 3 (2): 145–159.

Röpke, Wilhelm. 1950a. "Germany: The economic problems." *Time & Tide*, April 8: 339.

Röpke, Wilhelm. 1950b/1982. "Ist die deutsche Wirtschaftspolitik richtig ? / Is the German Economic Policy the Right One?" In Standard Texts on the Social Market Economy: Two Centuries of Discussion. Edited by Horst Friedrich Wünsche, translated by Derek Rutter, 37–48. Stuttgart: Gustav Fischer Verlag.

Röpke, Wilhelm. 1956. "The place of economics among the sciences." In *On Freedom and Free Enterprise: Essays in Honor of Ludwig von Mises*. Edited by Mary Sennholz, 111–127. Princeton: Van Nostrand.

Röpke, Wilhelm. 1963. *Die Lehre von der Wirtschaft / Economics of the Free Society*. Based on the 9th German edition. Chicago: H. Regnery.

Rothschild, Kurt W., ed. 1971. *Power in Economics: Selected Readings*. London: Penguin Books.

Rothschild, Kurt W. 1989. "Political economy or economics? Some terminological and normative considerations." *European Journal of Political Economy* 5 (1): 1–12.

Rueff, Jacques. 1949. *Epître aux dirigistes*. Paris: Gallimard.

Rüstow, Alexander. 1932/1982. "Liberal intervention." In *Standard Texts on the Social Market Economy: Two Centuries of Discussion*. Edited by Horst Friedrich Wünsche, translated by Derek Rutter, 183–186. Stuttgart: Gustav Fischer Verlag.

Rüstow, Alexander. 1942. "General sociological causes of the economic disintegration and possibilities of reconstruction—Appendix." In *International Economic Disintegration*. By Wilhelm Röpke, 267–283. London: W. Hodge.

Rüstow, Alexander. 1951/2017. " Sozialpolitik oder Vitalpolitik / Social policy or vitalpolitik." In *Birth of Austerity: German Ordoliberalism and Contemporary Neoliberalism*. Edited by Thomas Biebricher and Frieder Vogelmann, translated by Daniel Steuer, 163–177. London: Rowman & Littlefield International.

Rüstow, Alexander. 1956. "Welfare state or self-responsibility." [Liberaal Archief] 7th Meeting of the Mont Pèlerin Society: Berlin, Germany.

Rüstow, Alexander. 1980. *Freedom and Domination: A Historical Critique of Civilization*. Princeton: Princeton University Press.

Rutherford, Malcolm, and Mary S. Morgan, eds. 1998. *From Interwar Pluralism to Postwar Neoclassicism*. Vol. 30. History of Political Economy (Annual Supplement). Durham: Duke University Press.

Ryner, Magnus. 2015. "Europe's ordoliberal iron cage: Critical political economy, the euro area crisis and its management." *Journal of European Public Policy* 22 (2): 275–294.

Sally, Razeen. 1996. "Ordoliberalism and the social market: Classical political economy from Germany." *New Political Economy* 1 (2): 233–258.

Sauermann, Heinz. 1979. "On the economic and financial rehabilitation of Western Germany (1945–1949)." *Journal of Institutional and Theoretical Economics* 135 (3): 301–319.

Say, Jean-Baptiste. 1828/2010. *Cours complet d'économie politique pratique*. Edited by Emmanuel Blanc, Pierre-Henri Goutte, Jean-Pierre Potier, and André Tiran. Œuvres complètes, vol. 2. Paris: Economica.

Schabas, Margaret. 2009. "Constructing 'the economy.'" *Philosophy of the Social Sciences* 39 (1): 3–19.

Schäfer, David. 2016. "A banking union of ideas? The impact of ordoliberalism and the vicious circle on the EU Banking Union." *Journal of Common Market Studies* 54 (4): 961–980.

Schäuble, Wolfgang. 2014. "Keynote speech by Wolfgang Schäuble on the strategy for European recovery given at the Fifth Bruges European Business Conference on Thursday, 27 March 2014." http://www.bundesfinanzministerium.de/Content/EN/Reden/2014/2014-03-27-bruges.html.

Schefold, Bertram. 1995. "Theoretical approaches to a comparison of economic systems from a historical perspective." In *The Theory of Ethical Economy in the Historical School*. Edited by Peter Koslowski, 221–249. Berlin: Springer.

Schefold, Bertram. 1996. "The German Historical School and the belief in ethical progress." In *Ethical Universals in International Business*. Edited by Prof Dr F. Neil Brady, 173–196. Berlin: Springer.

Schefold, Bertram. 2003. "Die Deutsche Historische Schule als Quelle des Ordoliberalismus." In *L'ordolibéralisme allemand: Aux sources de l'économie sociale de marché*. Edited by Patricia Commun, 101–118. Cergy-Pontoise: CIRAC/CICC.

Scherf, Harald. 1986. *Enttäuschte Hoffnungen: Vergebene Chancen: Die Wirtschaftspolitik der Sozial-Liberalen Koalition 1969–1982*. Göttingen: Vandenhoeck & Ruprecht.

Schmidt, Karl-Heinz. 2011. "German Historical School and the question of liberalism." In *Freedom and Happiness in Economic Thought and Philosophy: From Clash to Reconciliation*. Edited by Ragip Ege and Herrade Igersheim, 105–118. London: Routledge.

Schmoller, Gustav von. 1902. *Politique sociale et économie politique (questions fondamentales)*. Translation revised by the author. Paris: Giard & Brière.

Schneider, Dieter. 1993. "Schmoller and the theory of the corporation and of corporate control." *History of Economic Ideas* 1/2 (3/1): 357–377.

Schumpeter, Joseph A. 1942/2006. *Capitalism, Socialism, and Democracy*. New York: Routledge.

Schumpeter, Joseph A. 1954/1981. *History of Economic Analysis*. London: Routledge.

Schwartz, Ivo E. 1957. "Antitrust legislation and policy in Germany. A comparative study." *University of Pennsylvania Law Review* 105 (5): 617–690.

Schweitzer, Arthur. 1970. "Typological method in economics: Max Weber's contribution." *History of Political Economy* 2 (1): 66–96.

Screpanti, Ernesto, and Stefano Zamagni. 2005. *An Outline of the History of Economic Thought*. Translated by David Field, 2nd edn. Oxford: Oxford University Press.

Senn, Peter R. 1996. "Heinrich von Stackelberg in the history of economic ideas." *Journal of Economic Studies* 23 (5/6): 15–39.

Senn, Peter R. 2012. "The scientific contributions of Heinrich von Stackelberg." In *Handbook of the History of Economic Thought*. Edited by Jürgen G. Backhaus, 565–579. New York: Springer.

Shackle, George L. S. 1967. *The Years of High Theory: Invention and Tradition in Economic Thought 1926–1939*. Cambridge: Cambridge University Press.

Shapiro, Peter D. 1962. "The German law against restraints of competition." *Columbia Law Review* 62 (1): 1–48.

Siems, Mathias, and Gerhard Schnyder. 2014. "Ordoliberal lessons for economic stability: Different kinds of regulation, not more regulation." *Governance* 27 (3): 377–396.

Simonin, Laurence. 1999. "La doctrine ordolibérale et la politique économique allemande de 1948 à 1966." Thèse de doctorat, Université de Nancy 2.

Simons, Henry C. 1936. "Rules versus authorities in monetary policy." *Journal of Political Economy* 44 (1): 1–30.

Simons, Henry C. 1948. *Economic policy for a Free Society*. Chicago: University of Chicago Press.

Slobodian, Quinn. 2018. *Globalists: The End of Empire and the Birth of Neoliberalism*. Cambridge: Harvard University Press.

Smith, Adam. 1776/1981. *An Inquiry into the nature and causes of the wealth of nations*. Edited by R. H. Campbell and A. S. Skinner. Vol. 1. Indianapolis: Liberty Fund.

Sohmen, Egon. 1959. "Competition and growth: The lesson of West Germany." *American Economic Review* 49 (5): 986–1003.

Solchany, Jean. 1997. *Comprendre le nazisme dans l'Allemagne des années zéro: 1945–1949*. Paris: Presses Universitaires de France.

Solchany, Jean. 2003. *L'Allemagne au XXe siècle: Entre singularité et normalité*. Paris: Presses Universitaires de France.

Solchany, Jean. 2015. *Wilhelm Röpke, l'autre Hayek: Aux origines du néolibéralisme*. Paris: Publications de la Sorbonne.

Solchany, Jean. 2018. "Wilhelm Röpke: Why he was a conservative." In *Wilhelm Röpke (1899–1966): A Liberal Political Economist and Conservative Social Philosopher*. Edited by Patricia Commun and Stefan Kolev, 165–173. Cham: Springer.

Sombart, Werner. 1929. "Economic theory and economic history." *Economic History Review* 2 (1): 1–19.

Sraffa, Piero. 1926. "The laws of returns under competitive conditions." *Economic Journal* 36 (144): 535–550.

Stackelberg, Heinrich F. von. 1934a. "Nationalsozialistische Wissenschaft: Rede anlässlich der ersten Veranstaltung der Kölner Dozentenschaft." *Völkischer Beobachter* 4 (1): 4–5.

Stackelberg, Heinrich F. von. 1934b/2010. *Marktform und Gleichgewicht / Market Structure and Equilibrium*. Translated by Damien Bazin, Lynn Urch, and Rowland Hill. Heidelberg: Springer.

Stackelberg, Heinrich F. von. 1938. "Probleme der unvollkommenen Konkurrenz." *Weltwirtschaftliches Archiv* 48: 95–141.

Stackelberg, Heinrich F. von. 1935/2001. "Der typische Fehlschluss in der Theorie der gleichgewichtslosen Marktformen (Ein Beitrag zum Seinsgebundenheitsproblem der Wissenschaft) / L'erreur dans la théorie des formes de marché sans équilibre: Une contribution au problème de la subjectivité de la science." Translated by Christian Rentzsch and Michel Hollard in *Cahiers d'Économie Politique* 37: 331–344.

Stackelberg, Heinrich F. von. 1940. "Die Grundlagen der Nationalökonomie. Bemerkungen zu dem gleichnamigen Buch von Walter Eucken." *Weltwirtschaftliches Archiv* 51 (2): 245–286.

Stackelberg, Heinrich F. von. 1948/1952. *Grundlagen der Theoretischen Volkswirtschaftslehre / The Theory of the Market Economy*. Translated by Alan T. Peacock. New York: Oxford University Press.

Stackelberg, Heinrich F. von. 1949. "Möglichkeiten und Grenzen der Wirtschaftslenkung." *ORDO: Jahrbuch für die Ordnung von Wirtschaft und Gesellschaft* 2: 194–206.

Staudenmaier, Peter. 2014. "The politics of the unpolitical: German anthroposophy in theory and practice before 1933." In *Between Occultism and Nazism*. 64–100. Leiden: Brill.

Steiner, Yves. 2007. "Les riches amis suisses du néolibéralisme. De la débâcle de la revue Occident à la Conférence du Mont Pèlerin d'avril 1947." *Traverse* 14 (1): 114–126.

Steiner, Yves, and Bernhard Walpen. 2006. "L'apport de l'ordolibéralisme au renouveau libéral, puis son éclipse." *Carnets de bord en sciences humaines* 11: 94–104.

Stigler, George J. 1957. "Perfect competition, historically contemplated." *Journal of Political Economy* 65 (1): 1–17.

Stolper, Wolfgang F., and Karl W. Roskamp. 1979. "Planning a free economy: Germany 1945–1960." *Journal of Institutional and Theoretical Economics* 135 (3): 374–404.

Strassel, Christophe. 2009. "Le modèle allemand de l'Europe: L'ordolibéralisme." *En Temps Réel* 39: 1–24.

Streit, Manfred E. 1992. "Economic order, private law and public policy: The Freiburg School of law and economics in perspective." *Journal of Institutional and Theoretical Economics* 148 (4): 675–704.

Taylor, Fred M. 1929. "The guidance of production in a socialist state." *American Economic Review* 19 (1): 1–8.

Temin, Peter. 1991. "Soviet and Nazi economic planning in the 1930s." *Economic History Review* 44 (4): 573–593.

Temin, Peter, and David Vines. 2015. "Keynes and the world economy today." *Challenge* 58 (5): 386–397.

Thompson, Grahame. 1992. "The evolution of the managed economy in Europe." *Economy and Society* 21 (2): 129–151.

Tietmeyer, Hans. 1999. *Économie sociale de marché et stabilité monétaire*. Translated by Sylvain Broyer. Paris: Économica.

Tobin, James. 1981. "The monetarist counter-revolution today: An appraisal." *Economic Journal* 91 (361): 29–42.

Tooze, Adam. 2001. *Statistics and the German State, 1900–1945: The Making of Modern Economic Knowledge*. Cambridge: Cambridge University Press.

Tooze, Adam. 2006. *The Wages of Destruction: The Making and Breaking of the Nazi Economy*. London: Allen Lane and Penguin Press.

Tribe, Keith. 1995. *Strategies of Economic Order: German Economic Discourse, 1750–1950*. Cambridge: Cambridge University Press.

Tribe, Keith. 2001. "The 1948 currency reform: Structure and purpose." In *50 Years of the German Mark: Essays in Honour of Stephen F. Frowen*. Edited by Jens Hölscher and Stephen F. Frowen, 15–51. Houndmills: Palgrave Macmillan.

Tribe, Keith. 2009. "The political economy of modernity: Foucault's College de France Lectures of 1978 and 1979: Review article." *Economy and Society* 38 (4): 679–698.

Triffin, Robert. 1940/1947. *Monopolistic Competition and General Equilibrium Theory*. Cambridge: Harvard University Press.

Uebel, Thomas. 2008. "Calculation in kind and marketless socialism: On Otto Neurath's utopian economics." *European Journal of the History of Economic Thought* 15 (3): 475–501.

Uterwedde, Henrik. 2007. "Les programmes de la CDU et du SPD: Convergences de fond." *Regards sur l'Économie Allemande* 84: 5–12.

Uterwedde, Henrik. 2009. "L'économie sociale de marché: La jeunesse d'un référentiel." *Regards sur l'Économie Allemande* 91: 23–30.

Van Horn, Robert. 2009. "Reinventing monopoly and the role of corporations." In *The Road from Mont Pèlerin the Making of the Neoliberal Thought Collective*. Edited by Philip Mirowski and Dieter Plehwe, 204–237. Cambridge: Harvard University Press.

Van Horn, Robert, and Matthias Klaes. 2010. "Intervening in laissez-faire liberalism. Chicago's shift on patents." In *Building Chicago Economics*. Edited by Robert Van Horn, Philip Mirowski, and Thomas A. Stapleford, 180–207. Cambridge: Cambridge University Press.

Vanberg, Viktor. 1988. "Ordnungstheorie as constitutional economics: The German conception of a 'social market economy.'" *ORDO: Jahrbuch für die Ordnung von Wirtschaft und Gesellschaft* 39: 17–31.

Vanberg, Viktor. 1998. "Freiburg School of law and economics." In *The New Palgrave Dictionary of Economics and the Law*. Edited by Peter Newman, 172–179. London: Macmillan.

Vanberg, Viktor. 2001. *The Constitution of Markets: Essays in Political Economy*. London: Routledge.

Vanberg, Viktor. 2006. "L'école de Fribourg: Walter Eucken et l'ordolibéralisme." In *Histoire du libéralisme en Europe*. Edited by Philippe Nemo and Jean Petitot, 911–935. Paris: Presses Universitaires de France.

Vanberg, Viktor. 2013. "Hayek in Freiburg." In *Hayek: A Collaborative Biography: Part 1. Influences from Mises to Bartley*. Edited by Robert Leeson, 93–122. Hampshire: Palgrave Macmillan.

Vanberg, Viktor. 2014. "Ordnungspolitik, the Freiburg School and the reason of rules." *Rivista i-lex* 9 (21): 205–220.

Vatiero, Massimiliano. 2010. "The Ordoliberal Notion of Market Power: An Institutionalist Reassessment." *European Competition Journal* 6 (3): 689–707.

Vatiero, Massimiliano. 2015. "Dominant market position and ordoliberalism." *International Review of Economics* 62 (4): 291–306.

Vaughn, Karen I. 1980. "Economic calculation under socialism: The Austrian contribution." *Economic Inquiry* 18 (4): 535–554.

Vogelgsang, Tobias. 2016. "Cognitive artefacts: Remaking economies, 1917–1947." PhD dissertation, London School of Economics and Political Science.

Wakote, Reine. 2016. "Hans Großmann-Doerth, un cofondateur méconnu de l'École de Fribourg." In *L'ordolibéralisme, aux origines de l'École de Fribourg-en-Brisgau*. Edited by Hugues Rabault, 127–160. Paris: L'Harmattan.

Wala, Michael. 2004. "The Marshall Plan and the origins of the Cold War." In *The United States and Germany in the Era of the Cold War, 1945–1990*. Edited by Detlef Junker, 73–77. Cambridge: Cambridge University Press.

Walpen, Bernhard. 2004. *Die offenen Feinde und ihre Gesellschaft: Eine hegemonietheoretische Studie zur Mont Pèlerin Society*. Hamburg: VSA-Verlag.

Walras, Léon. 1898/1992. *Études d'économie politique appliquée*. Edited by Jean-Pierre Potier. Œuvres économiques complètes, vol. X. Paris: Economica.

Walther, Julien. 2016. "Prométhée enchaîné ou la puissance maîtrisée. Le 'lien générique' entre droit privé et concurrence dans l'œuvre de Franz Böhm (1895–1977)." In *L'ordolibéralisme, aux origines de l'École de Fribourg-en-Brisgau*. Edited by Hugues Rabault, 95–126. Paris: L'Harmattan.

Wandel, Eckhard. 1979. "Historical developments prior to the German currency reform of 1948." *Journal of Institutional and Theoretical Economics* 135 (3): 320–331.

Ward, Benjamin N. 1972. *What's Wrong with Economics?* London: Macmillan.

Warlouzet, Laurent. 2008. "Europe de la concurrence et politique industrielle communautaire La naissance d'une opposition au sein de la CEE dans les années 1960." *Histoire, Économie & Société* 27 (1): 47–61.

Weber, Max. 1904/1949. "'Objectivity' in social science and social policy." In *Max Weber on the Methodology of the Social Sciences*. Edited by Henry A. Finch, translated by Edward A. Shils, 50–112. Chicago: Free Press.

Weber, Max. 1905/2001. *The Protestant Ethic and the Spirit of Capitalism*. Translated by Talcott Parsons. London: Routledge.

Weber, Max. 1906/2012. "Roscher and Knies and the logical problems of historical economics." In *Max Weber: Collected Methodological Writings*. Edited by Hans H. Bruun and Sam Whimster, translated by Hans H. Bruun, 3–93. London: Routledge.

Weber, Max. 1917a/1968. "Le sens de la 'neutralité axiologique' dans les sciences sociales et économiques." In *Essais sur la théorie de la science*. Translated by Julien Freund, 399–478. Paris: Plon.

Weber, Max. 1917b/2009. "Science as a vocation." In *Essays in Sociology*. Edited by Hans H. Gerth and C. Wright Mills, 129–156. London: Routledge.

Weber, Max. 1956/1978. *Economy and Society: An Outline of Interpretive Sociology*. Edited by Guenther Roth and Claus Wittich. Berkeley: University of California Press.

Weidmann, Jens. 2013. "Krisenmanagement und Ordnungspolitik." Walter-Eucken Vorlesung/Discours du 11/02. https://www.bundesbank.de/de/presse/reden/krisenmanagement-und-ordnungspolitik-710712.

Weikart, Richard. 1993. "The origins of social darwinism in Germany, 1859–1895." *Journal of the History of Ideas* 54 (3): 469–488.

Weisz, Jean-Daniel. 2001. "A systemic perception of Eucken's foundations of economics." In *Institutional economics in France and Germany: German Ordoliberalism Versus the French Regulation School*. Edited by Agnès Labrousse and Jean-Daniel Weisz, 129–156. Heidelberg: Springer.

Wohlgemuth, Michael. 2013. "The Freiburg School and the Hayekian challenge." *Review of Austrian Economics* 26 (2): 149–170.

Wolf, Holger C. 1993. "The lucky miracle: Germany 1945–1951." In *Postwar Economic Reconstruction and Lessons for the East Today*. Edited by Rudiger Dornbusch, Wilhelm Nölling, and Richard Layard, 29–56. Cambridge: MIT Press.

Wörsdörfer, Manuel. 2010. "On the economic ethics of Walter Eucken." In *60 Years of Social Market Economy Formation, Development and Perspectives of a Peacemaking Formula*. Edited by Christian L. Glossner and David Gregosz, 20–41. Sankt Augustin: Konrad Adenauer Stiftung.

Wörsdörfer, Manuel. 2011. "Die normativen und wirtschaftsethischen Grundlagen des Ordoliberalismus." PhD dissertation. Frankfurt am Main: Johann Wolfgang Goethe-Universität.

Wörsdörfer, Manuel. 2012a. "Freiburg School of law and economics, Freiburg (Lehrstuhl-) Tradition and the genesis of norms." *Working Paper Series, Cluster of Excellence* "The Formation of Normative Orders."

Wörsdörfer, Manuel. 2012b. "Walter Eucken on patent laws: Are patents just 'nonsense upon stilts?'" *Economic Thought* 1 (2): 36–54.

Wörsdörfer, Manuel. 2013a. "Individual versus regulatory ethics: An economic-ethical and theoretical-historical analysis of German neoliberalism." *Œconomia. History, Methodology, Philosophy* 3/4: 4–31.

Wörsdörfer, Manuel. 2013b. "Von Hayek and ordoliberalism on justice." *Journal of the History of Economic Thought* 35 (3): 291–317.

Wörsdörfer, Manuel. 2014. "The 'societal crisis of the present' as a neoliberal leitmotif." *History of Economic Thought and Policy* 3 (2): 77–109.

Wren-Lewis, Simon. 2016. "Unravelling the new classical counter revolution." *Review of Keynesian Economics* 4 (1): 20–35.

Wright, Claire. 2016. "The 1920s Viennese intellectual community as a center for ideas exchange: A network analysis." *History of Political Economy* 48 (4): 593–634.

Yeager, Leland B. 1994. "Eucken on capital and interest." *Journal of Economic Studies* 21 (4): 61–75.

Yeager, Leland B. 2005. "Walter Eucken (1891–1950)." In *The Elgar Companion to Law and Economics*, 2nd edn. Edited by Jürgen G. Backhaus, 508–518. Cheltenham: Edward Elgar.

Young, Brigitte. 2013. "Ordoliberalismus—Neoliberalismus—Laissez-faire-Liberalismus." In *Theorien der Internationalen Politischen Ökonomie*. Edited by Joscha Wullweber, Antonia Graf, and Maria Behrens, 33–48. Berlin: Springer.

Young, Brigitte. 2014a. "German ordoliberalism as agenda setter for the euro crisis: Myth trumps reality." *Journal of Contemporary European Studies* 22 (3): 276–287.

Young, Brigitte. 2014b. "The power of ordoliberalism in the eurozone crisis management." In *The Eurozone Crisis and the Future of Europe*. Edited by Daniel Dăianu, Giorgio Basevi, Carlo D'Adda, and Rajeesh Kumar, 126–137. London: Palgrave Macmillan.

Young, Brigitte. 2015. "The battle of ideas in the eurozone crisis management." In *The Economic Crisis in Social and Institutional Context: Theories, Policies and Exit Strategies*. Edited by Sebastiano Fadda and Pasquale Tridico, 78–90. London: Routledge.

Young, Brigitte. 2018. "Contemporary Anglo-Saxon neoliberalism is not German ordoliberalism." In *The SAGE Handbook of Neoliberalism*. Edited by Damien Cahill, Melinda Cooper, Martijn Konings, and David Primrose, 179–189. Los Angeles: Sage.

Young, Brigitte, and Willi Semmler. 2011. "The European sovereign debt crisis: Is Germany to blame?" *German Politics and Society* 29 (1): 1–24.

Zimmermann, Reinhard. 2013. "L'héritage de Savigny. Histoire du droit, droit comparé, et émergence d'une science juridique européenne." *Revue Internationale de Droit Économique* 27 (1): 95–127.

Zmirak, John. 2001. *Wilhelm Röpke: Swiss Localist, Global Economist*. Library of modern thinkers. Wilmington: ISI Books.

Zweig, Stefan. 1943/1964. *The World of Yesterday: An Autobiography*. Lincoln: University of Nebraska Press.

# INDEX

*For the benefit of digital users, indexed terms that span two pages (e.g., 52–53) may, on occasion, appear on only one of those pages.*

The letter *f* following a page locator denotes a figure.

CPSIA information can be obtained
at www.ICGtesting.com
Printed in the USA
BVHW030455200922
647469BV00002B/6

9 780197 607800